To Jim
With love & best wishes
for a Very Happy Birthday

Aileen

Sept. 19, 2000.

KRIEGHOFF | Images of Canada

KRIEGHOFF | *Images of Canada*

DENNIS REID

with essays by

RAMSAY COOK

FRANÇOIS-MARC GAGNON

DOUGLAS & MCINTYRE Vancouver/Toronto

ART GALLERY OF ONTARIO Toronto

Copyright © 1999 by Art Gallery of Ontario
Individual texts copyright © 1999 by Ramsay Cook, François-Marc Gagnon, Dennis Reid,
Raymond Vézina

99 00 01 02 03   5 4 3 2 1

The Art Gallery of Ontario is funded by the Ontario Ministry of Citizenship, Culture, and
Recreation. Additional operating support is received from the Volunteers of the Art Gallery of
Ontario, the City of Toronto, the Department of Canadian Heritage, and the Canada Council.

Supported by the Department of Canadian Heritage Museums Assistance Program.

This book is published on the occasion of *Krieghoff: Images of Canada*, the exhibition organized
and circulated by the Art Gallery of Ontario, Toronto, and sponsored by the American Express
Foundation.

Douglas & McIntyre   Art Gallery of Ontario
2323 Quebec Street, Suite 201   317 Dundas Street West
Vancouver, British Columbia v5t 4s7   Toronto, Ontario m5t 1g4

CANADIAN CATALOGUING IN PUBLICATION DATA

Main entry under title:

Krieghoff

Co-published by: Art Gallery of Ontario.
Includes bibliographical references.
ISBN 1-55054-725-9 (bound) — ISBN 1-55054-754-2 (pbk.)

1. Krieghoff, Cornelius, 1815–1872. I. Krieghoff, Cornelius, 1815–1872. II. Reid, Dennis.
III. Cook, Ramsay, 1931– IV. Gagnon, François-Marc, 1935– V. Art Gallery of Ontario.
ND249.K7K74 1999   759.11   C99-910655-4

frontispiece:
CANADIAN AUTUMN, VIEW ON THE ROAD TO LAKE ST. JOHN, 1862 (detail of pl. 118)

ITINERARY

Art Gallery of Ontario, Toronto, 26 November 1999 – 5 March 2000
Musée du Québec, Quebec City, 14 June 2000 – 10 September 2000
National Gallery of Canada, Ottawa, 12 October 2000 – 7 January 2001
Vancouver Art Gallery, Vancouver, 17 February 2001 – 21 May 2001
McCord Museum of Canadian History, Montreal, 22 June 2001 – 8 October 2001

Design by George Vaitkunas
Editing by Alison Reid
Translation of François-Marc Gagnon's essay by Judith Terry
Translation of Raymond Vézina's chronology by Lucie Chevalier
Index: Laura Brown and Lucie Chevalier

Printed and bound in Canada by Friesens
Printed on acid-free paper

Douglas & McIntyre Ltd. gratefully acknowledges the assistance of the Canada Council and of
the British Columbia Ministry of Tourism, Small Business and Culture. The publisher also
acknowledges the financial support of the government of Canada through the Book Publishing
Industry Development Program.

Canadä

All dimensions of works of art are given in centimetres, height preceding width.

All plate numbers are catalogue numbers unless otherwise indicated.

CONTENTS

Sponsor's Foreword

Perhaps no other artist has influenced the way we see Canada more than Cornelius Krieghoff. His numerous images of everyday life of rural Quebec, First Nations people, and the landscape of the St. Lawrence River have provided us with a historical snapshot of nineteenth-century Canada.

The American Express Foundation is proud to partner with the Art Gallery of Ontario in bringing the first-ever full-scale retrospective of Krieghoff's works to the public. American Express believes that it is important that Canadians have access to a breadth of cultural and artistic experiences. For this reason, we extend our support to funding major exhibitions at some of Canada's leading galleries, such as the Art Gallery of Ontario, and to sponsoring significant performances and productions by performing arts companies and local music festivals.

We understand that as good corporate citizens, we have the responsibility and privilege of supporting and enriching the communities in which we do business. Arts and cultural heritage projects, initiatives that address education and training for young people, and the volunteer efforts of our employees are at the heart of our company's program of corporate citizenship.

The American Express Foundation will continue to support arts and cultural heritage projects that touch Canadians and expose new audiences to the sights and sounds of the arts. We are particularly honoured to lend our support to *Krieghoff: Images of Canada*.

Alan W. Stark
President and General Manager
Amex Canada Inc.

DIRECTOR'S FOREWORD

Which are the exhibitions we remember? Exhibitions that have about them the intimacy and engagement of a story well told, narratives that convey a sense of discovery (or rediscovery), presentations that engage the pleasures of looking and, ultimately, reinforce the idea that art lets us see the world in new ways.

Dennis Reid, the Art Gallery of Ontario's Chief Curator, has for many years explored the work of Canada's most important nineteenth-century painter, Cornelius Krieghoff. This exhibition celebrates his scholarly investigation. There is much new information here—reflections on the history of Canada and its peoples, factual data about Krieghoff and his work recorded for the first time, and attribution of paintings securely dated and placed within the artist's oeuvre—all of which reminds us that history and the history of art comprise both documentation and analysis, and change always through the convictions of the storyteller.

That Krieghoff now seems to us more ambitious, more painterly, and his work more engaged with the emergence of ideas of nationhood than ever before is a testament to the thoroughness of Dennis Reid's project, and to the contributions of the authors who have added their illuminating texts to this publication, Ramsay Cook and François-Marc Gagnon. The three essays show us that in many ways art reflects nothing less than the values of the time it was made—indeed, tells us more, that art can play a role in moulding such values in unique and specific circumstances.

That there has not been a Krieghoff retrospective in two generations surprises many. His work seems omnipresent and easily accessible to us. Perhaps, then, the greatest achievement of *Krieghoff: Images of Canada* is that by gathering work rarely on public view, and creating new contexts in which to see the paintings, this exhibition takes the seemingly familiar and tells us much we didn't know.

The American Express Foundation has generously supported the presentation of *Krieghoff: Images of Canada*. In their truly exemplary way, the American Express Foundation has enabled the Art Gallery of Ontario to ensure that Krieghoff's work will be appreciated by generations of Canadians.

Matthew Teitelbaum
Director
Art Gallery of Ontario

PREFACE AND ACKNOWLEDGEMENTS

Cornelius Krieghoff is the best-known but least-understood nineteenth-century Canadian artist. A prolific painter, he created images of Canada that were eagerly collected in his own time and that have become familiar icons of an idealized past in the more than 125 years since his death. This great popularity has been a mixed blessing, however. Because his paintings have always had currency with collectors, most have been brought to market a number of times, resulting in repeated restorations. Almost all have had their canvases reinforced by lining, and many are extensively, often clumsily, overpainted. In addition, his art was copied in his lifetime and has been the most popular Canadian target of forgers ever since. We've effectively lost sight of what an actual Krieghoff painting looks like up close.

The great popularity of Krieghoff's work has, ironically, also had the effect of diminishing his role in the history of Canadian art. Writers in English have followed his first significant biographer, Marius Barbeau, who interpreted the paintings as realistic glimpses of the everyday activities of his time. Writers in French have been influenced by the contrary view of Gérard Morisset, Barbeau's contemporary, that Krieghoff was a foreign-trained interloper whose disrespectful depictions of French-Canadian life bear little resemblance to reality. Clearly, much remains to be said. The last book on Krieghoff, by J. Russell Harper, was published twenty years ago. There has never been a critical retrospective exhibition.

Just after his book came out, I asked Russell Harper if he would organize such an exhibition for the Art Gallery of Ontario. He declined, saying the task would be too complicated. I kept my own interest in

Krieghoff alive, and growing, by leading a graduate seminar on the artist's work at the University of Toronto for one term every three years from 1981 to the present, which has resulted in a wealth of discussion and highly original papers from forty students. During most years when the seminar has been held, one class has been set aside for a visit to the remarkable collection of Krieghoff paintings assembled in Toronto by Kenneth Thomson. From those meetings a relationship developed that led to talk of a possible exhibition, and then to a generous expression of support from Mr. Thomson. I then proposed to my colleagues at the Gallery a long-term research project that would begin with systematic examination of the approximately 250 Krieghoffs in the Thomson Collection, then proceed to a similarly close physical examination of other important holdings of Krieghoffs in public and private hands, in concert with archival research to broaden our understanding of the artist's relationship to his times and the subsequent history of his works. We began in October 1995, and now, four years later, an exhibition has been selected based as much as possible on the condition and quality of individual works that will for the first time examine Krieghoff's entire career in detail, revealing his very considerable skills as a painter and his changing vision of Canada as it evolved from colony to nation. The publication you are now reading reproduces in colour all the works in the exhibition, and situates them within the broader context of Krieghoff's own times while interpreting their significance today. My essay focuses on Krieghoff as a major Canadian cultural figure in the years leading up to Confederation, showing him to be as much shaped by his new homeland as it was shaped in the public mind by his images. Ramsay Cook's essay presents a fresh reading of some of these familiar images in light of the underlying social attitudes and political issues of the day. François-Marc Gagnon's essay examines the sources of Krieghoff's images of French Canadians and Natives, and discusses how these images have been interpreted by the first important historian of the art of French Canada, Gérard Morisset. Arlene Gehmacher provides a detailed catalogue outlining the history of each work in the exhibition, while Raymond Vézina's chronology situates all the firm facts of the artist's life against the major events of his time. Laura Brown has produced a useful bibliography of the principal publications relating to Krieghoff.

To accomplish all this has required the collaboration of many people, and we'd like to acknowledge a number who have been particularly helpful. At Thomson Works of Art Limited, under which the Thomson Collection is incorporated, we've benefited from the commitment of Mr. Thomson's staff, specifically Anna Travascio, Administrator, and Heather McMichael and Vince Stekly, Assistants.

At the Musée du Québec, Quebec City, Mario Béland, Curator of Early Quebec Art, has been a key collaborator from the beginning of the project, and a number of his colleagues have also gone out of their way to assist my research, including Denis Martin, Curator of Graphic Arts and Photography, Claude Belleau, Conservator, and Lise Nadeau, Collections Archivist. Nathalie Thibault, Documentation Technician, Collections Management, has been helpful with photography.

René Villeneuve, Assistant Curator, Early Canadian Art, at the National Gallery of Canada has also been a constant support throughout, and Anne Ruggles, Senior Conservator, Susan Walker, Assistant Conservator, Cyndie Campbell, Head, Archives, Documentation and Visual Resources, and France Duhamel, Assistant to Reproductions, Rights and Sales, have helped at crucial junctures. At the National Archives of Canada, Ottawa, Anne Goddard, Archivist, Social and Cultural Archives Section, Manuscript Division, has been especially forthcoming, as have Jim Burant, Chief, Art, Photography and Philatelic Archives Section, Visual and Sound Archives Division, Jennifer Devine, Archivist in the same section, Gilbert Gignac, Preservation Custodian, Holdings Management Section, Preservation Division, Patricia Kennedy, Archivist, Economic and Public Archives Section, Manuscript Division, and Michel Poitras, Consultation Officer, Researchers Services Division. At the Canadian Museum of Civilization in Hull, Benoît Thériault, Reference Archivist and Archival Information Analyst, Library, Archives and Documentation Services, provided ready access to the Marius Barbeau Papers.

In Montreal, Rosalind Pepall, Curator of Canadian Art (1915–1970) at the Montreal Museum of Fine Arts, and Jean-Pierre Labiau, Curator of Canadian Art (before 1915), at the same institution, Rodrigue Bédard, Chief Conservator, Catherine O'Meara, Conservator, Danielle Blanchette, Documentation Technician, Archives, and Marie-Claude Saia, Technician, Photographic Services and Copyright, all assisted enthusiastically, as did the staff at the McCord Museum of Canadian History, particularly Conrad Graham, Curator of Decorative Arts, and Nora Hague, Cataloguer, Notman Archives, Suzanne Morin, Archivist, and Brenda Klinkow, Technician, Rights and Reproduction. At the Musée du Château Ramezay in Montreal Jean-François Royal, Manager, Collections, also deserves thanks.

At the Royal Ontario Museum, Toronto, essential help has been provided by Howard Collinson, Mona Campbell Curator of Decorative Arts; Carol Baum, Technician, Department of Western Art and Culture; Tricia Walker, Registration Coordinator; and Mary Allodi, Curator Emeritus, Department of Western Art and Culture. Tobi Bruce, Curator, Historical Art, at the Art Gallery of Hamilton, has also been especially responsive, as have Gemey Kelly, Director of the Owens Art Gallery, Mount Allison University, Sackville, N.B.; Dianne O'Neill, Associate Curator, Art Gallery of Nova Scotia, Halifax; Curtis Collins, Curator, Rachel Brody, Registrar, and Greg Charleton, Preparator, at the Beaverbrook Art Gallery, Fredericton, N.B.; and Catharine Mastin, Senior Curator of Art, and Ewa Smithwick, Conservator, Paintings, at the Glenbow Museum, Calgary.

In the private sector, Alan Klinkhoff of Galerie Walter Klinkhoff, Montreal, has been a constant source of valuable information, and William Tetley and Victor Isganaitis also introduced me to important collections. Paul Marechal, Assistant Curator, Art Collection, at the Power Corporation of Canada, Montreal, has been especially understanding of my research needs. Donald Sobey, Chairman of the Sobey Art Foundation, Stellarton, N.S., Mark Holton, Curator, and Brenda and Donald Gillis, Custodians, have all been generous with their time in giving me access to that notable collection of Krieghoffs. Paul Kastel and Anthony Nevin of the Kastel Gallery, Montreal, also have been helpful, as have Michel Moreault, Director of Galerie Dominion, Montreal, and Mariitta Maavara (who also made the papers of the former Continental Galleries available). Geoffrey Joyner, Joyner Auctioneers and Appraisers, Toronto, Christina Orobetz, Sotheby's Canada, Toronto, and John R.

Williams, Williams & Son, London, have responded eagerly to queries. Peter Winkworth, London, is another crucial and long-time supporter of the project, and Bill Tennison, Toronto, has also assisted greatly. Paul Ultsch of Schweinfurt, Germany, both in his writings and in conversation, has most graciously supplied vital information. The late Michel Doyon of Montreal provided me with stimulating hours of discussion of Krieghoff, freely offering the results of his own research. Ramsay Cook and François-Marc Gagnon both made useful suggestions to improve my text.

Over the past four years, thirteen undergraduate students at the University of Toronto have under my supervision surveyed mid-nineteenth-century Montreal and Quebec City newspapers for Krieghoff-related material, participants in a one-year credit course under the Research Opportunity Program. Their work has enriched the project, and one of them, Vincci Ching, has created a wonderful Krieghoff web-site, available at http://members.home.net/vincci2/. Du-Yi Leu, Fiona Valverde, and Fred Schaeffer have been extremely valuable research volunteers at the Art Gallery of Ontario.

Without the remarkable staff we have, the AGO could not even have contemplated undertaking a project of this scope. Everyone in the institution has contributed, or will contribute over the next few months, to its successful realization, and a number have performed beyond the expected professional standard. Among these are Sandra Webster-Cook, Conservator, who has worked closely with me for more than five years, examining many hundreds of Krieghoff paintings and helping me to understand his painting technique. Her observations have directly influenced the choice of works for the exhibition. John O'Leary, Senior

Framer, has very positively affected this process, both at the Gallery and afield. John O'Neill, Conservator, has assisted with works on paper, and Curtis Strilchuk, Deputy Registrar, Faye Van Horne, Resources Coordinator, Photographic Resources, and Carlo Catenazzi, Head Photographer, all assured that the movement and thorough documentation of the huge Thomson Collection, as well as the many other Krieghoff paintings we've scrutinized at the Gallery in the past few years, has proceeded smoothly. Joy Tyndall, former Curatorial Assistant, initially coordinated activities around most of the Thomson paintings and established a working bibliography and other basic research apparatus. Arlene Gehmacher, Curatorial Assistant, has refined this material, and catalogued all the works in the exhibition, achieving an impressive level of precise information in remarkably short order. Laura Brown, Curatorial Assistant, has, with remarkable efficiency, pulled together all the various images and texts that make up this publication. Lucie Chevalier, French Language Services Coordinator, as well as assuring that we will be proud of the French edition, has unhesitatingly given us the benefit of her expertise with the computer-related publishing process. Linda Milrod, Head, Exhibitions and Publications, is leading the production team. Catherine van Baren has provided her experienced editorial guidance. Karen McKenzie, Chief Librarian, and her staff in the Edward P. Taylor Research Library and Archives have assisted at countless points throughout the project, and although I'm writing this seven months before the exhibition opens, I know that George Bartosik, Manager, and his staff in Technical Services will install it brilliantly. The Krieghoff project has proceeded under three successive Directors at the

Art Gallery of Ontario, and I would like to thank Glenn Lowry and Maxwell Anderson for their understanding, but particularly Matthew Teitelbaum, who always encourages boldness but expects it to spring from a well-prepared position.

Brian Merrett, photographer, and Andrew Ornoch, paintings conservator, have both added with their services to the high standard of our publication and exhibition, as have Judith Terry, who translated François-Marc Gagnon's text, and Alison Reid (yes, my wife, Kog, to those of you who know us), who edited this publication with her usual great sensitivity and efficiency. Thank you also Scott McIntyre and Terri Wershler of Douglas & McIntyre for helping make our book as grand as it is, and George Vaitkunas for designing an object that is both dignified and ravishingly beautiful. Finally, my heartfelt thanks to Kenneth Thomson, who has been unequivocally supportive throughout, and without whom this project could not have been realized.

Dennis Reid
Chief Curator
Art Gallery of Ontario

PLATES 1–40

1. Étienne Sévère Filiatrault, 1840–41

watercolour on paper, 21.5 × 19.2 cm

Musée du Québec, Québec, purchased 1997, in memory of Jacques Labrecque, folklorist (97.10)

2. Madame Étienne Sévère Filiatrault, née Martine Brien dit Desrochers, 1840–41

watercolour on paper, 22.0 × 19.0 cm

Musée du Québec, Québec, purchased 1997, in memory of Jacques Labrecque, folklorist (97.11)

3. William Williamson and His Son Alexander, 1844

oil on canvas, 102.0 × 87.4 cm

Royal Ontario Museum, Toronto, purchased 1978, Sigmund Samuel Trust (978.289.1)

4. Margaret Erskine Williamson and Her Daughter Jessie, 1844

oil on canvas, 102.0 × 87.4 cm

Royal Ontario Museum, Toronto, purchased 1978, Sigmund Samuel Trust (978.289.2)

5. MARINE VIEW—MOONLIGHT (after Grolig), c. 1845

oil on canvas, 60.5 × 91.0 cm

National Gallery of Canada, Ottawa, gift of Dr. Max Stern, Montreal, 1983 (28426)

6. The Artist's Studio, c. 1845

oil on canvas, 44.7 × 54.0 cm

National Gallery of Canada, Ottawa, purchased 1902 (128)

7. The Winetasters (after Hasenclever), c. 1846

oil on canvas, 35.3 × 50.3 cm

The Thomson Collection (P-C-65)

8. STILL LIFE WITH FLOWERS, FRUIT AND CORN, 1846

oil on canvas, 97.7 × 78.0 cm

Montreal Museum of Fine Arts, purchased 1967, Horsley and Annie Townsend Bequest (1967.1549)

9. THE PLAINS OF BABYLON (after Staunton), 1846

oil on canvas, 32.5 × 41.0 cm

The Collection of Power Corporation of Canada, Montreal

10. An Officer's Room in Montreal, 1846

oil on canvas, 44.5 × 63.5 cm

Royal Ontario Museum, Toronto, gift of the Sigmund Samuel Endowment Fund, 1954 (954.188.2)

[11]

11. Breaking Lent (or A Friday's Surprise), 1847

oil on canvas, 36.3 × 54.3 cm

The Thomson Collection (P-C-672)

12. HABITANT SLEIGH, VIEW NEAR THE CANADA LINE, c. 1847

oil on canvas, 64.1 × 92.0 cm

The Thomson Collection (P-C-669)

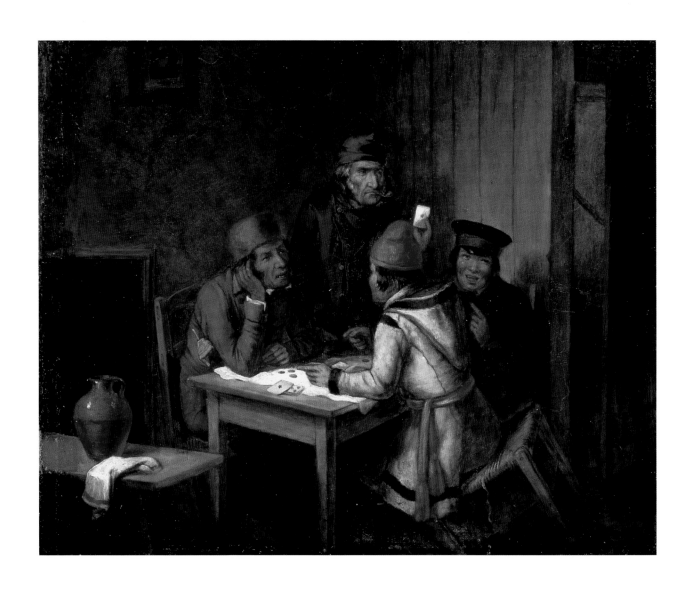

13. A GAME OF CARDS, 1848

oil on canvas, 26.3 × 32.6 cm

National Archives of Canada, Ottawa, gift of the Estate of Charles Murphy, Ottawa, 1938 (C-011003)

14. THE ICE BRIDGE AT LONGUE-POINTE, c. 1848

oil on canvas, 60.8 × 76.2 cm

National Gallery of Canada, Ottawa, gift of Geneva Jackson, Kitchener, Ontario, 1933 (4085)

15. CANADIAN INTERIOR, 1850

oil on canvas, 45.0 × 70.0 cm

Musée du Québec, Québec, gift of the Honourable Maurice Duplessis Estate, 1959 (59.629)

16. Habitant Family with Horse and Sleigh, 1850

oil on canvas, 46.0 × 67.5 cm

The Thomson Collection (P-C-584)

[17]

17. VILLAGE SCENE IN WINTER, 1850

oil on canvas, 66.5 × 92.7 cm

The Thomson Collection (P-C-74)

18. Cottage, St. Anne, c. 1850

oil on canvas, 46.0 × 67.0 cm

Musée du Québec, Québec, acquired before 1934 (34.257)

19. WHITE HORSE INN BY MOONLIGHT, 1851

oil on canvas, 101.1 × 124.7 cm

National Gallery of Canada, Ottawa, gift of Gabrielle Coste, Marie Louise Savon, and Eugene Francis Coste, 1971,

grandchildren of Thomas Dillon Tims, to whom this painting was given by the artist (16702)

20. FIDDLER AND BOY DOING JIG, 1852

oil on canvas, 38.2 × 32.4 cm

The Thomson Collection (P-C-777)

21. Sleigh Race on the St. Lawrence at Quebec, 1852

oil on canvas, 45.0 × 62.9 cm

The Thomson Collection (P-C-78)

22. Caughnawaga Indian Encampment at a Portage, 1844?

oil on canvas, 35.5 × 54.0 cm

Royal Ontario Museum, Toronto, gift of Dr. Sigmund Samuel, 1949 (949.39.20)

23. A Caughnawaga Indian Encampment, c. 1848

oil on canvas, 34.0 × 50.5 cm

Royal Ontario Museum, Toronto, gift of Dr. Sigmund Samuel, 1949 (949.39.17)

24. Indian Trapper on Snowshoes, c. 1849

oil on canvas, 38.7 × 30.5 cm

The Thomson Collection (P-C-81)

25. Caughnawaga Woman and Baby, c. 1849

oil on canvas, 38.8 × 30.5 cm

The Thomson Collection (P-C-80)

26. Chief Tanaghte, Delegate to Lord Elgin at Montreal, c. 1849

oil on canvas, 33.9 × 25.5 cm

The Thomson Collection (P-C-72)

27. CAUGHNAWAGA INDIAN, c. 1850

oil on board, 31.4 × 24.6 cm

National Archives of Canada, Ottawa, acquired 1937 (C-003139)

28. Indian Encampment by a River, c. 1850

oil on canvas, 57.5 × 70.0 cm

Kastel Gallery, Montreal

29. The Trader, 1850

oil on canvas, 45.5 × 60.6 cm

Art Gallery of Hamilton, gift of Mrs. C.H. Stearn, 1957 (1966.75.0)

30. HURON INDIANS AT PORTAGE, 1850

oil on canvas, 71.1 × 84.0 cm

Royal Ontario Museum, Toronto, gift of the Sigmund Samuel Endowment Fund, 1954 (954.188.3)

31. INDIANS AND SQUAWS OF LOWER CANADA, 1848

lithograph with watercolour on paper (Crehen), 34.4 × 47.4 cm (image)

Collection of Peter Winkworth, London

32. FRENCH CANADIAN HABITANS PLAYING AT CARDS, 1848

lithograph with watercolour on paper (Borum), 34.2 × 48.8 cm (image)

National Gallery of Canada, Ottawa, gift of Donald Maclaren, Ottawa, 1990 (30821)

INDIAN WIGWAM IN LOWER CANADA.

Published under the patronage of the Right Hon. the Earl of Elgin & Kincardine Governor General of British North America

33. INDIAN WIGWAM IN LOWER CANADA, 1848
lithograph with watercolour on paper (Borum), 34.4 × 48.5 cm (image)
National Gallery of Canada, Ottawa, gift of Donald Maclaren, Ottawa, 1990 (30820)

PLACE D'ARMES À MONTRÉAL.

Published under the patronage of the Right Hon the Earl of Elgin & Kincardine, Governor General of British North America

34. Place d'Armes à Montréal, 1848

lithograph on paper (Borum), 34.7 × 48.7 cm (image)

Collection of Peter Winkworth, London

35. Sledge Race near Montreal, 1848
lithograph with beige tint stone, on paper (Borum), 34.6 × 49.6 cm (image)
National Archives of Canada, Ottawa, purchased 1931 (C-013466)

ICE CUTTING.

36. ICE CUTTING, c. 1849

lithograph with watercolour on paper (Sarony & Major), 17.1 × 24.9 cm (image)

Collection of Peter Winkworth, London

SUGAR MAKING IN CANADA.

37. SUGAR MAKING IN CANADA, c. 1849

lithograph with watercolour on paper (Sarony & Major), 17.1 × 24.8 cm (image)

Collection of Peter Winkworth, London

38. Untitled (Hunter and Two Women), c. 1849

lithograph with watercolour on paper (Sarony & Major), 17.1 × 24.4 cm (image)

Collection of Peter Winkworth, London

39. UNTITLED (INDIAN PORTAGING A CANOE), c. 1849
lithograph with watercolour on paper (Sarony & Major), 17.1 × 24.6 cm (image)
Collection of Peter Winkworth, London

FRENCH CHURCH, PLACE D'ARMES, MONTREAL.

40. FRENCH CHURCH, PLACE D'ARMES, MONTREAL, C. 1850
lithograph with watercolour on paper (Sarony & Major), 44.2 × 33.4 cm (image)
National Archives of Canada, Ottawa, acquired from the W.H. Coverdale Collection of Canadiana, 1970 (C-040912)

CORNELIUS KRIEGHOFF:
The Development of a Canadian Artist

Dennis Reid

Canada made Krieghoff, shaped him as an artist. Not the Canada we know today, but a country changing so rapidly that it would have been hard to define even at the time. The largest part of the grouping of colonies known as British North America, the Province of Canada was created by the Act of Union in 1840 from two separate administrations—Lower Canada (today Québec), largely French, a community then with a history along the St. Lawrence of some two hundred years, and Upper Canada (now Ontario), a region opened to settlement only fifty years before. This union (which now comprised Canada East and Canada West), a response to rebellion that had broken out in 1837, was meant to encourage the assimilation of the French into a British community growing rapidly through immigration. It became as well a response to increasing demands for self-rule, demands that resulted near the end of Krieghoff's life in Confederation, the foundation of the modern Canadian state.

The Krieghoff who by chance arrived in Canada in 1840 had an interest in art, it seems, but no significant training. Like other ambitious aspirants in North America at the time, he found a way over the next few years to gain some European training, and soon after settling in Montreal early in

1846 began producing distinctive paintings that in a dignified and sensitive manner addressed the essential nature of his new home through depictions of the people he felt were most deeply rooted in the place: the Aboriginal inhabitants and the rural francophones. Changing fortunes took him to Quebec City seven years later, where he found a supportive group within the anglophone community who shared his artistic interests, and virtually all of whom had links with the wealth of the timber trade. His sense of place was profoundly affected by this association, and the forests became the central fact of his painting, not just as a background to life but as its source and sustenance.

Krieghoff's images of Canada are romantic, of another time, and in many ways about another place, a Canada that in part existed only in his vision, and presumably in the hopes and beliefs of those who encouraged him. Yet they are images that have survived now a century and a half or more, informing the imaginations of succeeding generations about the Canadian past and, inevitably, the present. It is important, then, that we understand the circumstances leading to their creation, something of the nature of their maker and of the place that shaped his vision. Some of those interested in how we became who we are as Canadians have been trying to understand Krieghoff and his work for a century now, a task made difficult on the one hand by the lack of almost any documentation regarding his life or thoughts, and on the other by the large number of often similar-seeming paintings. The history that has evolved over the years is an accretion of memories, small facts, speculations, and entertaining stories that burden us with a view of the man and his art as a static, even if substantial, milestone in the history of Canadian art. In the pages that follow, we will scrape back the layers of earlier narrative, revealing the few tiny flagstones of documentation that mark the path of a life. Situating dated paintings along that pathway we will gain a confident sense of the growth of this important Canadian artist, of the development of his skills and of his ideas. Along the way exploring what we can of his relations with family, friends, other artists, officials, business associates and collectors, we'll arrive finally at a better understanding of the complex genesis of Krieghoff's images of Canada.

EUROPE

Nothing in the records of Cornelius Krieghoff's earliest years or in what we know of his family's prior history portends his later career as an artist. The earliest document, a register of birth (he was born at six in the evening of 19 June 1815 at his parents' residence, Het Rokin no. 191, Amsterdam), lists his father's profession as *koffyschenkerknegt*, a waiter in a coffee house, and his mother as *zonder beroep*, without profession.[1] According to their register of marriage four years earlier, Johann Ernst Krieghoff, then also working in a coffee house, hailed from Ufhoven, near Langensalza, Thüringen, and Isabella Ludovica Wouters was from Ghent, in Flanders (then under French control).[2] By 1820, when their second son and fourth child, Johann Ernst, was born, the family was living in Düsseldorf on the Rhine (then part of Prussia), where Johann

Ernst the elder was employed as a *Tapeten-Fabrikant*, a manufacturer of wallpaper.[3] In February 1822 the family moved east again to the northern Bavarian city of Schweinfurt on the Main River, where Johann Ernst had contracted to run a wallpaper manufacturing business for a local industrialist, Wilhelm Sattler.[4] The manufactury, which employed more than one hundred people, was established in the common hall of a twelfth-century castle that Sattler had recently purchased at Mainberg, about five kilometres upriver from Schweinfurt. The Krieghoff family had an apartment in the huge structure, where they lived for more than twenty-five years.[5] Cornelius did not stay that long, of course, although we have no record of him until July 1837 when, in New York City, he enlisted in the United States Army.

This lack of documentation has not prevented historians from speculating about the nature of Krieghoff's education during the roughly fifteen years between the family's move to Schweinfurt and his departure for America. G.M. Fairchild, an early chronicler, writing in 1907 with information from Krieghoff's closest and most durable Canadian friend, John Budden, an auctioneer from Quebec City, describes Krieghoff as a professionally trained musician and accomplished performer on an array of instruments. Fairchild claims that Krieghoff studied painting and several of the natural sciences at Rotterdam, subsequently spending several years travelling "through the various states of Europe" supporting himself as a musician, painter, and student of natural sciences and languages.[6] A decade earlier, Budden, writing in response to a request from the portraitist Robert Harris for information about Krieghoff to be included in a history of Canadian art he was preparing for a proposed Canadian encyclopedia, described his late friend as a "Capital Musician" who "understood it in all branches, used to Play and Compose Music for hours Every day. He had the most wonderful faculty for Picking up Languages, Spoke & wrote English, French, Italian, Spanish, German & Dutch, Latin & Greek; was deep in Natural History—took away the finest Collection of Bird's Eggs, Skins & Coins which had ever been located at Quebec up to that time."[7] Fairchild's first piece on Krieghoff elicited a response from William Krieghoff, a grand-nephew of the artist and himself then an artist and illustrator for *The New York Herald*. Fairchild changed a few statements in a later version, notably asserting that he "studied music and painting in Düsseldorf," not Rotterdam, and was itinerant from about the age of eighteen, supporting himself with his music and painting.[8] The most recent and authoritative study, by J. Russell Harper, concludes that "Krieghoff's attendance at the Düsseldorf Academy must be assumed primarily because of his obvious familiarity with the work and the approaches to art prevalent there."[9]

Harper was unable to gain access to the student records of the Düsseldorf Academy. They are now available, and reveal that Krieghoff did not study there, nor was he involved with any of the informal student drawing groups or artists' associations related to the academy.[10] This is not surprising, for what appear to be Krieghoff's earliest artistic efforts, dating from the early 1840s, show no evidence of academic training.

They do indicate an intensity of observation and a refined sensibility, which could have been influenced by the various Sattler businesses as well as the special character of the Sattler family circle. Connection to that family was cemented when Wilhelm Sattler's son, Christian Wilhelm, married the younger Krieghoff daughter, Charlotta. Sattler's business interests were far-ranging, including a winery, sugar refineries, and other industrial processing plants, but a good portion were, like the wallpaper manufactury, of a decidedly artistic nature. The wallpapers produced at Mainberg were of the highest quality, often custom designed for particularly grand interiors. The family was respected for its patronage of the arts, and while Wilhelm's wife, Catharina, was an amateur artist of some ability, her sister, Margaret Geiger, was a professional portraitist.[11] It was a liberal, literate, culturally refined environment that clearly helped shape young Cornelius's interests.

THE UNITED STATES

The young man of twenty-two years who volunteered at New York for service in the United States Army on 5 July 1837 gave his occupation as "clerk."[12] Described as brown-eyed, with "light hair, and red complexion; height 5 feet 10½ inches," Krieghoff must have seemed, both to the recruiting officer and himself, suited for active duty, and he was "assigned to Battery 1, 1st United States Artillery," at that time deployed in the so-called Seminole Wars in Florida.[13] The United States government sought through treaties with the Native inhabitants adjacent to the

eastern seaboard to relocate them farther west, thereby opening traditional tribal lands for white settlement. When the Seminoles in the new territory of Florida resisted, war broke out in 1835, a war that reached a violent peak in 1836–7, necessitating the recruitment drive that attracted Krieghoff. Fairchild describes his army role as essentially that of a documentary artist who took field sketches and subsequently created a "large number of paintings for the U.S. Government.... The sketches which became the property of John S. Budden, Esq., were all destroyed in the great Quebec fire of June, 1881."[14] Information from William Krieghoff allowed Fairchild to add in his revised version of the following year that there were "several hundreds of drawings," and that he was commissioned to make "replicas of them for the War Department Archives, which he did in his studio at Rochester, New York, where he resided for several years."[15]

No trace of these commissioned paintings has ever been found, and it is difficult at this juncture to believe they ever existed.[16] Research in U.S. Army records over the years has also cast doubt on the story, and recently discovered evidence of Krieghoff's movements during the early 1840s reveals that Fairchild has radically telescoped the narrative. First, there is nothing in the army records to support the belief that Krieghoff functioned as a topographical or documentary artist. When discharged 5 May 1840 following his three-year tour of duty, he was described as an "artificer." Although it has been interpreted to mean some sort of artist, it is in fact a term that in nineteenth-century military parlance designates essentially a handicraftsman who constructs and repairs artillery bulwarks.[17] Krieghoff's military record also reveals that he immediately re-enlisted following his discharge (at Burlington, Vermont) and then appears to have deserted.[18] He did not then head for Rochester, however, but, it would seem, across the border to Lower Canada.

BOUCHERVILLE AND MONTREAL

At present, only three pieces of evidence document the next three years of Krieghoff's life. The first is the record of the baptism, 18 June 1840, of one Henry Krieghoff at the parish church of Ste-Famille in Boucherville, on the south shore of the St. Lawrence downriver from Montreal. Born some five weeks earlier, according to this document, "of the legitimate marriage of Cornelius Krieghoff and Émilie Gauthier of this parish," young Henry came into the world about ten days after his father left the army.[19] It is curious that his father was not present for the baptism (a Henry Gauthier, presumably the grandfather, witnessed the document), and that it was delayed so long following his birth. The next document sadly records his burial a year later in Montreal, 14 June 1841. His name was then Ernest, after his other grandfather and uncle, and his father is described as "*peintre*," a term likely the same as painter, which at the time meant house or decorative painter, not artist.[20] The third document is a notice in a Rochester, New York, newspaper, 30 May 1843, of an upcoming exhibition of Krieghoff's paintings in that city. Less securely fixed within this thin web of evidence is a daughter, with the same name as her mother but apparently spelled Emily, for whom no record of birth has

been found, but whose register of marriage in 1862 describes her as "of major age," at least twenty-one.[21] And there are three works of art we can identify with this earliest period. One is dated 1841, and the other two, although not dated, are of Boucherville subjects, and so probably precede it.

These two are small watercolour portraits of Étienne Sévère Filiatrault and his wife, Martine Brien dit Desrochers, who settled in Boucherville in 1839, where he was a schoolteacher, and where she died in 1843 (see pls. 1 and 2). Both are signed and remained in the family until their recent sale to the Musée du Québec. Undoubtedly Krieghoff's work, they are in certain respects unlike anything else we know. They are watercolours, and although numerous other watercolours are attributed to the artist, many clearly are not his, and all are to a degree suspect. These two are neoclassical in style, with sharply outlined, fully modelled, simplified forms, and are somewhat awkward, even naive in character. Étienne's hand holding the book, for instance, is entirely out of scale, the result of an imperfect understanding of foreshortening. These two earliest known do nonetheless relate to later works.

The signed work of 1841, which presumably could have been painted at Boucherville or Montreal, or even in Rochester, depending on when Krieghoff moved there, is an oil called *The Fiddler* (fig. 1, page 48). It too is awkward and naive, and on close examination shares other characteristics with the Filiatrault portraits. The conception of the head in three-quarters view is very similar, as is the finely observed mouth and the way the eyes

Figure 1
THE FIDDLER, 1841
oil on canvas, 61.5 × 46.5 cm
Confederation Centre Art Gallery and Museum,
Charlottetown, Prince Edward Island, gift of
Dr. Max Stern, Montreal, 1982 (82.14)

relate to the bridge of the nose. The cursory ears of the two men are the same, as is the treatment of the fiddler's cloak bunched up on his thigh and the lower portion of Mme Filiatrault's dress. *The Fiddler*, with wonderfully observed informal still lifes squeezed into each of its four corners, is the work of an essentially untrained artist of talent, not unlike scores of other painters of the period who eked out livings travelling from one small city or town to the next throughout the settled portions of North America. The growing communities along the St. Lawrence and around the Great Lakes, linked directly to one another by water, attracted a number of such itinerants, and we shouldn't be surprised that Krieghoff might have wanted to join their ranks.

ROCHESTER

Exactly when he left Montreal, however, and whether he visited communities other than Rochester and Toronto (Buffalo is also sometimes mentioned by his brother's descendants) we do not know.[22] Rochester certainly would have been a desirable destination. Situated at a large waterfall upstream from the mouth of the Genesee River, midway along the south shore of Lake Ontario and right on the Erie Canal, it was an essential transportation link to the rapidly expanding Midwest, and a major centre for the production of flour. Widely recognized in the 1830s as the fastest-growing city in America, it had attracted the portraitist Jean-Baptiste Roy-Audy (1798–by 1848) from Montreal in the middle of that decade, was the home base for the highly successful American itinerant Alvah Bradish (1806–1901) from about 1837 through most of the forties, and a destination in 1841 for the well-travelled James Bowman (1793–1842), who died there the following year.[23] Krieghoff was close to Bowman, and in that May 1843 newspaper notice of his exhibition of "some splendid historical pictures" announced his intention "to appropriate most of the proceeds of this exhibition to raise a monument to his friend."[24] Bowman's death had been reported in *The Daily Democrat* on 1 June 1842, so Krieghoff must have been in Rochester some time before then for a friendship to develop. Bowman, who billed himself as both a history and portrait painter, would have shared with Krieghoff memories of his experience of two years at Quebec (1831–3), some fifteen months in Montreal (1833–4), and six months or so in Toronto (1834–5), as well as his other travels.[25] Bowman also allowed Krieghoff to copy at least one of his paintings, a *Portrait of the Sculptor Thorwaldsen*.[26] A note in *The Daily Democrat* of 8 June 1843 sheds no more light on what Krieghoff may have shown in tribute to Bowman, describing the collection in the typical rhetoric of the time as "in subject and number superior to any previous exhibition in this city."

There are at least two more paintings known today from Krieghoff's years in Rochester, both dated 1843. One, *Portrait of a Notary*, is likely also copied from one of Bowman's works. The other is a small painting of a young woman holding a little girl, the latter wearing a portrait miniature of a man around her neck.[27] Both works reveal a better grasp of composition than *The Fiddler*, and because they are more spare and are executed with more thoughtful brushwork seem to demonstrate a firmer grasp of form. But they are still what we would call primitive or naive. We know Krieghoff wasn't relying on his art for a living. A letter of May 1843 from his father to Wilhelm Sattler gives the news that both Cornelius and his brother, Ernst, are in Rochester, and Ernst is working during the busy season in Cornelius's upholstery business.[28]

TORONTO

William Krieghoff told Fairchild that his great-uncle had moved to Toronto after Rochester to join his brother Ernst, and established a studio there.[29] There is no record of either of them in the Toronto city directories of 1843–4 or 1846–7, the two published during this period. There is, however, an advertisement that appeared in the Toronto *Banner* from 26 January to 16 February 1844: "D. KREIGOFF, ARTIST, Eleve of the Royal Sapon Academy at Dresden, and Fellow of the Royal Academy of Holland. Specimens to be seen at Mr. Thompson's Store, King St., and at his studio, in Mr. Goodal's house, in rear of Messrs. Jacques & Hays Cabinet Warehouse, third door from Bay Street." Remarkably full of errors even in light of the lax standards of the time (though "Sapon" was corrected to "Saxon" in later editions), the ad is surprising as well for its exaggerated claims for artistic training and affiliation. Was he anticipating competition? He probably knew that Alvah Bradish was painting a grand portrait of nearby Hamilton's most prominent citizen, Sir Allan MacNab, leader of the Tory opposition in the Legislative

Assembly, and later that year to be named speaker.[30] But there were few artists then resident in the city, only a couple of drawing masters and two portraitists, Hoppner Meyer (active 1833–60), who worked in pencil and watercolour, and Peter March (active 1842–52), a decidedly local talent who painted in oils. We should also note that Jacques & Hays was the principal furniture manufacturer in Canada West, patronized by society's discerning, and doubtless offered employment to upholsterers.

Krieghoff received one major commission in Toronto, a pair of double portraits of *William Williamson and His Son Alexander* and *Margaret Erskine Williamson and Her Daughter Jessie* (pls. 3 and 4). Williamson was a law clerk with a family home in Ancaster, a small town near Hamilton, who owned several houses on Church Street in Toronto. Krieghoff depicts them in three-quarters face, similar in the conception of the features to the Filiatrault portraits (even to the cursory ears), but much more finely finished and full of sympathetically observed character. While we are drawn immediately to the intensity of the eyes and the finely worked noses and mouths, the splendour of these works resides in their grand scale and imaginatively conceived romantic settings. Mr. Williamson and Alexander sit against rich swags of drapery by a window looking out upon a lake backed by hills. Mrs. Williamson and Jessie are in a porch or gazebo, under an ivy bower of richly intricate detail, with again a view out to a romantic setting, in this case a small cottage with mountains beyond. The forms are all roundly modelled and slightly idealized in what can still be described as a provincial neoclassical style. Somewhat sober,

the figures nonetheless swell with human feeling in a manner Krieghoff may have learned from the portraits of James Bowman. They are at the same time positively tactile with a reverence for the materiality of things, a characteristic of the Biedermeier taste prevalent in Munich and elsewhere in the German-speaking world in the early decades of the century.

Jessie Williamson was born in November 1842, Alexander in March 1841, so it seems likely these portraits were painted during the summer of 1844. Once again, however, we are unsure of Krieghoff's movements until early October, when in Paris he registered to copy at the Louvre. He had been there for at least a short while by then, for he had a lodging, at 102 rue du Bac, on the Left Bank near St-Germain-des-Prés, and had a teacher, Michel-Martin Drölling (1786–1851).[31] There is no record of what he copied, nor do we know how long he stayed. He surfaces next sixteen months later, back in Montreal.

MONTREAL

Marius Barbeau, the author of the first book-length study of Krieghoff, published in 1934, was skeptical of reports of his residence at Rochester and Toronto, unaware of the trip to France, and convinced as well that the artist's "habitant" family was the inspiration for his Canadian work. Believing that the wife, daughter, and in-laws in fact sat for most of the early pictures, he insists that Krieghoff lived in Longueuil, just across the river from Montreal, with Émilie's parents until the end of the 1840s.[32] Subsequent writers have followed suit, despite the lack of any evidence establishing either Krieghoff or the Gauthier family as resident in Longueuil. The Krieghoffs likely did live outside the city when they returned to Montreal in late 1845 or early 1846, since they weren't listed in the directory for another three years, but Cornelius certainly had a studio in town, as we can read in a neat, direct advertisement that appeared in *The Pilot* from 10 February to 24 November 1846. "CORNELIUS KRIEGHOFF, ARTIST," it states, with none of the pomposity of the Toronto ad of two years earlier, and only one typographical error, in his name, "No. 60, Bonaventure Street, Second Door above Prince Edward Lane."[33] We should expect that Krieghoff would have settled in Montreal. It was the largest city in British North America (about 45,000 in 1844), although the cultural significance of that figure was diminished by the fact that the population was divided almost six to four between the majority anglophones and francophones, communities that mingled least of all in matters of culture. It had been the commercial centre of the British portion of the continent for decades, with the fur trade based there, and in 1843 had become the capital of the Province of Canada. There were few artists in Montreal in 1846 (only two are listed in the city directory for 1845–6), but during the year they formed an association and organized an exhibition that opened in rooms at 25 Great St. James Street on 11 January 1847.

THE MONTREAL SOCIETY OF ARTISTS

The Montreal Gallery of Pictures, as the exhibition was called, provides both an evocative glimpse of artistic aspirations in the city at that moment and revealing evidence of Krieghoff's rapid development as an artist over the previous three years.[34] The organization, the Montreal Society of Artists, consisted of seven members and two honorary members when the exhibition opened in January 1847, and welcomed on its walls the work of eight other artists, mainly amateurs. Among the members were Krieghoff, James Duncan (1806–1881), a topographical artist and drawing master born in Coleraine, Londonderry, Ireland;[35] William F. Wilson (active 1842–54), an English-born landscape and portrait painter; William Sawyer (1820–1889), born and raised in Montreal, a portrait and genre painter;[36] and Martin Somerville (1796/7–1856), a drawing master, landscape and genre painter born in England, who settled in Montreal in 1839, and who at least as early as January 1846 was installed in rooms at 25 Great St. James Street, where the exhibition was held.[37] The two honorary members were Dr. Andrew A. Staunton (d. 1847), a topographical artist and portraitist who was an assistant surgeon in the British Army assigned to the Montreal garrison, arriving in September 1845 following a posting in Arabia, and Maj. Henry S. Davis (active 1818–47) of the 52nd Regiment.[38] All in all, the seventeen participants represented virtually the whole of the Montreal artistic community of the day. They were all anglophones (except Krieghoff, we might say), and, indeed, there is no evidence of any francophone artists in the city at the time.

Only three reviews have been located.[39] One, in *The Gazette*, is short, another in *La Minerve* shorter still. The latter simply mentions some names and lauds the idea of supporting art; the former singles out a few artists for specific praise, particularly Krieghoff, whose interiors, it is remarked, show "a great deal of merit" and especially his "officer's apartment…in which there is much skilful and characteristic grouping of inanimate objects, and great soundness and transparency of colouring, which, indeed, seems to be his leading characteristic."[40] The piece in *The Pilot*, in the form of a letter to the editor from a doctor who signs H.N., is much longer and more reflective. It devotes more attention to Krieghoff than to any of the others, remarking that even his numerous copies have been securing for him "the highest praise of the connoisseurs." In addition, his interiors are "the truest representations of home scenes in the room," and though his two subjects from Sir Walter Scott's "Abbott" are apparently unfinished, his *View near Boulogne* is "the best picture in the room."[41]

Turning to the catalogue, we can see that there were a large number of copies in the show and a relatively narrow range of subjects.[42] There were Canadian interiors by another artist as well as Krieghoff, and additional genre scenes by Somerville, Duncan, and Sawyer. *The Chief's Daughter* by Somerville appears to have been the only Native subject. A number of scenes depicted the rural French-Canadian habitants. Topographical views of the tropics by Davis and scenes of Mesopotamia by Staunton were balanced by a fair number of Canadian landscapes. Krieghoff exhibited forty-eight pieces (only four for sale), more than twice as many as anyone else. They included at least one painting from Rochester, the *Portrait of Thorwaldsen* after Bowman, and a fascinating group of works he

copied in Paris 1844–5. In the collection of contemporary art at the Musée du Luxembourg he had found *Romulus and Remus* by Champmartin, *Strolling Actors…* by Biard, *German Winter Scene…* by Wickenberg, and *Marine View— Moonlight* by Grolig, and at the Louvre he copied *Lot's Daughters* by Rubens, *Approaching Storm* by Ruysdael, *The Harvesters of the Roman Marshes* by Robert, and an elaborate fruit-and-flower piece based on several paintings. He also showed four paintings worked up from sketches by Dr. Staunton, and three copies after prints from the portfolio *Sketches in the Canadas* by Coke Smyth (an artist who accompanied Lord Durham to the Canadas in 1838), probably made the fall of 1846.[43] Then there are about six works listed as copies, including *The Alchymist* after Isabey, *Guitar Player* after Teniers, and *The Winetasters* after Hasenclever, that are not located to specific collections and likely are after prints. Finally, there are a number of other works, such as *The Artist's Studio*, *German Forester*, *Lighting His Pipe*, and *Italian Flower Girl*, that likely are based substantially or in part on popular prints.

A number of works by Krieghoff that were in the exhibition are known today, including *The Artist's Studio* (pl. 6), one of the copies after Staunton, likely *The Plains of Babylon* (pl. 9), a splendid original piece, *An Officer's Room in Montreal* (pl. 10), *Marine View—Moonlight* (after Grolig) (pl. 5), and *The Winetasters* (after Hasenclever) (pl. 7). In addition, an ambitious still life now in the Montreal Museum of Fine Arts (see pl. 8) likely is *Flower and Fruit Piece*, and another work can perhaps be identified with one of Krieghoff's original compositions in the exhibition, *Canadian*

Interior; a Friday's Surprise (see pl. 11). A closer look at some of these will demonstrate how much he learned while copying in Paris. *Marine View— Moonlight*, after a painting by Curt Grolig (1805–1863), who exhibited in the Paris Salon 1844–6, precisely when Krieghoff was there, offered a challenge to extend his skills. He developed proficiency in the use of glazes to maintain a broad and subtly shifting range of tone in dark areas, while also learning to register the precise "temperature" of light sources, distinguishing clearly among brilliant moonlight, partly filtered by clouds, and its reflection off water in one instance, or off the limp, heavy sails of a becalmed ship in another, or off the wet gunwhale of a rowboat in a third. This orchestration of cool silver is enhanced by a tiny counterpoint of weak, warm light glowing from a lantern in the bow of the boat, reflecting back on the upper body and face of the sailor who holds it. Although not yet what one could call a virtuoso performance, this skill in handling light will be exercised in later works with increasing confidence and ever more impressive effects.

The work that must have enthralled most visitors, however, was an original composition, *An Officer's Room in Montreal*. As Russell Harper has demonstrated, it depicts Dr. Staunton ensconced in his study, which he had creatively, if somewhat obsessively, arrayed with a multitude of fascinating objects that reflect his travels and other pursuits, both intellectual and physical. This sort of depiction of three sides and the floor and ceiling of a room, slightly splayed like a stage, which is then dressed with the accoutrements appropriate to a particular inhabitant, had

enjoyed a long tradition in Europe back to medieval times. Krieghoff's own fascination with the genre is reflected in a number of pieces in the 1847 exhibition, including *The Artist's Studio*, *The Alchymist*, *The Antiquarian*, and the series of Canadian interiors that would come to constitute a significant branch of his work in Montreal. The richness of *An Officer's Room...*, however, the almost overwhelming array of closely observed detail, puts it at the head of the list. Associates of the artist or of his subject would have discovered numerous fascinating conceits in the painting. At the most immediate level we see ample evidence of Staunton's interest in riding, hunting, and fishing, as well as his literary and artistic pursuits. A closer look reveals more specific information. The bust of Shakespeare, as Harper has pointed out, is associated with both Staunton's and Krieghoff's membership in the Shakspeare [*sic*] Club, a local dramatic, literary and debating society.[44] The stuffed birds in the upper reaches suggest an involvement in ornithology, and the number and quality of the Native artifacts displayed indicates more than an idle interest in souvenirs. An even closer look provides identification of the paintings on the walls.[45] A number of Arabian figures and landscapes are either by Staunton himself or are the Krieghoff copies shown in the 1847 exhibition. The middle picture in the stack of three on the left side over the bookcase, for instance, is a work shown in the exhibition as *The Plains of Babylon*. It has been suggested that the painting high on the wall above Staunton is *View of the City of Montreal from the Mountain* by Krieghoff, also in the exhibition.[46] Numerous other pieces seem to be

Krieghoffs (the large one on the left wall relates to his copy of the Wickenberg *German Winter Scene...* in the exhibition). Very attentive viewers would have been thrilled, certainly, to discover *An Officer's Room in Montreal* itself depicted in the painting in a place of prominence resting on the moose antlers high above the mantelpiece, as well as the clue to the owner of it all in the embroidered initials A.A.S. on the gloves on the floor at the corner of the desk. A demonstration of the fascination objects hold for us, of the power of possessions, it is as well in its loving, exquisite portrayal of such commonplace belongings as boots and skates and slippers a celebration of the intense pleasure to be found in close observation.

An *Officer's Room in Montreal* was one of six Canadian interiors shown by Krieghoff. Although we cannot now identify any others with certainty, they each were titled generically "Canadian Interior," and so we might imagine they were meant to be typical or characteristic rather than particular rooms. One was titled slightly more generously *Canadian Interior; a Friday's Surprise*, and perhaps can be identified with one of Krieghoff's most accomplished figure scenes of the time, a work known today as *Breaking Lent* (pl. 11). Presented in the form of a domestic stage, much like *An Officer's Room in Montreal*, it differs in the scale and number of figures and in its emphasis on dramatic narrative rather than the elaborate "dressing" of the set. The depiction of objects is important, nonetheless, but they are arranged into relatively discrete still-life groupings that, while conveying information about the inhabitants' domestic practices,

function as little virtuoso eye-pleasers on their own. The array of washing utensils in the lower right, for instance, the beautifully lit blanket coat lower left, and the pitcher positioned so exquisitely on the stove in thoughtful relationship to a small informal grouping of wall-hung objects are just the most obvious examples. We are drawn to linger pleasurably over a range of contained spaces in a similar fashion, each one, such as the enclosed transom to the left, the back passageway to the right rear, and the permeable space beneath the table and chairs, a complex visual poem articulated through the play of light, shade, and delicately nuanced colour. As pleasing as these elements are, however, they are but enrichments of the main focus of the painting, a domestic drama of the highest order as an obviously powerful, officious priest encounters a rustic French-Canadian family breaking the tradition of fasting during Lent. The interrelationship of the figures is skilful, as is the depiction of facial features, reflecting the range of responses to being caught in transgression. There is some humour in the scene, certainly, but it is far from broad, and we finally are left pondering authority and its place in the everyday world.

MONTREAL IMAGES OF HABITANTS

These "Canadian Interiors" remained an important theme in Krieghoff's work for at least the next three years. Many are relatively small, such as *A Game of Cards* of 1848 (pl. 13), and usually depict a simple room setting with little evidence of time or skill expended on creating either still-life

Figure 2
THE JEALOUS HUSBAND, c. 1847
oil on board, 36.2 × 27.8 cm
The Thomson Collection (P-C-538)

arrangements (there are usually only one or two carefully observed accoutrements) or ancillary spaces. The focus is very much on the figure groupings, of usually only three or four in these small pictures, and the narrative is consequently simpler, more emphatic, often broadly comic, as with the card player here revealing his hand to us while two of his companions dispute the game, or when an outraged father or a jealous husband comes upon a daughter or wife in the arms of a British soldier (see fig. 2). Such emphatic dramas demand more extreme facial gestures, of course, and these at times verge on caricature, combining exaggerated expressions with ethnic or class stereotypes.[47] Genre scenes of this sort were particularly popular in Britain, the United States, and much of northern Europe during the first half of the nineteenth century, reflecting the rise to prominence of the middle class, whose taste for such subjects extends back to seventeenth-century Holland. Positioning the work of American genre painters like William Sidney Mount (1807–1868) and Francis W. Edmonds (1806–1863), the art historian Elizabeth Johns has remarked that such paintings enjoyed their greatest popularity "during periods of economic and social change," when "new patrons and classes were on the move as well."[48] Krieghoff certainly was aware of this widespread interest, and in the late 1840s made a very polished copy of a small interior by the most famous genre painter of the day, the Scottish painter Sir David Wilkie (1785–1841) (see fig. 3).[49]

He was at times more ambitious with these interiors, and the most ambitious of all, the culminating work in the series, *Canadian Interior* of

Figure 3
THE CARD PLAYERS (after Wilkie), c. 1848
oil on board, 20.3 × 27.9 cm
Art Gallery of Ontario, Toronto, gift of Mrs.
Lorraine Dingman, Toronto, 1975 (74/387)

1850, in the Musée du Québec, is large, dramatically complex, and unique among his paintings in its clever play with shadows (pl. 15). It unfortunately was badly overcleaned in an early restoration, but we can still appreciate the creative imagination and painter's skills it once showcased so effectively. There are four sources of light in the picture—the candle on the table, the reflection of glowing coals in the iron stove, moonlight through the window, and behind the wall to the right the smoking ember at the tip of the wick of a recently snuffed candle, each influencing a portion of the painting with its distinct temperature, and each with its random reflections and dancing shadows contributing to the shifting, amorphous sense of the space of the room. The large shadow on the back wall dominates the image, at first absorbing our attention but then leading us to observe and reflect on the range of evening activities depicted that gives this particular interior its special quality of intimacy.

The other important habitant theme of Krieghoff's Montreal period is the sleigh scene, in which one or two country sleighs are shown stopped in a winter landscape while usually four or five, but sometimes as many as six or eight, travellers converse. Marius Barbeau's belief that Krieghoff lived with his wife's parents in what he perceived to be the rustic habitant setting of Longueuil during the first few years in the Montreal region, drawing on his immediate family for subject matter, has led some later writers to assume a high level of both documentary precision and personal revelation in these works. Russell Harper, for instance, seems to go even further than Barbeau in affirming that "the lively

Longueuil record, when isolated as a unit, is one of the most introspective documentations of life, society, customs, and topography of any single Canadian village."[50] Both Barbeau and Harper centred their conviction on a painting in the National Gallery of Canada, *The Ice Bridge at Longue-Pointe* of about 1848 (pl. 14), that until recently was known as *The Ice Bridge at Longueuil* (the church to the right has been identified from a nineteenth-century watercolour as the one at Longue-Pointe).[51] It was believed to be Longueuil because it was once owned by Henry Jackson, who worked for the St. Lawrence and Atlantic Railway, whose western terminus was there. Doubtless because Jackson (who was the grandfather of the Group of Seven painter A.Y. Jackson) is thought to have known Krieghoff personally, it has been surmised that some of the figures are depictions of the artist's immediate family.[52] We have as little reason to believe they are his relatives as we had to imagine the church was at Longueuil. That's not to say these are entirely imaginary landscapes, for their flat, open nature is characteristic of the region and the background is almost always recognizably the St. Lawrence River, and often, as is the case in *The Ice Bridge...*, with the familiar profile of Mount Royal and such prominent features of the Montreal skyline as the twin towers of Notre-Dame visible on the far shore. Unlike *An Officer's Room in Montreal*, these paintings are not about particular people or a specific place but about a particular kind of people in a localized region. The landscape and the climate, it should be stressed, are meant to provide an appropriate atmosphere for the presentation of the figures, and particularly their clothing, their sleighs and equipment, their horses, and their dogs. Just as much as the interiors, these outdoor scenes derive from a seventeenth-century tradition that was enjoying a vigorous revival throughout northern Europe, Britain, and settled North America. We know Krieghoff's model for these winter sleigh scenes, however—a painting now in the Louvre that he copied in the Musée du Luxembourg in Paris and showed at the Montreal Gallery of Pictures in January 1847 as *German Winter Scene: A Prussian Forester Talking to Children in a Sleigh*, by Petter Gabriel Wickenberg (1812–1846), a Swedish artist active in Paris when Krieghoff was there. Laurier Lacroix of the Université du Québec à Montréal, who traced the Wickenberg in the Louvre, where it is now known as *Winter Scene* (fig. 4), has also pointed out that what appears to be a depiction of Krieghoff's copy in *An Officer's Room in Montreal* shows only "the central part" of the original image, bringing the sleigh and figures into greater prominence.[53] That is more or less the scale of *The Ice Bridge...*, while *Habitant Sleigh, View near the Canada Line*, perhaps as early as 1846, shows an even more prominent sleigh and figures, though retaining a cottage and starkly bare tree to the right that is remarkably like the original (pl. 12).[54] It also shows a rock smashed in the ice, effectively rendered cracks and frozen bubbles, and broken blocks of ice scattered about, just like those we see in the Wickenberg, as does *Habitant Family with Horse and Sleigh* of 1850 (pl. 16). *Village Scene in Winter*, also of 1850, introduces a significant variation in the setting while retaining something closer to the scale of the original (pl. 17). What we have in them all, as exemplified in *...View near*

Figure 4
Petter Gabriel Wickenberg
WINTER SCENE, 1841
oil on canvas, 130.0 × 195.0 cm
Musée du Louvre, Paris, purchased from the
Salon of 1841 (8527)

the Canada Line, is a low horizon, vast sky, snow-covered, open landscape framed by rustic buildings and spare trees, in which is presented a very carefully described country sleigh, a typical horse of the region and its harness, and a number of figures displaying a variety of traditional Canadian headgear, types of habitant coats (two in this case), a woman's cloak, children's clothing, and a fur blanket. Once engaged by one of these paintings, we're fascinated by the information it provides and delighted by the graceful poise of its composition, its lucid, vibrant colour, the clarity of its forms, and the magnificently rendered sky providing an informing mood that compensates for the relative lack of interaction among the figures.

Krieghoff did not limit himself in his depiction of habitants outdoors to these groupings around sleighs, although they dominate his view of the subject. He also produced small pictures of typical tradesmen or seasonal labours, such as hauling blocks of river ice to storage for summer cooling (see fig. 22, page 159). And there are a few paintings from the Montreal period that focus on a particular type of rural structure, describing characteristic activity around it. The lovely *Cottage, St. Anne* of about 1850 in the Musée du Québec, a rare example of a summer scene, shows a family unloading a cart just returned from town or the fields and storing the supplies or produce in a cellar (pl. 18). The spectacular *White Horse Inn by Moonlight* of 1851, one of the largest paintings of the period as well as one of the most romantically dramatic, depicts a commercial coach on runners stopped at a rural inn at night to change horses and

refresh the passengers (pl. 19). Expressively moody, it is also rich with small incidents and carefully observed detail. Considerably more sophisticated in its depiction of the reflection of moonlight off various surfaces as well as of light from a number of sources than the copy after Grolig of some six years earlier, it also reveals a growing sophistication in the deployment of figures through a complex of interrelated spaces as passengers and inn staff are shown moving around the coach and horses and in and out of the inn and attached stable.

IMAGES OF NATIVES IN MONTREAL

We noted earlier that there appears to have been only one painting of a Native subject in the 1847 Montreal Gallery of Pictures exhibition, a work called *The Chief's Daughter* by Martin Somerville. Three years later, however, scenes of Native life had become almost as important a part of Krieghoff's production as his paintings of habitants. All his Native subjects seem to be from the period after the January 1847 exhibition, and none may date from before 1848. Natives were part of the life of Montreal, particularly Mohawks from the Caughnawaga (Kahnawake) Reserve on the south shore of the St. Lawrence at Lachine, about eleven kilometres upriver from the city. Women from Caughnawaga brought basketry, beadwork, and other traditional fine women's work into Montreal to sell, and a painting of the period that has been attributed to Krieghoff, but that may be by Somerville, shows such a vendor offering a pouch and highly decorated moccasins for sale in front of the building

Figure 5
A RED INDIAN WOMAN OUTSIDE THE
ARTIST'S STUDIO, c. 1849
oil on canvas, 31.8 × 23.5 cm
Collection of Peter Winkworth, London

in which both artists had their studios (see fig. 5).[55] François-Marc Gagnon discusses elsewhere in this volume the importance of images of Natives within both the francophone and anglophone communities in Canada, an importance that invariably reflects the interests of the image maker, of course, not of the subject. Occasionally Natives were able to place their issues before the public, however, and there was one such occurrence in March 1848 when a deputation of three Montagnais leaders from the Saguenay region, accompanied by interpreters and the local member of the Legislative Assembly, called on the governor general, Lord Elgin, with a petition decrying the state of poverty to which they had been reduced following the destruction of their traditional hunting and fishing grounds by lumbering and settlement. Their meeting with Lord Elgin and their specific demands, which included the designation of tribal lands and the receipt of some financial benefit from the three trading posts in the region, were reported in detail in the newspapers and extensively discussed. The reports in the French press also noted that Théophile Hamel (1817–1870), who had established his studio in the city just a few months earlier following three years of study in Europe, had painted a group portrait of the Montagnais delegation, a subject, as one said, that is "*palpitant d'intérêt*."[56] The painting, which was acquired by Lord Elgin at the time, shows the three Montagnais delegates and their interpreter, three of the four looking directly at the viewer, the central figure holding the petition face out so the text can be read (see fig. 6). Each of the Montagnais wears a Victoria medal on a ribbon around his

Figure 6
Théophile Hamel
MONTAGNAIS DELEGATION TO LORD
ELGIN, c. 1848
oil on canvas, 44.0 × 34.5 cm
Private collection

neck but otherwise no ceremonial garb. Dressed in blanket coats and the traditional soft pointed hats of their people, they appear far from exotic, and their features are portrayed sensitively with attention to their individuality.[57]

The earliest securely dated Native scene by Krieghoff is a print, a lithograph he had made after one of his paintings in New York in 1848 that was released for sale by its Montreal publisher probably late that summer.[58] *Indians and Squaws of Lower Canada*, as it was titled, shows quite large figures of a male hunter with a woman and baby stopped in a winter landscape in conversation with two other women, one of whom carries moccasins for sale. A dog, prominent in the foreground, looks on, three other figures in the distance move off to the right carrying loads, one pulling a toboggan, and in the far distance we see what appears to be the St. Lawrence with Mount Royal beyond (pl. 31). The image is in concept similar to the habitant sleigh scenes in which a chance encounter is the device to assemble a group in a characteristic landscape with the purpose of displaying a range of typical costumes and artifacts. Here the cradleboard and snowshoes are featured, as well as intricate details of the clothing. Two of the women are positioned so we see them full face, but in a manner that still connects them to the group. A number of oils of this theme survive, with variations in the positioning of the figures, their costumes and accoutrements, and as with the habitant sleigh scenes, the scale of the figures varies, although they usually are larger in their landscapes than are the habitants (see fig. 36, page 229).

The depiction of the native figures as essentially manikins for the display of exotic costumes relates these images to a practice widespread in Europe since the early eighteenth century of showing peasants of the various regions in their local costumes, a practice with which Krieghoff would have been familiar. This same practice had been applied to the depiction of Native North Americans for some time as well, most famously by Charles Bird King (1785–1862) and George Catlin (1796–1872) in the United States. The Toronto painter Paul Kane (1810–1871), inspired by Catlin, was in 1848 completing a tour of western British North America, systematically collecting images of the various Aboriginal nations, and although Krieghoff certainly didn't meet Kane when he lived in Toronto in 1844 (Kane was then residing in Mobile, Alabama), he likely would have read the news of his western trip that appeared in a Montreal paper in July 1848.[59]

Krieghoff's approach to the depiction of Natives was not as focused on either the portrayal of prominent leaders or the systematic cataloguing of different nations as was the work of King, Catlin, or as Kane would be. His few small paintings of individuals were seldom portraits. One splendid pair, in fact, resembles illustrative plates from a travel book, with the figures positioned to give the clearest description of clothing and gear (see pls. 24 and 25). We can see exactly how snowshoes are fastened, how moccasins are sewn, the details of a magnificent "octopus" pouch on the man's belt, the way a tumpline is used to carry a load, how mittens are fashioned, the details of basketry, both of birchbark and the woven variety, and a lovingly decorated cradleboard. The faces are generalized types. The occasional painting of a Native conveys more sense of individuality, such as the woman subject of *Caughnawaga Indian* with her red gemstone ring (pl. 27). But even when, more than a year after Hamel, Krieghoff took the opportunity of a visit of another Native delegation to Montreal to paint a portrait, he emphasized ceremonial costume rather than personality, and made no reference to the reason for the visit. Three Chippewa leaders from the north shore of Lake Superior called on Lord Elgin late in the spring of 1849 to protest the unlawful sale by the government of some of their traditional lands to copper and silver mining companies whose operations were driving out the game. We know from a report in *The Illustrated London News* that includes a reproduction of a drawing of the three delegates by Martin Somerville that Krieghoff's small oil is of *Nabunagoging (The Eclipse)*, although it is inscribed verso on the stretcher "Tanaghte/Young Chief from Lake Superior/Copper Mines," and is titled today *Chief Tanaghte, Delegate to Lord Elgin at Montreal* (pl. 26).[60] Only six years later *The Illustrated London News* published a reproduction of a painting by Krieghoff that is this image of Nabunagoging, with his red crane crest and large silver heart pendant, but wearing the headdress of one of the other delegates and carrying the club of the third in place of his ceremonial pipe. He is identified simply as "Iroquois Chief," and the accompanying article retails the story of the three delegates to Lord Elgin with the significant alteration of the nationality of the complainants from Chippewa to Iroquois.[61] Krieghoff's image evidently conveyed none of the specificity of Hamel's.

His most ambitious Native scenes of the Montreal period depict family groupings around a fire in summer, the Native equivalent, in a manner, of the Canadian Interior series. There is a group of these, and though only a couple are dated, they appear to run from about 1848 to 1850. The exception is *Caughnawaga Indian Encampment at a Portage*, which bears the date 1844, although that cannot be right: close examination shows that the date has been reinforced, and at whatever time that was done was misread (pl. 22). The purpose of the composition—large figures grouped about a campfire in front of an unconvincing wigwam in a forest setting that opens out to a distant view—is to present typical Natives of the Montreal region in a natural setting to emphasize their attachment to the land. The figures are stiff and manikin-like, as in the winter scenes, serving simply to support the display of clothing and artifacts. As in the habitant interiors, there are small still lifes here and there—a wonderfully crafted basket full of berries in the foreground near the dog, for instance—but also always focused studies of groupings of plants, as in the lower left corner here, or around the base of the tree against which the cradleboard leans. These are like virtuoso still lifes as well.

Writers have over the years speculated about where Krieghoff would have encountered Natives camping in this fashion in the Montreal region. Although we know from a convincing depiction of *Montreal from the Indian Encamping Ground* (fig. 7) in a print by James Duncan of 1844 that such scenes were certainly available a few years earlier, nothing in any of the Krieghoff paintings indicates that he worked from sketches

Figure 7
James Duncan
MONTREAL FROM THE INDIAN
ENCAMPING GROUND, 1844
lithograph, 25.6 × 37.0 cm (image)
Royal Ontario Museum, Toronto, gift of Dr.
Sigmund Samuel, 1950 (950.29.3)

done in the field. The settings themselves, as much as they contain close-ly observed plant life, are flat and contained, like an interior, but even more like a museum diorama, offering just enough space for the effective arrangement of the display. Also militating against the suggestion that these scenes are directly of nature is the fact that both the seated man and the little girl with the bird on a string in *Caughnawaga Indian Encampment at a Portage* are borrowed from Coke Smyth's portfolio *Sketches in the Canadas*, the former from the print titled *Indians Bartering*, the latter from *Zity a Huron Indian*.[62] The idea for *The Trader* of 1850 (pl. 29) also comes from Smyth's *Indians Bartering*, whose trader has the same hat, same coat, and is similarly kneeling while showing a blanket, although he is present-ed in three-quarters view from the front. The dog in the 1848 print is an exact copy of the one in Smyth's *Moos Hunter*. (Krieghoff also copied entirely another of Smyth's prints, *Indians of Lorethe*.)[63] The ridiculously frail branch supporting the heavy iron pot over the fire in *Caughnawaga Indian Encampment at a Portage* also belies direct experience, as does the flimsy twist of twigs fulfilling the same function in *A Caughnawaga Indian Encampment* of about 1848 (pl. 23), or the single twig in *Huron Indians at Portage* of 1850 (pl. 30). This last is the largest and, it would seem, culmi-nating image of the series. There is, as in all of them, intense delight in the foliage details (the ivy hanging from the rock at the left, for instance), and great pleasure to be had in examining the minutely described baskets, cradleboard, rifle, and here a fascinating whirligig held high by the eldest child. At this stage in the series, the landscape also is opening up, taking on more prominence. It clearly is no longer a broad symbol of nature but reflects knowledgeable observation in its convincingly portrayed mix of coniferous and deciduous trees on the distant hills.

THE MONTREAL PRINTS

By 1850 Krieghoff appears to have been producing a steady supply of paintings, quite a few of impressive scale. We don't know how many works he was selling. Barbeau was convinced that he "could hardly make a living with his work," and that his financial situation steadily declined in Montreal.[64] Beginning in 1848 he arranged the production of prints after his work, and ten in all were issued during the Montreal years from 1848, when, as we noted, the lithograph *Indians and Squaws of Lower Canada* appeared, until about 1850. That first print was published and distributed by a bookseller who also handled art supplies, John McCoy on Great St. James Street, and was printed by the firm of G. & W. Endicott in New York, having been transferred to the lithographic stone by C.G. Crehen. We don't know if Krieghoff travelled to New York to arrange this or if it was all set up by McCoy. At the same time Krieghoff had made arrangements to have the bookseller and print dealer R. & C. Chalmers, also on Great St. James Street, publish a set of four lithographs after his work. These were transferred to stone by A. Borum in Munich, one of the principal European centres for lithography, and were printed there by Thomas Kammerer. It doesn't seem possible that Krieghoff attended, although we can imagine he might have returned to Schweinfurt for a

visit after Paris in 1845, and perhaps gone on to Munich to establish contacts that were useful later. The first two of the four arrived in mid-October,[65] the other two a month later. Complete sets were offered in black and white or hand coloured.[66] It is a very grand production and was "published under the patronage of the Right Hon. the Earl of Elgin & Kincardine Governor General of British North America," as was proudly printed at the bottom of each impression and emblazoned across the top of the title card at the front of the portfolio (see fig. 45, page 283).[67] The four prints in the set include a Native scene, *Indian Wigwam in Lower Canada*, a typical summer scene with particularly strange wigwams (pl. 33), *French Canadian Habitans Playing at Cards*, a many-figured interior (pl. 32), *Sledge Race near Montreal*, which Harper claims actually shows Lord and Lady Elgin and two friends in a spectacularly elegant sleigh drawn by a team of four just leaving the south shore at Longueuil to cross the ice bridge to Montreal (pl. 35),[68] and *Place d'Armes à Montréal*, a splendid view across the central square of the city to the new Bank of Montreal building, with an array of elegant sleighs in the foreground (pl. 34).

The title card for *Scenes in Canada* notes at the bottom Krieghoff's intention to publish the following year a second series of lithographs after his paintings. Although no newspaper announcement has yet been found, Peter Winkworth, the author of the standard study of the prints, argues convincingly for their appearance in 1849.[69] While the prints of *Scenes in Canada* are grandly elegant in appearance and one imagines would have appealed to civic pride as well as to the souvenir-seeking tourist, this next set of four is more humble. Only two of the four bear letterpress, telling us they were produced by Sarony & Major of New York. No credit is given for the transfer to stone, but the work is loose, almost sketchy, so different from the firm, well-modelled forms of Borum but not unsuited to their much more modest scale. The two titled works show seasonal labour, *Ice Cutting* and *Sugar Making in Canada* (pls. 36 and 37). The other two show yet another Native scene, in winter again but with only three figures (see pl. 38), and a Native man portaging a canoe (see pl. 39). They usually are found hand coloured.

Krieghoff's last Montreal print, *French Church, Place d'Armes, Montreal*, returns to the grand scale of the Borum lithographs (pl. 40). Produced again by Sarony & Major in New York before 1857, when the firm changed its name, and likely in 1850 or the following year, it is quite a bit tighter in rendering than the four smaller scenes. Depicting the great parish church built from 1823 to 1829, the largest religious structure in North America at the time, that sits across Place d'Armes from the Bank of Montreal, the print was probably popular with a fairly broad range of the citizenry of the city, although another view of the church had been published in Montreal about three years earlier.[70]

BUSINESS PARTNERS, PATRONS, AND FRIENDS IN MONTREAL

Krieghoff's ambitious print production (far more over that period of two years or more than that of the two or three other artists in the city who issued prints) was paralleled, it seems, by his efforts to sell paintings. *The Winetasters* (after Hasenclever), which was first shown in the Montreal Gallery of Pictures exhibition, was offered by the bookseller Campbell Bryson just before Christmas 1847, although this may have been a resale, as Krieghoff's name is not mentioned in the advertisement.[71] It's more likely he took the initiative earlier in the year, in April, to include three of his paintings in the exhibition of the Toronto Society of Arts, and then to have works left for sale in that city with the book and print dealers Scobie and Balfour.[72] His work was included in a sale by the Montreal auctioneer John Leeming for the first time, it seems, in February 1848, two paintings, *The Astrologer* and *An Old Habitant*, but it is not clear from the advertisement that Krieghoff himself consigned them.[73] A relationship had developed with Leeming by the fall of 1849, and "about twelve" of Krieghoff's paintings were offered at a sale in November, certainly by arrangement with the artist.[74] In February 1850 Leeming showed thirty-one Krieghoffs at the Eighth Annual Festival of the Montreal Mechanics' Institute. If he was thought to be anything other than Krieghoff's agent by this point, all doubts would have been dispelled when he offered forty pieces in a sale devoted exclusively to the artist just seven days later.[75] Perhaps as a marketing device the advertisement concludes with this cryptic statement: "In consequence of arrangements entered into by Krieghoff, these will, in all probability, be the last of his works which can be procured in Montreal."

Krieghoff participated in the Provincial Industrial Exhibition held in Montreal in October 1850, showing "a fine display of oil paintings...

representing the Indians of Canada, in various groups and employments, also sleighing, marketing, and other scenes familiar to the inhabitant of Canada."[76] These paintings seem not to have been in competition, although Krieghoff did win a prize in another category, for painting on cast-iron tables![77] Although Leeming was the Montreal secretary for the Provincial Industrial Commission that organized the exhibition, it is likely that Krieghoff took the initiative to participate, just as he certainly had when he contributed a work to the Western Art-Union in Cincinnati, Ohio, the year before.[78] A year after the Provincial Industrial Exhibition, in September 1851, it was clear that Leeming no longer represented Krieghoff when the cast-iron table was offered with "a collection of Paintings and Sketches in Oil, by 'Krieghoff,'" and numerous prints from his collection and crayon drawings by Frederick W. Lock in an exclusive sale by Scott & Glassford Auctioneers in a hall above the famous Dolly's Chop House on Great St. James Street.[79] This was followed in early October by the inclusion of "a number of paintings by Mr. Krieghoff not disposed of at his last sale" in a general art auction held by Fisher & Armour.[80] The same firm handled what was his last Montreal sale, in June 1852, when it was advertised that "Mr Krieghoff's stock will on this occasion surpass any former one in design."[81] As unclear as this phrase is, it at least attests to the high profile Krieghoff enjoyed at this point, as does in its own way the fact that a few months later, in September 1852, the mother of a former mayor of Toronto proudly displayed in an exhibition showcasing local collections in that city a work by Krieghoff that we now know is a fake.[82]

That Krieghoff clearly enjoyed a level of celebrity in Montreal by 1852 was not simply the consequence of the aggressive marketing of his prints and paintings but acknowledgement of his status as a respected cultural figure. To understand him better in that role we must look more closely at the special connections that flowed from his commissions, both public and private, and his more immediate circle of friends and business associates. Chief among these latter must be numbered the other artists in the city, and as we've noticed, Krieghoff appears to have enjoyed a close relationship with Martin Somerville over the years, with their studios in the same building and both apparently teaching part-time at the Misses Plimsolls' young ladies school from about 1847 to 1850.[83] Of the other members of the Montreal Society of Artists, only James Duncan and William Sawyer were still in the city by the end of 1848, and Sawyer was away for long periods travelling from Quebec to Toronto as an itinerant portraitist.[84] There were new artists, of course, including the already mentioned Théophile Hamel from Quebec, and Frederick W. Lock (active 1843–60). An English-born landscape artist and portraitist who worked mainly in watercolour and pastel, he settled in the city probably late in 1849, just in time to be included in the 5 February 1850 Mechanics' Institute Festival, where his work attracted attention.[85] Krieghoff made copies of some of Lock's views of Niagara Falls, and they were featured together in the September 1851 sale over Dolly's Chop House. But the artist Krieghoff was most closely involved with by this time was Duncan. The advertisement for that sale with Lock noted, "As Mr. Krieghoff is preparing to commence painting the *Panorama of Canada* and must necessarily relinquish the painting of minor subjects, the above sale will be the last opportunity which the public will have of purchasing the works of this artist." This panorama had been announced in mid-July as a joint venture of Krieghoff and Duncan, a huge painting that was meant to present all the principal scenic sites along the St. Lawrence and on the Great Lakes.[86] Panoramas, either wrapped around part of a large hall or on great rolls that could be spooled out for the viewing of a seated audience during an evening, were extremely popular at that moment, what could be called a public craze. Famous panoramas toured the continent, and a number passed through Montreal, including in June 1850 Brewer's moving panorama that featured views of Niagara and the Mammoth Caves of Kentucky, as well as scenes along the Nile, Lewis's Colossal Panorama of the Mississippi in May 1851, Bayne's Gigantic Illuminated Panorama, *A Voyage in Europe*, in September 1851, and Craven's moving panorama of August 1852, which with sound and lights transported its audience from Philadelphia to the West Indies, on to Brazil and around Cape Horn, and up the Pacific coast to the California gold fields.[87] It was probably Lewis's Mississippi panorama that gave Krieghoff the confidence to launch such a project himself, as he had assisted with repairs to it in June, contributing "considerable improvement in the Indian sketch," as was reported at the time.[88] We hear no more in Montreal of Krieghoff and Duncan's panorama plans, however, after September 1851.

More important to Krieghoff during the Montreal years than the panorama project proved to be were the numerous associations he established through private commissions and the more public commissions these connections inevitably assisted. Among the earliest must have been when in 1846 he painted for the Hon. Edward Hale "portraits" of Sleepy Hollow, the house he had built a dozen years earlier on the St. Francis River near Sherbrooke, and three other Hale homes; the Seigneury at Sainte-Anne-de-la-Pérade, which his father, the Hon. John Hale, had acquired about 1790, and where Edward had been in part raised; the Plantation, Yorkshire, built by Gen. John Hale for his bride about 1763, and where the Hon. John Hale was born; and King's Walden, Hertfordshire, where Gen. John Hale was born. The Hale family was remarkably well connected within the British military and colonial administration, both in Britain and in Canada, where they decided to settle. Edward entered colonial service as a young man, serving as secretary to his uncle, Lord Amherst, when he was governor general of India, returning to Canada to become justice of the peace, later receiving an appointment to the Legislative Council, and ultimately elected speaker. He was a good person to know. The four paintings, now in the McCord Museum of Canadian History, vary considerably in quality. Only one is signed (and dated), the *Seigneury at Sainte-Anne-de-la-Pérade* (pl. 41). It is painted in a fine, delicate style, with the foliage of the impressive elm that dominates the image rendered extremely well. Almost as fine is *King's Walden, Hertfordshire* (pl. 42). Although not signed, it is undoubtedly Krieghoff's work. The

Figure 8
JUDGE JOHN FLETCHER, c. 1848
oil on canvas, 33.0 × 27.3 cm
Private collection, Ottawa

same cannot be said for the other two paintings. All four houses were painted from prints or drawings, the *Seigneury* from sketches made by Edward's mother, Elizabeth (1774–1826), who was a competent topographical artist active in Quebec City garrison circles in the previous generation.[89]

There are a number of "portraits" of fancy sleighs and their owners that date from the Montreal period as well, and Harper has concluded from their provenance that Krieghoff also enjoyed the patronage of, among others, Col. Augustus Heward, a wealthy local merchant, and the Hon. John Molson, one of the most influential Montreal businessmen of the time.[90] He seems not to have sought, or at least not to have enjoyed, much patronage as a portraitist in the usual sense. There is, in fact, only one portrait from life of the Montreal period we can be sure was commissioned, of *Dr. Daniel Arnoldi*, ordered in 1847 by the newly created College of Physicians and Surgeons of Lower Canada to honour him as its first chancellor. Slightly larger than the portraits of the Toronto Williamsons, it approaches them in conception if not quite in finish.[91] Another 1847 portrait, of Lord Metcalfe, who had served in Montreal as governor general (1843–5) but only briefly owing to illness, is a stiff copy of an 1844 print after a portrait by Alvah Bradish that may have been a commission, although Harper makes a case for it being the means by which Krieghoff gained membership in the Shakspeare Club (see pl. 44).[92] Two modest but engagingly intimate paintings, *Judge John Fletcher* and *Mrs. Fletcher and Her Great-Niece, Emily Fletcher*, not a pair but presumably commissioned close together, are probably from 1848 (figs. 8 and 9).

Figure 9
MRS. FLETCHER AND HER GREAT-NIECE, EMILY FLETCHER, c. 1848
oil on canvas, 39.4 × 30.5 cm
Private collection, New York

Figure 10
JOHN BUDDEN, 1847
oil on canvas, 58.4 × 73.7 cm
Private collection, Toronto

A pair of roughly the same size as the Fletcher paintings, which I haven't seen, of John Leeming and his wife, Sarah, probably date from 1849 or '50.[93] These latter two may have been painted in payment for services, or in friendship. Also of ambiguous motive is another small work of 1847, a full-length portrait of *Lt. Robert McClure*, who would go on to fame and knighthood a decade later for his service in the high Arctic (pl. 43). He had been to the Arctic already in 1836, followed by service on the Great Lakes in the wake of the rebellion, and so his connection with Krieghoff likely was through the Montreal garrison. What is curious is that his bulky fur coat, sealskin trousers, fur hat, muffler and bear-like fur gloves, and the St. Lawrence looking like an Arctic wasteland, evoke both his earlier experience there and his future exploits. The only reference to Montreal is the "octopus" pouch he wears. It's not clear what the Bavarian long-stemmed meerschaum pipe alludes to.

The one great portrait of the Montreal period also dates from 1847. Of the Quebec City auctioneer John Budden, it is informal yet classically elegant (see fig. 10). In an oval format, Budden is shown in hunting gear, sitting on the ground with his legs extended and one arm behind, his body turned three-quarters away from the viewer, his face in profile. His dog sits on his far side, and a wonderful still life of beaver hat, gun, and hunting sack secures the lower left. The details of his footwear and clothing, as well as his features, are superb. The landscape setting is cursory yet warmly earthy. Budden is clearly a man content within himself and comfortable in nature. If this was Krieghoff's answer to a commission, it was brilliant, but it seems more likely to have been a response to a friend.

One of the reviews of the 1847 Montreal Gallery of Pictures exhibition mentions that Krieghoff was "now engaged completing a picture of Queen Victoria, intended for the Legislative Assembly," which was expected to be ready in time to hang in the exhibition for a few days.[94] We don't know if it was in the exhibition, but it seems to have been installed in the reading room of the Legislative Council by July, when the Montreal correspondent of the *Journal de Québec* took exception to its poor quality.[95] A copy of a famous painting of Victoria in her coronation robes by Sir George Hayter (1792–1871), it apparently was donated to the government by a nephew of James McGill,[96] the Scottish-born philanthropist whose fortune originated in the fur trade. That would be Peter McGill, who was president of the Bank of Montreal, the widely acknowledged unofficial leader of the Montreal business community involved in a range of enterprises, including railways (he was Molson's competitor), and member of the Legislative Council, elected speaker in May 1847. The portrait hung in the Parliament Buildings until the evening of 25 April 1849, when a Tory mob in opposition to the Rebellion Losses Bill, which, more than ten years after the rebellion, sought to compensate all citizens for loss regardless of political stripe, rioted and burned down the Parliament. It subsequently was decided to move the seat of government out of Montreal, and in a peculiarly Canadian compromise the decision was made to alternate it between Toronto and Quebec until a permanent capital was chosen. Toronto was first, and the government officially moved in November in preparation for a mid-May opening of the legislature. Needless to say, panic struck Montreal.

Just how intensely concerned some of the artists were with the loss can perhaps be taken from the response to a news item in the Montreal *Gazette* of 25 October 1849, in which Hamnett Pinhey of Bytown (Ottawa) announced his intention to use £100 awarded him as a local official in appreciation for his service to commission a copy of the portrait of Queen Victoria that had been rescued from the burning Parliament. He meant a painting by Sir John Partridge (1790–1872) that hung in the Legislative Assembly, and whose rescue from the flames was reported in the newspapers. The next day both Duncan and Krieghoff wrote Pinhey, each offering Peter McGill as a reference. Krieghoff pointed out that "two paintings were saved, the one I painted almost without damage and the one painted by Partridge very much damaged." He went on, "I can copy either & from my being knowing throughout Canada, I need not say that I think my self qualified." With what we already have discovered is a typical Krieghoff pressure tactic, he concluded, "For want of employment I was to leave next week for N. York; if therefore my services may be desirable I would request respectfully to send your answer to Mr. McCoy Bookseller, Great St. James Street."[97] Duncan had also sent a letter to McGill, who dutifully wrote to Pinhey in his support, but the commission went to George Theodore Berthon of Toronto.[98]

The advertisement for the big Leeming sale of Krieghoff's work in February 1850 had similarly ended with a note of urgency, suggesting circumstances were shaping up that would remove his work from the Montreal market. Certainly he must have been considering any number of options, although he kept working in Montreal at least until early 1852, latterly, presumably, on the panorama. He is listed in the 1852 Montreal city directory, "corrected in May," resident at Barclay Place. *White Horse Inn by Moonlight* is one of only two known works dated 1851.[99] Did the panorama project, of which no trace has survived, consume all his energy? His parents were visiting during this period, arriving possibly as early as the summer of 1850 and leaving likely spring 1852, which would have taken up some time.[100] There are only four known works dated 1852. One is a copy after the fashionable English artist John Frederick Herring (1795–1865).[101] The second, a painting now called *Fiddler and Boy Doing Jig*, which surfaced some years ago in Germany, is reportedly inscribed on the back of the canvas "Montreal 1852, von onkel [from uncle] Cornelius Krieghoff" (pl. 20).[102] Uncharacteristic in the size of its figures and its high degree of finish, it may have been painted expressly for his parents to take back to Schweinfurt. The third and fourth paintings are *Montmorency Falls in Winter, Quebec* (fig. 26, page 161), and *Sleigh Race on the St. Lawrence at Quebec* (pl. 21). That Krieghoff was travelling again in the early 1850s there can be no doubt. Whether it was simply down the St. Lawrence to gather images for the Panorama of Canada or farther afield we can't say.[103] There is a Krieghoff listed in the 1853 Montreal city directory in a house on Aylmer, but only the surname is given. Could this be his brother, or perhaps his wife and daughter

alone? Even if it is our artist, we know he soon would move yet again, to Quebec, where he is recorded in that city's directory in May 1854.

QUEBEC

The main outline of the story of Krieghoff's Quebec years that has come down to us derives from John Budden's reminiscences to Fairchild a half-century after the fact. Perhaps as a consequence, Budden looms very large in the tale. It was at his "instigation" that Krieghoff moved to Quebec "about 1853," we read in the 1907 version, "and both took up their residence in a most picturesque little cottage at Mount Pleasant."[104] In his last word on Krieghoff, published in 1962, Barbeau was even more emphatic than Fairchild regarding Budden's role: "The prevailing influence on him from now on no longer remains Louise [as Barbeau understood his wife Émilie's name to be], who vanishes almost completely from the scene. The role is transferred to John Budden, his patron and friend with whom he enjoyed a gay existence from 1855 to 1864."[105] Budden very likely did encourage Krieghoff to move to Quebec. While we must remain skeptical of Barbeau's reading of Émilie and her family at Longueuil as the essential subject of the Montreal period habitant scenes, there is much evidence, as we will see later, that the Budden social circle became both Krieghoff's own circle and the subject of a significant portion of his art. At the same time, he probably would have moved to Quebec even without Budden's encouragement. The city was in 1853 attractively picturesque, with even then an air of antiquity unusual for

North America. Almost as large as Montreal at a population of some 58,000, close to 40 per cent anglophone (as opposed to the then slightly more than 50 per cent anglophone component of Montreal's population), it was the military headquarters for British North America, the centre of the all-important timber trade with Britain, the location of a burgeoning new shipbuilding industry, and since October 1851 had been the seat of government for the Province of Canada, a position it would retain until the capital moved again to Toronto early in 1855. And Krieghoff already had a certain presence in Quebec, as his full-length portrait of Queen Victoria (after Hayter) hung to the right of the governor general's throne in the Council Chamber of the newly renovated and sumptuously furnished Legislative Building, opposite a *George IV* after Sir Thomas Lawrence by Joseph Légaré (1795–1855) that hung to the left.[106]

LANDSCAPE IN QUEBEC

That at least one trip to Quebec, which we earlier noted documented in two paintings, was probably in pursuit of images for the Panorama of Canada project is borne out by a notice in a Quebec newspaper more than three years later. "Mr Krieghoff," it reports, "an artist who has resided in Canada for some years, and has attained considerable celebrity, from his happy mode of treating Canadian subjects generally, and particularly his sketches of Indian life, sleighing, and other incidents peculiar to our climate and habits, is now preparing a Panorama, which will embrace the whole of the prominent points of the scenery on the St.

Lawrence, from Lake Erie to the Saguenay."[107] The following February he addressed a formal petition to the government, seeking financial aid to complete the "Panorama and a series of Tableaux in oil descriptive of Canada, and containing views of the principal cities and picturesque spots along the St. Lawrence, Ottawa and tributaries Richelieu St. Maurice St. Francis Saguenay, and the Lakes."[108] The project when complete would "comprise no less than two hundred and fifty pictures, many of which he has already finished, or is on the point of finishing," as well as a publication "containing many illustrations and giving a description both historical and statistical of this country." He concluded by underlining "the advantages which will accrue to Canada from the exhibition in England, France, Germany and other European states of Paintings of this nature, shewing as they will the various public works of this Province, large lumbering establishments, the various branches of industry of its inhabitants, and thus calling the attention of a better class of Emigrants to a country so rich in resources and yet so little known to Foreigners." This was not the first such petition the government had received from an artist. In the mid-forties an intermediary sought financial assistance for Hamel to complete his studies at Rome, and Légaré hoped to sell a portrait of Queen Victoria, and in 1850 and again the following year Kane sought help to finish a great cycle of paintings of Native life in the northwest.[109] Krieghoff's petition was tabled in the Legislative Assembly 3 March 1856, but was never acted on. That same session there was discussion whether Kane had complied with the conditions of the grant he had been given five years earlier, which may have affected consideration of Krieghoff's request, as would the decision that was also made to subscribe to 140 copies of W.S. Hunter's "Ottawa Scenery," the first volume of a series on Canadian scenery this artist was planning.[110]

Krieghoff never did publish his proposed volume, and as mentioned earlier, no trace of the panorama has ever been found.[111] He did, however, turn a considerable portion of his energies in Quebec to landscape, both as a more prominent component of his habitant and Native scenes and as a pursuit in and of itself. Very soon after settling in the city, he declared his ambition in this direction with a spectacular canvas, one of the largest he would ever paint, of the ice cone at Montmorency Falls, a winter phenomenon that formed from the mist that rose from the open, rushing falls on the frozen St. Lawrence just below Quebec. It was a favourite gathering spot for those enjoying a sleigh ride on a bright winter day, and the festive nature of the scene had been attracting artists since before the turn of the century. More recently a local artist named Robert Todd (1809–1866) had made something of a specialty of "portraits" of fancy sleighs in front of the Montmorency cone, but Krieghoff's picture, not only by its size but in its sense of scale—the number and variety of figures and the care devoted to the expansive landscape setting—was calculated to outdo all the competition (see pl. 45).[112]

Also not long after settling in Quebec Krieghoff turned his hand to another long-favoured scene of the region, a wide view of the city from the Pointe-Lévis shore across the river. The image must have been popular because he painted two versions that year and two more later in his decade in Quebec. We don't know which of the first two, *Quebec Viewed from Pointe-Lévis*, now in the Musée du Québec (pl. 46), or *Quebec from Pointe-Lévis*, in the Royal Ontario Museum in Toronto (pl. 47), he painted first. The former was acquired by Lt. Alfred Torrens of the 66th Regiment probably not long after it was painted. The early provenance of the other is unknown. The topographical portions of the two paintings—the actual view of the city with all its principal structures picked out in brilliant light—is virtually identical, as are the general proportions of sky to middle ground to foreground. The arrangements of the ships on the river are similar, with only small variations here and there, and the basic conception of the landscape is the same in both as well, with bands of dark alternating with light, bridged by dark trees that pull us into the picture.[113] The foregrounds, roughly the lower third of each canvas, are dissimilar, however. Both employ traditional picturesque elements and structure, but the dominant framing tree is on the left side of one and on the right of the other, and the "staffage," or small figures to set scale, are entirely different. Virtually every element of the foregrounds reflects a rethinking.

Such views of the city and nearby sights would have appealed to both visitors and residents, and Krieghoff had prints made of both Montmorency and his city view, one at the beginning of his Quebec decade and the other at the end. He also continued to paint the expected scenes and numerous versions of every waterfall within visiting distance are known, reflecting a touristic canon that by the mid-fifties was securely established.[114] His *Falls of Lorette, near Quebec* (pl. 48), an 1854 view of the small village situated on the edge of a rushing wide arc of falling water that was at the heart of the Huron reserve northwest of the city shows a bourgeois couple, clearly visitors, standing at the preferred vantage point taking in the full force of the spectacle. A superb pair of paintings in close to original condition recently acquired by the National Gallery of Canada show the falls on the St. Anne River, one from above, where the water is sucked into a deep crevice (see pl. 50), the other from below, the falls viewed from across the chasm as the water splashes its way in myriad paths to collect as a river again at the bottom (see pl. 51). A bourgeois couple is shown enjoying the scene above, while a local habitant builds a small fire at the far right, perhaps to prepare refreshment. In the view below the falls a tiny figure of an artist, his portfolio tucked under his arm, leans against a blasted tree on the edge of the precipice, better to absorb the sublime power of the experience.

Later in the decade Krieghoff moved on to waterfalls farther afield, and there is a group of such works painted in expansive oval formats that may have been conceived as a series. These include *The Artist at Niagara*, as one of 1858 is now called (pl. 54), *The Chaudière*, also of 1858 (pl. 55), depicting the "Big Kettle" on the Ottawa River at Ottawa, and *Jam of Sawlogs, Shawinigan Falls* of 1861 (pl. 59), the "upper most fall in the little Shavanagan R.," as an inscription on one spandrel reads, "near the Great falls at Shavanagan St. Maurice 25 miles above Three Rivers,

Canada." The first two show their respective cascades against spectacular sunset skies, each with a tiny solitary figure in the lower left, an artist in both cases, recording the spectacle for posterity. The third view shows a sport fisherman in a similar position, but intent on the task at hand rather than appreciating the powerful torrent. He is oblivious even, it seems, to the wreckage of sawlogs, some near him of enormous size, that litter the shore and rocks precariously all around. The bush bordering the river is painted in minute detail, yet composed in broad movements of light and dark and laced through with intricate depictions of the specific hue and texture of various species in a magnificent orchestration of natural effects.

One painting that is a "pure" landscape with no figures at all, *The Passing Storm, St. Féréol* of 1854 (pl. 49), is a waterfall too, an early example. It has survived in particularly fine condition, allowing us to appreciate fully the painting skills Krieghoff had developed by this time. The brushwork in the rocks should be noted for the way it combines a descriptive function—sensitively following forms in nuanced detail—with an expressive intent. We can't but empathize with the artist's struggle to achieve the essence of a particular surface's texture and indeed the rich proliferation of detailed descriptions—of the fallen branch in the lower left or the trapped log in the river lower right, for instance—constantly brings us to an awareness of the artist's hand as much as to delight in the "actuality" of an object or focused situation caught in complex confluence of space and time. When we step back, the whole composition works similarly with its broad sweeps of light and shadow creating an engaging interrelationship of forms that is both descriptive and expressive, expertly capturing that exquisite mix of fear and pleasure that the late eighteenth century defined as "the sublime." Add to this the complex colour harmonies he achieves, here largely in brown and tan and green and red, all played through a remarkably broad range of tones, and we have a work of art that barely acknowledges the topographical function in its pursuit of pure delight in colour, form, and texture.

Krieghoff became more deeply engaged by the formal aspects of his landscape paintings after the middle of the decade, but seldom with the emotive dimension found in *The Passing Storm, St. Féréol*. We can, in fact, distinguish a whole category we might call decorative landscapes, not works of a lesser artistic order necessarily, but paintings meant to please primarily with the richness of their visual effects. There are always figures in these, but their scale is reduced and their narrative role too is diminished to that essentially of staffage. In a painting like *In the Jardin de Caribou, below Quebec* of 1856 (pl. 53), we're caught up immediately with the strong lines of tree trunks, upright and fallen, of intersecting hills, and of fractures in the ice, that, playing off the decorative circular "tondo" shape of the painting, concentrate our gaze on the tiny figures that are held, and with none of the threatening connotations my image evokes, like a butterfly in a spider's web. They are decorative elements too, and though we are delighted with such touches as the colourful horse blanket, our eyes are soon drawn back into the endlessly engaging, sustaining, complex order of the surrounding landscape.

A later version of the theme, *In the Jardin de Caribou, 50 Miles below Quebec* of 1861 (pl. 58), although with its beautifully executed figures engaged in a slightly more complex narrative, works in essentially the same way. This time the painting is rectangular rather than circular; being only slightly taller than wide, it is still pleasingly decorative, and the strong lines in the composition play off the shape in a manner that is just as involving as in the tondo. The most ambitious of these decorative landscapes is also rectangular, and fairly large, almost a metre wide. Called now *Landscape with Deer and Doe* (pl. 61), it is almost a pure landscape, although the dramatic nature of its little narrative, with the startled animals caught just before they take flight, places a lot of tension at one spot in the composition, tension that is reinforced by the dominant lines, and that finally is just barely balanced by the luminous atmospheric effect across the lake to the right. Krieghoff himself probably would not have seen these decorative landscapes as a distinct aspect of his work. His scenes of habitant and Native life of the Quebec period also reveal growing interest in the formal elements of picture making. One of the most unabashedly decorative of all his paintings is in fact a rendering on a platter-like oval support of one of the more popular of his Native themes, the portage at Grand'Mère Falls, with the picture set in the centre of a tilt-top table, surrounded by a wreath of preserved autumn maple leaves (see pl. 57).[115]

Another trend in his landscapes of the mid-fifties to early sixties is the increasing representation of evidence of human industry, the antithesis, really, of the idealizing of nature inherent in the decorative urge. Krieghoff could have found ample evidence of such industry around Montreal in the late forties, but chose not to represent it, and it crept into his work slowly. There is what could be one stranded sawlog perched on a table rock to the left in *The Chaudière*, only the slightest acknowledgement of the wealth of timber that flooded down the Ottawa every year and that had already by 1858 resulted in structures that significantly altered the appearance of the river. *Jam of Sawlogs, Shawinigan Falls* of 1861, a picture of a site in another major centre of the lumber industry, reflects that reality more directly.

The *Falls of Lorette...* includes prominently in the upper right a depiction of the mill that was one of the main reasons for the location of the village at the falls, and certainly *The Tubular Bridge at St. Henry's Falls* of 1858 is as much, if not more, about the Grand Trunk Railway bridge that crosses the Etchemin River so dramatically just above the falls than it is a picture of the falls itself (pl. 56). The third and fourth views of Quebec that were mentioned earlier show an even more dramatic change in Krieghoff's approach to industry, although it is clearly a response to actual change in the landscape. Little more than a year or so after the completion of the two 1853 views, in November 1854, a railway station was opened at Pointe-Lévis to serve a line that had been constructed by the Grand Trunk Railway to Richmond on the St. Francis River in the

Eastern Townships, there to link with the old St. Lawrence and Atlantic (by then leased by the Grand Trunk) running between Longueuil and Portland, Maine, on the Atlantic coast. *View of Quebec from the Grand Trunk Railway Station at Pointe-Lévis* of 1856 is hardly a view of Quebec at all (pl. 52). The Citadel and city below have slipped into the background, become simply one of a ring of natural features to set off the sunbathed docks of the terminus at the centre of the painting. The station was destroyed by fire in December 1856, and the adjacent hotel in April 1859, so his fourth version of the theme, *View of Quebec City from Pointe-Lévis* of 1863, is different again (pl. 64). The hotel, station, and adjacent docks are all larger and extend over a greater area, and as though to soften their impact Krieghoff has blocked our view of a portion of the switching yard with foreground trees and moved the Citadel and Quebec forward slightly into the light, a little more into the picture.[116] The upper corners were once arched, which would have enhanced the sense of the reintegration of the city with its transportation hub on the opposite shore, while still leaving no doubt where the heart of the business beat.

PATRONS, FRIENDS, AND BUSINESS ARRANGEMENTS IN QUEBEC

Although we don't know their early provenance, it seems not unreasonable to imagine one or both of the later Quebec views were commissioned by railway interests. Another painting that certainly would have been commissioned is *The Steamship Quebec* of 1853 (pl. 65), of a ship that plied between Montreal and Quebec for the Royal Mail and People's Line.[117] A powerful image of progress in transportation technology, it is at the same time a celebration of Quebec's place in the modern world (we see the trademark Citadel exquisitely picked out on the far horizon), and a bold announcement of Krieghoff's arrival in his new home. It is a remarkably fresh effort at a highly conventional form, the marine view or ship's portrait, and in another commission within the first year and a half or so of his arrival he demonstrated his skill with yet another conventional form, the equestrian portrait. *Fraser, with Mr. Miller Up* (pl. 67) was commissioned by a W. Kirwin, probably following his horse's win of the hurdle race on the Plains of Abraham, upriver of the Citadel, in August 1854.[118] As with the marine, Krieghoff has demonstrated his considerable painting skills in a variety of textures, and in the convincing delineation of forms, while conveying as well a remarkable sense of locale. In addition he has served up candid portraits of both Fraser and Mr. Miller.

Krieghoff had some prior experience with equestrian portraits (as he also did, through copying, with marines), with the painting of sleighs and their equipage and owners on the St. Lawrence ice in front of Montreal in the late forties, and that practice continued in Quebec. A modest but very fine example was commissioned by Lt. Alfred Torrens of the 66th Regiment, probably shortly after his marriage in 1854 to Caroline-Anne Price, whose father was an important figure in the timber trade (see pl. 66). Lieutenant Torrens also acquired at about the same time the *Quebec Viewed from Pointe-Lévis*, and Krieghoff enjoyed the patron-

age in Quebec of a number of British military officers, likely more even than in Montreal. Capt. John Walker, another officer in the 66th Regiment, for instance, commissioned Krieghoff in 1857 to paint him with his dog and two ladies in front of a country property he was acquiring (see pl. 72).[119] Not so different in conception from the Hale commissions of a decade earlier, this "estate portrait" does reveal a greater concern for the specific natures of the various foliage and consequently a more convincing sense of place.

Krieghoff presumably received commissions of the sort just outlined without the agency of John Budden. There are a considerable number of pictures that reflect his involvement with the Budden circle, however, and they provide evidence that his interests in Quebec were shaped, or at the least supported, by their influence. Krieghoff probably maintained his studio near or with Budden until 1858, when the city directory records the painter at 11 Grande-Allée without a separate business listing. There is no evidence that his wife ever lived in Quebec, but none showing her resident elsewhere. One document and some reports place their daughter in the city in the early sixties, but nothing suggests she was there before that time (she would have been at least twelve or thirteen in 1853). Harper, apparently based on information in a letter that another of Krieghoff's close friends, Christopher O'Connor, wrote to Robert Harris about 1897, has him staying "first in an upstairs room at Mr. Philip's boarding house on Angel Street, in the old quarter near the Ursuline Convent, where Budden also had rooms," at which time Budden began to introduce him to a circle of friends.[120] An informant of Barbeau's relates that "Krieghoff boarded for years with a family named Clerihue," and that "Budden and the Clerihues were friends," and were involved together in a theatre group.[121] The Quebec Dramatic Club, established in 1850, included among its members Budden, O'Connor and his brother Robert, John P. Bickell, and Denis Gale, who were also associated with Krieghoff.[122] Krieghoff may not have been involved with this club, which lasted only three seasons, but could have played with the Histrionics, as they called themselves, a group formed in 1854 from the core of the earlier club that lasted thirteen years.[123] There is no record that he joined, but his involvement with the Shakspeare Club in Montreal encourages us to assume he did. And in 1854 he painted the portrait of one of the members, a lumber and ship's supply merchant in his business life, and his wife.

Elizabeth Bickell and *John Palmer Bickell* make an attractive couple (pls. 68 and 69). Their head-and-shoulders portraits appear in oval formats, spare and direct, with most of Krieghoff's skills turned to their faces, particularly their eyes, noses, and mouths. The way the features are drawn follows his earlier portraits, even to the reddish lumps that pass for ears. John Bickell's hair, on the other hand, is handled beautifully, as is the black lace trim of Elizabeth's dress. Another portrait reflecting friendship, or at least close relations, is of *Andrew John Maxham* (pl. 71), who was Budden's partner in the auction firm A.J. Maxham & Co., and who would represent Krieghoff's interests in the 1860s. This too is an informal, relatively modest oval with most of the labour expended on

the face. The features are particularly detailed yet warmly represented, and the hair and flesh are realized especially well. We know Krieghoff didn't often paint portraits, but in December 1860 he gave the O'Connors a picture of their dogs, "in token of regard & friendship," as he inscribed on the back. *The Pets and the Materials* is a souvenir of good times, showing the two lap dogs on a table amid an array of wines and spirits, a partly consumed melon, cigars, a pipe, and an issue of the English satirical newspaper *Punch* (pl. 76). Even Budden is brought in, with his calling card poking out of a magnificent moose-foot pouch that hangs on the door frame, and of course Krieghoff is fully there in the care he has lavished on depicting the groupings of objects.

Theatre, art, and good conversation brought these friends together, but they also shared a love of hunting, fishing, and the outdoors, and that too is reflected in a surprising number of Krieghoff's paintings of the Quebec period. This sportsmen's camaraderie is celebrated in the most glorious fashion in a painting of 1859 titled *The Narrows on Lake St. Charles* (pl. 73). The lake, which is about thirty kilometres northwest of Quebec, was one of a number within relatively easy reach of the city, including Lake Beauport, frequented by Budden, the O'Connors, and James Gibb, a prominent lumber merchant and banker, whose father was a shipbuilder, among others.[124] Although many of these lakes were settled in the early decades of the century, mainly by retired soldiers, farming was barely viable, and they were well along to reverting to their wild state by the fifties (see pl. 75) and were considered choice locations within the anglophone community for summer cottages and fishing and hunting resorts. *The Narrows on Lake St. Charles* shows "Old Gabriel" Teoriolen, a guide, to the left, John Budden in the centre, Krieghoff, with his portfolio, seated back to us, and James Gibb, as identified in Krieghoff's hand on the original stretcher. They're at a favourite fishing spot off Campbell's Point, named after a notary, W.D. Campbell, who had a cottage there.[125] Gibb seems to have first owned the painting. Another major canvas of 1859, *Death of the Moose at Sunset. Lake Famine South of Quebec*, shows the three friends with two Native guides hunting in winter on a lake near the Maine border (pl. 74). Krieghoff is in the centre this time, standing facing out, a perfect tiny self-portrait, armed only with his sketching portfolio. Gibb is to the right, and the third figure, with his back to us, must be Budden, who first owned the painting.[126] It is near the end of a short winter day, so shadows are long and the sky is spectacular with the setting sun. Both paintings have arched tops, which lends dignity to their appearance, and the landscapes in both are beautifully handled, among his very best. They clearly were important to the artist and to that small circle of friends that represented the core of his patronage in Quebec.

There are a number of other paintings of sportsmen, including the impressive nocturne *Sportsmen at Jacques Cartier Falls* of 1861 (pl. 77), that evidently portray identifiable figures. (In this case the man with sideburns standing nearest the fire looks like John Maxham.) None other shows Krieghoff himself so well as *Death of the Moose...*, however, and it

is all the more valuable a document because, although he often places a small figure of an artist in his pictures, as we've seen, there is only one actual *Self-Portrait* known (pl. 70). Signed and dated 1855 near the lower left side, it once was in the shape of a perfect circle. Krieghoff himself seems to have enlarged the image to fill the rectangular canvas and signed it a second time lower right. He turned forty in 1855, and comparing the canvas with a photograph Budden told Fairchild was taken about five years later (see fig. 11), we can see that at the time of the painting he applied heavy pomade to his hair to flatten and darken it and shaped his beard to lengthen and narrow his face. His friends recalled him to be an affable companion, outgoing and active, but he presents himself here as intense, contained, smouldering deep inside.

The patronage in this circle of friends and the few private commissions he received would have accounted for only a relatively small part of Krieghoff's income during the Quebec years. As he did in Montreal, he painted speculatively, producing work for an emerging middle-class market that in Britain and the United States, certainly, but also in parts of Europe was not only encouraging the commodification of art but was reshaping its content.[127] Krieghoff's habitant and Native imagery changed during the Quebec years, and so did the ways he sold his art. He did not, as he had in Montreal, associate with other artists to open a gallery. In fact he seems to have had little to do with other artists in the city. This was in part because the principal artists were securely established within the francophone community, and by the time he moved to Quebec

Krieghoff quite clearly was functioning within English-speaking circles. The three most important artists in the city essentially constituted a dynasty. The oldest, Joseph Légaré, had undertaken many commissions for the Catholic Church and was active politically (on the Patriote side in the rebellion, later in municipal politics, and appointed to the Legislative Council just before his death). His apprentice, Antoine Plamondon (1804–1895), was also successful with Church commissions, by and large, and enjoyed a reputation as a portraitist. And his apprentice, Théophile Hamel, who had returned to Quebec from Montreal in 1851, took over the practice.[128] With Plamondon's retirement to the country in 1851, where he continued to paint (not on commission) and to fulminate periodically on artistic matters, and Légaré's death in 1855, Hamel became unassailable. He is frequently designated "*notre peintre national*" in the newspapers of the day, and effectively became official government portraitist when he was awarded a commission in 1853 to paint the portraits of all past and the present speakers of both the Legislative Assembly and Legislative Council, a role that, while it took him to Toronto for a while when the government moved there again in 1856, nonetheless strengthened his position in Quebec.[129] Even though Krieghoff and Hamel initially had studios within a couple of blocks of each other on St. John Street in Quebec, they had entirely distinct clientele, as Raymond Vézina has remarked, and we have no reason to believe they communicated.[130]

Martin Somerville moved from Montreal to Quebec about the same time as Krieghoff, and they latterly had studios in the same little development

Figure 11
Ellison & Company
CORNELIUS KRIEGHOFF, c. 1860
albumen print, 8.75 × 5.75 cm
Musée de la civilisation, Québec,
fonds d'archives du Séminaire de Québec
(Ph. 1988-1374)

at Mount Pleasant, so must have spent time together. Somerville, however, died in the late spring of 1856.[131] Only a few other artists, all minor, were resident in the city during the period, including Frederick F. Minee (active 1854–56), John Murray (1810–c. 1868), Samuel Hawksett (1827–1903), and Joseph Dynes (1825–1897), so there was not, then, much of a basis for association, nor was there the need there had been in Montreal in 1846.[132] A provincial agricultural and industrial exhibition was staged annually, with prizes in a number of artistic categories. It was held in Montreal in 1853, where Krieghoff took first prize for a Canadian subject in oil (we don't know what it was), and Plamondon won first overall in oils for his *Wild Pigeon Hunting*; and in Quebec in 1854 (his friend James Gibb was president of the association that staged this fair), Krieghoff took two prizes, first for landscape in oil ("Canadian winter scene"), and first for an oil study "of a cart horse," while Légaré took firsts in historical painting and still life.[133] The prizes were small (between about £1 and £2), and the exposure probably not significantly greater than a shop window on St. John Street. It seems he didn't participate in the Provincial Exhibition for the next few years. He had his sights on new territory made available by the Grand Trunk Railway line, and in 1857 made arrangements to establish a presence in Philadelphia. Fairchild mentions a firm, Messrs. Thomas & Co., that purchased "a number of large pictures, representative of Canadian life," several of which he claims subsequently were reproduced as lithographs.[134] No such lithographs have yet turned up. There are records, however, of Krieghoff works being shown regularly at the Pennsylvania Academy of the Fine Arts' annual exhibitions in Philadelphia from 1857 to 1862, a total of fourteen works. These were not submitted by the artist but by dealers or collectors, and a number of the canvases stayed in Philadelphia.[135]

There are two rare letters from 1860 and 1861 in Krieghoff's hand to John Young, one of his more important Quebec patrons, one, in June 1861, passing on the charges of a Philadelphia frame maker, identified in an earlier invoice as "Mr. Earle," doubtless of the firm James Earle & Son, prominent Philadelphia framers and art dealers.[136] The other note to Young refers to an imminent trip to New York, and in 1860 one of his "Merrymaking" pictures, probably the large one now in the Beaverbrook Art Gallery, was offered at the Lyceum Gallery, a well-known New York outlet for contemporary American and foreign art, in company with pieces by such noted American genre painters of the day as G.H. Durrie (1820–1863), Lily Martin Spencer (1822–1902), and Arthur F. Tait (1819–1905).[137] That same year his work was featured in the Provincial Exhibition in Montreal, billed the "Great Exhibition" and housed in a new "Crystal Palace" built expressly for the annual displays of provincial accomplishment, a smaller version of the elaborate glass structure that had caused a sensation at the Great Exhibition of the Works of Industry of all Nations in London in 1851.[138] The art display had been organized by the newly formed Art Association of Montreal, and Krieghoff's old friend and agent, John Leeming, was one of five members of the founding committee. At the end of 1861 he had a piece in an exhibition in Buffalo, and in 1863 another in the recently organized Buffalo Fine Arts Academy exhibition, and three at the end of that year in an exhibition in Rochester.[139]

In Quebec Krieghoff did not use auctions regularly to sell his work the way he had in Montreal, but when he decided to leave the city in the early sixties he put everything under the hammer. He did try to raffle a collection of his paintings in January 1855; it is not clear he sold enough tickets to follow through.[140] And in the June 1861 letter to John Young he mentioned he was "trying to raffle a painting of Montmorenci at Dawson's," and would appreciate the collector's support. There may have been other such instances that we have not yet discovered, but it seems that the hundreds of paintings sold to both local buyers and British soldiers and colonial officials, who took them to England when they returned home, were sold mainly out of the studio or through the agency of Budden.[141]

THE QUEBEC PRINTS

The first print he issued in Quebec, *The Ice Cone at the Falls of Montmorency near Quebec, Lower Canada*, in 1853 (pl. 79), he published himself through one of the largest London firms, Ackermann & Co. Krieghoff's image was transferred to the stone by W. Simpson, and printed by Day & Son. The next effort, a pair of chromolithographs of an old beggar shown knocking on a lawyer's door with the supplication *"Pour l'amour du Bon Dieu?"* and then cursing *"Va au Diable!"* when rejected, appears to have been published by the Montreal firm of framer dealers B. Dawson & Son (pls.

80 and 81).[142] This doubtless is the same "Dawson's" with whom he was trying to raffle a Montmorency painting in the early summer of 1861.

Krieghoff's involvement with prints during the Quebec decade was not as ambitious as it had been in Montreal. The first he brought out— *The Ice Cone...*, dated December 1853 by Ackermann and available in Canada in the spring of 1854, and the last, *View of Quebec, Canada: From the Railway Station Opposite Quebec, the City*, published 24 January 1862 by Moore, McQueen & Co. of London and available in Canada that spring (pl. 83)—are very grand, the largest of all his prints at about 60 cm width. The first is based on one of his most ambitious canvases, the large *Montmorency Falls* (pl. 45), and the Quebec view, which is very rare, known only by this one impression, is based on the 1856 version (pl. 52). The latter published in black and white but sold hand coloured, the former printed with colours, they have an open, airy quality of considerable elegance. The beggar pair, on the other hand, are fairly crude chromo-lithographs, small ovals apparently published without letterpress. The work of "one of the best London establishments," according to Dawson's advertisement, they probably arrived in Canada in the spring of 1860. At least in some cases embossed to simulate brushstrokes, they are usually found varnished and framed in imitation of oil paintings.

In addition to the 1862 *View of Quebec...* (which may not even have been circulated in Canada), there are only two other prints of the Quebec decade, both published by John Weale, London, in 1860, as illustrations in a volume celebrating the completion of the great Canadian engineering feat of the day, the Victoria Bridge at Montreal.[143] Built to bring the railway across the St. Lawrence to Montreal, the bridge was six and a half years under construction and was officially opened by Edward Albert, Prince of Wales, in August 1860. The prints—*Indian Chiefs* (pl. 78) and *Passengers and Mail, Crossing the River* (pl. 82)—are delicate colour lithographs with two tintstones, which were available only in the book, issued in a regular edition and a deluxe with larger margins. Based on two themes Krieghoff already had painted in a number of versions, they functioned in the publication as images of life in Canada before the bridge. Likely through Dawson's, Krieghoff had sold a number of paintings to Alexander McKenzie Ross, the chief engineer on the construction of the bridge, and that perhaps led to his connection with the publisher.[144]

SINGLE-FIGURE PAINTINGS

We know from a letter of March 1859 that Krieghoff wrote to the minister of finance of the day, Alexander Galt, that he was discouraged by a 15 per cent duty that applied to all imported prints, both his own and others he might bring in as a collector or for resale.[145] Although the import duty may have been a deterrent, Krieghoff was less reliant on prints in Quebec to reach buyers of modest means because he had followed Martin Somerville's lead in Montreal and developed a line of small inexpensive canvases of single emblematic figures. He produced hundreds of these during the Quebec years, mainly of Native subjects, but occasionally of habitants. Certain subjects, such as the Native hunter on snowshoes (see pl. 84), he produced very frequently, sometimes in virtually identical versions, like *The Trapper* (pl. 87), but usually with significant variations in the landscape, the clothing, accoutrements, or direction of movement of the figure (see pls. 93 and 101). As common as the Native hunter is the Native woman with baskets, moccasins, or other women's work for sale, travelling to town in the summer (see pl. 85), or winter (see pl. 86), or perhaps stopping in a country lane to show some particularly fine objects (see pl. 90). There is a whole category of head-and-shoulders studies of habitant "types" (see pls. 88 and 89), and less often three-quarters or full-length figures of habitants engaged in characteristic tasks, such as *The Woodcutter* (pl. 91), or *The Berry Seller* (pl. 100). Such images have always been a staple of genre, the figures representative of a particular class, ethnic group, or region, so laden with telling characteristics as to border on caricature. Krieghoff's single figures are stereotypes certainly, but in the portrayal of habitants he not infrequently strives to capture a specific quality of personality rather than a general type (see pls. 98 and 99). On the other hand, the single Native figures that stand apart from the rest are those in which the detail of costume or trade objects is particularly fine.

QUEBEC IMAGES OF NATIVES

Native images did not dominate in his larger canvases to the same degree, but they remained a major part of his work throughout the Quebec period. The earliest works quite naturally reflect many of the characteristics of the Montreal period. *Indian Encampment at Big Rock*, for instance, of about 1853, has many characteristics that suggest it could be a late Montreal painting (pl. 103). The figures are quite large in a diorama-like setting, and there are the expected carefully observed still-life arrangements of Native gear (the grouping at the right, of rifles, backpack, and propped-up cradleboard with bundled baby, is splendid), as well as the heavy iron pot suspended from a spindly twig. But the figures are more natural than in the Montreal pictures, with an easy interaction, exemplified by the hatted woman's animated conversation with the smoking man. And the big rock against which they've camped is a clever device to create a stage-like space while allowing vistas for virtuoso landscape painting both on the left and in a minor note in the upper right. There is a rapid change from this point, however, a steady development, with the figures growing ever smaller and less closely observed in an increasingly important landscape.

There was a Native presence in Quebec in the mid-fifties, probably as much as Krieghoff had earlier experienced in Montreal. Micmac and Montagnais from New Brunswick and the north shore of the St. Lawrence camped every summer at Indian Cove on the Lévis side of the river until at least the mid-nineteenth century, according to George Gale, selling trade goods throughout the season and collecting their treaty payments before departing in the early fall.[146] And the Huron village at Lorette was only about thirteen kilometres to the northwest of Quebec up the St. Charles River. It had been established in 1697 by the Jesuits for converts

who had fled the Iroquois attacks on Huronia (east of Georgian Bay). The mill was in operation at Lorette by 1751, and by the mid-nineteenth century there was a small factory producing snowshoes, toboggans, paddles, beadwork and basketry for sale in Quebec. Unlike the Mohawks of Caughnawaga, the men of Lorette continued to hunt and trap, passing every fall at a reserve just to the west of the village, and after 1851 at a much larger one deeper into the hinterlands northwest. These are the Natives Krieghoff knew, hired by him and his friends as guides for hunting and fishing trips, men like Gabriel Teoriolen, who appears in the group portrait in *The Narrows on Lake St. Charles* (pl. 73). The only other identified portrait of a Native of the Quebec period is also of a Huron, Thomas Seweet (Sioui), also shown at Lake St. Charles, which is just beyond Lorette (see fig. 12, page 84).[147] With few exceptions, such as the little painting on board of 1855 of *Indians Dancing*, with its quirky air of observed reality (pl. 106), the Native subjects are subsumed to a larger vision of place. The painting now called *Taking Shelter from the Storm* (pl. 108) reveals little interest in details of a way of life. The figures are mere staffage to help us experience more fully the sublime force of the storm, the exhilarating freshness of the landscape, and its bountiful capacity to shelter its creatures.

By the late fifties and early sixties the work shows none of the diorama-like space of the Montreal pictures. Even in paintings where the figures are somewhat large, their clothing more carefully described, and there is still the sense of a stage, as in *Indian Hunters on the St. Maurice*

Figure 12
THOMAS SEWEET, LAKE ST. CHARLES,
1854
oil on canvas, 28.7 × 23.7 cm
Private collection, Montreal

River of 1860 (pl. 113), the richly orchestrated landscape dominates with its shifting, permeable background alluding everywhere to infinite space, and its elaborately conceived composition of vertical and diagonal lines racing our eyes round the image to enjoy the array of visual delights while focusing us finally on the central image of hunting. *Chippewas on Lake Superior* (pl. 114), also of 1860, has at its centre a respectful if nonetheless romantic depiction of nomadic life with the portrayal of dignified discussion at an ordained place. This simple, idealistic message is framed by the most extravagantly sumptuous landscape. The depiction of the various species of tree, the goldenrod in the foreground right, the delicate ferns is a virtuoso performance, yet is saved from pedantry by the subtle sweeps of light and shadow that crisscross the scene. Again, the composition moves us around and through the myriad delights while grounding us repeatedly in the core image. *Chippewas on Lake Superior* is the closest canvas to the lithograph *Indian Chiefs* and, like it, is meant to offer a glimpse of times past. As we move into the sixties the images become even more intensely pleasurable and at the same time increasingly remote. We are usually privileged with a moment caught forever, as in *After the Kill* (pl. 116). An essential act of human survival is frozen at a point of intensity, to be examined endlessly in its complex yet harmonious setting, like a ritual. One of the great later Native images, *On Lake Laurent* of 1863, sets the ritual on a vast stage, the tiny figures acting out the drama against a backdrop of searing, transitory ecstasy only moments before the descent to freezing darkness (pl. 119). It is an instant caught in *Shooting the Rapids* of 1861 as well, the tiny figure stopped forever this time at the bottom of the exhilarating run of the shoot, deep in the midst of an Edenic paradise of gold and red, rusts, browns, and greens (pl. 117).

QUEBEC IMAGES OF HABITANTS

It was two or three years after moving to Quebec before Krieghoff returned with any real interest to habitant scenes, but in 1856 a series of ambitious canvases began to appear. In *The Habitant Farm* of that year we can see their derivation from the so-called Longueuil images (pl. 120). The picture is centred on a gathering around a sleigh, but the Laurentian Shield landscape of the Quebec region imposes quite different terms on the composition from the flat river plains of the Montreal area. Vistas are now an essential component of the image, and there is a present aware-ness of the bush, of wilderness. The conifers massed to the left of the house, for instance, have received a great deal of attention from the artist. The figures are smaller than they generally are in the Montreal pictures, and this enhances our sense of their harmony with the natural setting. And they are positioned to emphasize the harmony within the small fam-ily unit as well. It is a home of some age, built of square timbers with a mud or plaster facade. There is a good-sized barn down the hill.

Settler's Log House, also of 1856, shows a farm at the end of its first or second year (pl. 122). The house is built of round logs and there are few windows. There are no outbuildings and the area of cleared land is not large. There is no horse or sleigh, just an ox and sledge, and there is no well. Water is taken from a hole in the ice on a nearby stream. The family is not simply represented as a compatible grouping but as though it were a well-trained troupe, with the father, unloading a fresh load of firewood, at the hub of a wheel, everyone else revolving around him, in a designated place, at a task: the son getting water with the dog, the older sister play-ing with a younger, the mother at the door of the house with the baby. A huge pine tree immediately behind the house, seeming to shelter it, exem-plifies the strength of this "natural order." A brilliant sky celebrates it.

These two images represent not just farmsteads of different ages but the beginning of a broadly supported settlement program in Canada East. As the relatively limited traditional farming areas along the St. Lawrence began to fill up, thousands of landless young people were immigrating to New England to work in the mill towns, or to the Ameri-can West to homestead, and in fear of losing a sizable proportion of the francophone Catholic population, the government opened crown lands for settlement in the regions of the Saguenay, the St. Maurice River above Trois-Rivières, along the Gatineau River north of Bytown, and in parts of the Eastern Townships. Such *colonisation*, as it was known in French, was vigorously supported by the Church, as well as the govern-ment, and thousands sought to start new lives on often marginal land. Krieghoff would have encountered *colons* up the St. Maurice and Shawinigan Rivers, and likely in the hinterlands far up the Montmorency and beyond Lake St. Francis, probably most often in the manner he encountered Natives, while on hunting or fishing trips. It remained one of his central themes throughout the balance of the Quebec period.

Bringing in the Deer of about 1859 shows a residence of some three or four years' duration, judging by the improvements (pl. 126). There is no well, but the bank of the stream has been shored up at a convenient spot for dipping. There are simple outbuildings, and there is a horse. Fences surround cleared fields, and a rustic cross presides at the gate. Family harmony is apparent, as is a harmonious relationship with nature; game remains an important source of food. *Clearing Land near the St. Maurice River* of 1860 shows the process at the end of the first summer season, before the snow (pl. 130). The figures here are even smaller, nature even more the subject, with two stately, surviving trees the focus of the composition, even as smoke billows from a clearing fire behind, and one settler attacks a birch with an axe. The two big trees are right in the middle of a fenced-in corn plot beside the log house, which makes no sense. Early photographs of such settlers' homes show that clear-cutting was the first step in creating farmland from wilderness (see fig. 13). The magnificent sheltering trees we see in Krieghoff's paintings reflect his values, not the *colons*. By 1863 and a painting like *Winter in Laval Mountains near Quebec*, he is celebrating this ethos of life in the wilderness in harmony with nature in monumental terms (pl. 138). The area around Laval had been settled for some time by then, but it was in the Laurentian Shield and so had the necessary wilderness qualities. The encounter at the stopped sleigh is the focus, but the setting is the real subject, a

setting presented with such scale and dignity, and with such precise compositional articulation of form and line, that it becomes like a large, open church, with nave, transverse aisle, and side chapels. The habitant figures are not entirely subsumed to this landscape as the Native figures of the period are, largely because evidence of their mark on nature is everywhere. In this sanctified landscape, the tall dead tree at the centre of the picture becomes a symbol of ultimate sacrifice around which the whole system evolves.

So the scenes of both Natives and habitants in the Quebec period reflect a world view that Krieghoff may have thought was that of his subjects but that was in fact his and his patrons' alone. The same assumptions about Tyrolean peasant life can be seen in Bavarian painting of the day, and there are many instances from the United States of paintings of pioneering that idealize what most often was a harsh struggle for survival (see fig. 14).[148] Such idealization served a higher, national goal, it might be argued, whereby individual suffering was deemed an acceptable cost of progress, of national consolidation or expansion. In light of this, it's a delight to occasionally encounter in Krieghoff's work a candid, usually puzzling, image such as *Log Cabin, Winter Scene, Lake St. Charles*, of about 1862, a variant on the theme that bends the mould (pl. 133). The structure here is very rough, with a smoke hole instead of a chimney. It is one of the very few scenes of apparent Native-habitant interaction, so appropriately located at Lake St. Charles. Should we read wariness in the way the Native woman is met, with all eyes on her? Or is

this a home reflecting mixed heritage, as the tied poles of a wigwam-like structure beyond the horse suggests, and is expectation the emotion we're meant to experience?

There are numerous habitant canvases of the period after 1855 that are more artful than candid, but that similarly play on an intensely emotional moment, though usually of a more obvious sort. *Winter Scene, Blizzard*, of 1856, is a good example of one such theme, where the composition skilfully emphasizes the perilous nature of winter travel, reflecting the hesitancy of the horse, and the anxiety of the driver and passenger (pl. 121). There is another group of small canvases of sleighs showing habitants going to town or returning (see pls. 127 and 131). They derive from the desire evident in the Montreal work to depict characteristic horses, vehicles, clothing, and so on, but these Quebec versions are often more imaginatively presented, and they are moving, not static. And sometimes, as in *Sleigh Race across the Ice* of 1861 (a theme we first saw in an 1852 scene, pl. 21), we get not only an interesting array of accoutrements but an exciting element of competitive contrast between social classes, and perhaps ethnic groups (pl. 132). Would everyone in Quebec have enjoyed seeing habitants besting "gentlemen," or would some have enjoyed it only as irony? One of Krieghoff's most popular themes of the period shows habitants rushing past a tollgate, taunting a lame tollkeeper (see pl. 136). Ramsay Cook in his essay elsewhere in this volume explains how this image would have touched on a number of concerns of the day. There is one response to an earlier version of the theme that is part of

Figure 13 (top)
Alexander Henderson (1831–1913)
FARMING IN CANADA/THE CLEARING,
FIRST SHANTY, AND SUBSEQUENT FARM
HOUSE, c. 1865
albumen print, 11.4 × 19.2 cm
National Archives of Canada, Ottawa, gift of the
Estate of Andrew Merrilees, 1983 (PA-181769)

Figure 14 (bottom)
Thomas Cole (1801–1848)
HOME IN THE WOODS, 1847
oil on canvas, 111.8 × 167.6 cm
Reynolda House, Museum of American Art,
Winston-Salem, North Carolina, gift of
Barbara B. Millhouse, 1978 (12-20-78)

an extended appreciation of two paintings by Krieghoff that were on display early in 1858. It is a rare text because there are few reflective contemporary writings on Krieghoff's work, and rarer still because it is the only extended contemporary critical response in French. This critic admired Krieghoff's paintings as honest reflections of "the French-Canadian way of life and the beauty of the landscape on the shores of the St. Lawrence," works that "are outstanding for their effect; but distinguish themselves by their meaning." The version of *Cheating the Toll Man* he saw delighted him because it presented a humorous confrontation between "three merry comrades from the countryside" and "*John Bull* (probably an old pensioner)," outraged because the only payment he received was "a caribou-mittened thumbed nose by way of a *Franco-Canadian* protest against the imported English tollgates. It's subtle, attractive, delightful; it's almost history, which is not always as cheerful."[149]

The other painting this critic admired was *Les Gens des noces*, which we know today as *Breaking Up of a Country Ball in Canada, Early Morning* (pl. 125). He describes it in every detail, delighting in the incidents portrayed, and identifying with the figures in the overturned sleigh. "It is charmingly delightful," he concludes, "subtle and colourful." It is one of a major group of pictures of the later fifties in which Krieghoff presents a more complex social dynamic. One of the earliest of these is *Playtime, Village School* (pl. 124). The scene is apparently set at "Canadien Lorette," a white community near Huron Lorette.[150] An encounter around a sleigh is at the centre of the image, but it is circled by a range of lively vignettes. To the right a couple prepares a bake oven in spite of the snow, for instance, and there are other signs of village life here and there. The main action is from the village school, as the children tumble out for their play break in the snow. It is the only theme of the Quebec period set in a village, and the school also brings a note of modernity, of actuality, to an otherwise picturesque scene.

The other paintings in this important group of the later fifties depict the breakup of an all-night revel at a country inn. Like that of the large *Montmorency Falls*, this theme allowed the representation of a cross-section of Canadian society, and as in the paintings of sportsmen it allowed Krieghoff to portray friends and patrons. One of Barbeau's informants identified the inn in two of the versions, *Breaking Up of a Country Ball in Canada, Early Morning* and *Merrymaking* of 1860 (fig. 29, page 223), as Gendron's, situated on the Beauport coast about two and a half kilometres from Montmorency Falls. Harper reproduces a photograph of this inn as it was in the 1930s that establishes it as the model.[151] It would be better to describe Gendron's as the inspiration rather than the model, however, for there are numerous differences between the inns in these two versions, not the least being in scale, the later one grander to suit a larger canvas and more numerous figures. And it should be added as well that in spite of the fact that so many of the characterizations in these pictures seem particular enough to be portraits—the mustachioed man on the spirited bay horse at the centre of *Breaking Up of a Country Ball...*, for instance, who seems to be the same man shown helping a woman into a sleigh pulled by a striking mixed team that is the focus of the first canvas on the theme, *After the Ball, Chez Jolifou* of 1856 (pl. 123)—none of the figures has been identified. To seek that degree of specificity is to follow a false trail anyway, because it would seem these paintings are meant to address broader human values: celebration, conviviality, the inclusiveness of bonhommie. Certainly it is those qualities that attracted the interest of the critic writing for *Le Courrier du Canada* in 1858. And the theme, which in a sense can be taken back to Pieter Bruegel's scenes of peasant feasts in the early sixteenth century, was of particular interest in the mid-nineteenth century, in the guise of country weddings or other festive gatherings of a representative social spectrum, in Britain, the United States, and in Europe.[152] All three of Krieghoff's merrymaking scenes of this period are beautifully painted, with particular attention to depicting the end of a moonlit night on one side of the canvas and the first glimmer of the rising sun on the other, with all the subtle lighting variations in between that that range implies. The usual set-piece still lifes are also very well executed. But the principal pleasure is in the detailed observation of the complexly interrelated groups of figures. Each grouping is complete in itself, effectively melded together in light and colour harmonies like one of his still-life details. Then either the gesture of a figure or the strong lines of a compositional device leads us to another group, where we become absorbed with its internal intricacies, to be led soon on to another, and so on. Three of these paintings, all except the largest and last of the Quebec period, *Merrymaking*, ended

up in Philadelphia collections.[153] It is a measure of his potential stature as an artist in the late fifties, surely, and clear evidence of his striving for both a market and recognition beyond Quebec and Canada.

THE YEARS ABROAD

The earliest evidence that Krieghoff was planning to leave Quebec is in an advertisement for a sale with A.J. Maxham & Co. in August 1861 of the artist's personal collection of prints, engravings after the likes of Frith, Herring, Landseer, and Turner, chromolithographs, and some old engravings. Krieghoff was leaving Canada, the advertisement noted.[154] He had made no mention of this in his short letter to John Young in June, when he told him about the raffle of the Montmorency painting at Dawson's but did say he would be visiting New York in September in connection with a "picture enterprise." It seems to have been to acquire paintings for resale in Quebec, as he concluded to Young, "The paintings will sell best here before Christmas." Then in mid-November a Maxham advertisement appeared in the newspaper for a sale on the 19th of contemporary paintings and copies of Old Masters, "carefully selected by a well-known artist and connoisseur from various studies in France and Germany during the past year."[155] A month later another appeared, for a huge sale of about a hundred Krieghoff paintings to be held at some point in the near future.[156]

Nothing happened for four months, but in March the Maxham advertisement appeared again, announcing that on the afternoon of

9 April 1862 Krieghoff's entire collection would be put on the block, including *Merrymaking*. An article the day of the sale reported "an immense number of visitors" to the preview, and singled out *Merrymaking* for particular praise, although remarking generally "the native brilliancy of sky and forest which is the leading characteristic of Mr. Krieghoff's pictures."[157] Interest was piqued even more, doubtless, by a note in the advertisement that this would be "the last and only opportunity" to acquire his work "as he leaves shortly for Europe."[158] Why then at the beginning of March had he leased a new house for a year farther out on the Grande Allée?[159] We'll probably never know the reason for this apparently contradictory behaviour, but it may have had to do with his daughter's marriage to Lt. Hamilton Burnett on 18 March.[160] That December there was a second sale, two days before Christmas, of thirty paintings that had not been sold in April, and with a note in the advertisement that there would be another shortly of the artist's furniture, his collections of stuffed birds, coins, and Chinese and other curiosities, and his magnificent library of some twelve hundred volumes.[161] With the lease coming up on 44 Grande Allée at the end of April 1863, his son-in-law in February arranged to rent a cottage even farther out on the Grande Allée for one more year, then sublet it in May only one day after taking possession.[162] The sale of Krieghoff's household effects meanwhile took place at his residence at 44 Grande Allée on 29 April. We don't know where the family lived for the next few months, but on 21 August 1863 Krieghoff signed power of attorney to Andrew Maxham, the next day

Burnett sold his commission and left the army, and within the week the artist, at least, had left Quebec, "on account of ill health," as it was noticed in the Toronto *Globe*, "to reside in Italy or France."[163] Was Krieghoff ill? We simply don't know. There are also unsubstantiated reports that Burnett died soon after his marriage, and that Emily took up with a mysterious Russian Count de Wendte, who lured Krieghoff to Chicago in 1864.[164] One of Barbeau's informants recalled that Krieghoff and his daughter passed the summer of 1864, she thought, together at Lac Larron (Laurent), just beyond Lake St. Charles, and that there was a German woman there as well who seemed to be his wife.[165]

Despite the personal reasons Krieghoff may have had to leave the country, it is probably not surprising that he had decided to leave Quebec. In 1858 the permanent capital of the Province of Canada had finally been chosen, and to many, particularly those in Quebec, the choice of Ottawa was inexplicable. Parliament returned to Quebec from Toronto in May 1859, where it remained until 1865, when new facilities were ready in Ottawa, but the die had been cast. Business was beginning to decline not only because of the pending move of government but because both the growth of the railways and the increased use of steamships on the St. Lawrence diminished Quebec's usefulness as a port. And to make matters worse, the great timber trade had begun to diminish, and the shipbuilding.

We can't be sure where in Europe Krieghoff passed the next seven years, but he certainly maintained a degree of presence in Canada and probably returned on more than one occasion. He clearly had set up a number of arrangements before departing. We know about the one with Maxham, which probably helped keep Budden involved in his interests as well. Dawson's continued to represent him in Montreal and placed three pieces in the Art Association of Montreal annual exhibition in 1864.[166] He also seems to have had some sort of arrangement with Denis Gale, one of his friends from the early days with the Quebec Dramatic Club and the Histrionics. Gale was employed in the lumber business but began painting in watercolours about 1865, often inspired in his subjects by Krieghoff.[167] Gale placed three or perhaps four Krieghoffs in an exhibition organized by the Toronto Mechanics' Institute in March 1865, and although four shown at the Hamilton Mechanics' Institute in May were lent by others, Gale may ultimately have been behind them too.[168] And in August there is a report from Halifax of an exhibition of "a fine collection of paintings and artistic photographs," including a number of Krieghoffs, that Gale was touring. This was his second visit, following a successful exhibition the year before.[169]

The Halifax newspaper refers only to original works by Krieghoff, but by 1865, and even the year before, some of Gale's "artistic photographs" could have been of our artist's paintings. At the end of April 1864 Krieghoff had taken the unusual step for the day of registering photographs of thirteen of his paintings with the government for copyright protection. These included some large prints as well as the smaller "carte-de-visite" format, although presumably it was the image that was pro-

tected, regardless of its size.[170] The first recorded public exhibition was in 1865, when nine large coloured photographs and twenty coloured carte-de-visite photographs of his paintings by the Quebec firm of Ellison & Co. were included in the Canadian section of the International Exhibition of Arts and Manufactures that opened in Dublin in May.[171] That same year the Montreal photographer William Notman included beautiful albumen prints of seven Krieghoffs from Budden's collection in a sumptuous volume of photographs of works of art and "from nature" (see pl. 143).[172] Krieghoff also seems to have sold photographs himself, as quite a few are known marked with a blindstamp "C. Krieghoff copyright." There is a lovely album that once belonged to Budden of carte-sized photographs that, according to Barbeau, were taken by Ellison.[173] Barbeau records another carte-de-visite album that he believed Krieghoff assembled for James Gibb, made up entirely of photographs bearing the stamp of the Paris firm Moulin, all "said to be" hand coloured by the artist himself.[174] Yet a third album contains hand-coloured cartes, some bearing the Krieghoff blindstamp, others the Moulin stamp, and some with none at all (see pl. 148). Presumably, then, such photographs were available from a number of sources and could be coloured by anyone, and numerous examples are known of subjects not among the thirteen copyrighted. It is doubtful that Krieghoff profited directly from them all, and we don't know if he received royalties on any.[175]

He certainly didn't benefit financially from every aspect of the market for his work that continued so vigorously through the sixties, but with the arrangements he had set up there must have been significant returns, which presumably flowed through Maxham. Someone seems to have been representing his interests in upstate New York as well, as he continued to show at the Buffalo Fine Arts Academy, with five works for sale in 1865, and then again in 1867 and '68 with paintings loaned by local collectors, and he had two single figures for sale with the Utica Art Association in 1867.[176] Eleven of his paintings were included in a sale by the Cincinnati firm of auctioneers Jacob Graff & Co. in May 1866 of a collection from a Philadelphia gallery.[177]

About this time Krieghoff changed Montreal dealers. William Scott, a carver and gilder who in 1867 set up a new, expanded business as a picture-frame and looking-glass manufacturer, that year submitted three Krieghoffs to the Art Association of Montreal annual exhibition, one of which was for sale.[178] Scott likely also was instrumental in securing Krieghoff a central presence in the Canadian display at the Exposition Universelle in Paris the summer of 1867. It was widely understood that the Canadian presentation at Dublin in 1865 fell far short of what it should have been because of the "hurried way in which every thing connected with the preparing of the...contributions...had...to be carried on," as was explained in the catalogue.[179] Preparations for Paris began far in advance, and first news of the artistic component appeared in April 1866, when it was announced that nine new William Notman photographs representing caribou hunting would be included.[180] By December it was clear when the list of participants was released that the emphasis would be again, as in Dublin, on photographs; this time all were "from nature," with contributions not only from Notman but also the three Quebec firms of Livernois, Smeaton, and Ellison, who would show images of Quebec and the surrounding region. In addition, it was mentioned that Krieghoff would be contributing "an oil painting illustrative of lumber trade."[181] We know Krieghoff's contribution from an old photograph that was first described in 1919 but then dropped from sight until rediscovered a few years ago (see fig. 15).[182] It is more than one painting, of course, although the central canvas dominates the whole. It is a painting known today as *Sillery Cove, Quebec* (pl. 140), representing one of the great square-timber depots where the ships were loaded for Britain. Surrounding it is the most elaborate frame, set into which are eight much smaller views of different stages in the lumber industry, from stocking the remote camps, through the steps of preparation for the spring flood when the logs were floated downstream to the St. Lawrence to be formed into rafts for the final leg to Quebec; there the square timbers were graded, sorted, and stored in floating piles for loading into ships. At the top is a carved garland of maple leaves surmounted by a crown, the symbol of the Province of Canada. At the bottom is a small plaque that reads "Painted by C. Krieghoff/Quebec/Framed by W. Scott/Montreal Canada East." As splendidly extravagant as this looks today, it did not seem to draw much attention either in Paris or back home. The only reference to it in reports of the exhibition that so far have been discovered is one line: "Mr. Kraighoff's [sic] painting, superbly framed by Mr. Scott (of Montréal) is exhibited in the Canadian section amid photographs."[183] Canon Scott, who first discovered the photograph, did not know the grouping was part of the Canadian display at Paris. He believed it to have been installed above the speaker's chair in the Legislative Assembly at Quebec. It may have been, following its return from Paris, although it then would have to have been fitted into the plans for refurnishing the chamber as the legislature of the new Province of Quebec, following Confederation, and there is no evidence other than Scott's contention that it ever was.[184]

At some point probably in the late sixties Krieghoff undertook another project with the Scott firm. A pair of embossed chromolithographs of Native single figures was published by the dealer; they were sold varnished and framed to approximate the appearance of paintings as closely as possible. More pleasing to the eye than the pair of chromos of the beggar of almost a decade earlier, *Calling Moose, "Huron" Indian* (pl. 146) and *In Doubt of Track, "Iroquois" Indian* (pl. 147) nonetheless were similarly aimed at a popular market. They were probably Krieghoff's last prints.[185] It is apparent from the number of known paintings dated between 1863 and 1870 that his production was greatly reduced from the previous decade. One small group of undated paintings of new themes of large-figured sportsmen hunting must belong to this period between 1867 and 1870, as they clearly were inspired by the Notman studio photographs of hunters that were shown with Krieghoff's *Sillery Cove, Quebec* at Paris in 1867. The rack and head of the moose in the painter's *Moose*

Figure 15
"SILLERY COVE, QUEBEC" AS EXHIBITED
IN PARIS, EXPOSITION UNIVERSELLE, 1867,
before 1883
albumen print, 21.5 × 28.0 cm
Musée de la civilisation, Québec, fonds d'archives
du Séminaire de Québec (Ph.1987-0669)

Hunters is copied directly from Notman's *Death of the Moose*, the guide kneeling at the moose's head is taken from Notman's *Trapping the Beaver*, and details in some of the other paintings in the group also derive from the Notman set.[186] If Krieghoff didn't see the photographs in Paris, he could have encountered them in a book the photographer published the year before, *Sports, Pastimes, and Pursuits of Canada Photographed from Nature by W. Notman*. They would have interested him particularly because his friend Budden posed for some of the photographs, Col. William Rhodes, a prominent sportsman of the Quebec region Krieghoff had included in a painting of 1853 is featured in most of them, and the man whose image Krieghoff took from *Trapping the Beaver* was François Gros-Louis, a Huron guide he would also have known.[187]

Most of the other paintings of the period are variants of earlier pictures. *Chippewa Indians at Lake Huron* of 1864 (pl. 141), for instance, is the latest of at least twenty-three versions of this same scene of Native hunters stopping to camp and dress a freshly killed caribou at the base of a huge rock. It is one of the more ambitious variations, with lovely detail in the costumes and a splendid foliage foreground to the left showing delicate white flowers in the water near the shoreline with a wonderful stand of goldenrod behind. It is virtually identical in most details to *Canadian Autumn, View on the Road to Lake St. John* of 1862 (pl. 118) but omitting the spectacular gnarled roots of an upended tree behind the canoe of the earlier example, and treating the left foreground vegetation differently. *Winter Scene in the Laurentians—The Laval River* of 1867 (pl. 145),

at a later point in this roughly seven-year period he spent outside Canada, also compares well with its earlier variant (see pl. 138). Although the image is not quite so grand in scale, there is no apparent diminishing of ambition, with the snow-filled canoe to the left and the spectacularly rendered waterhole that has been smashed into the ice, raising this painting above the ordinary. *Sillery Cove, Quebec*, however, is the great painting of the period. Also a variant—a version dated 1862 is likely one of a group illustrating aspects of the timber trade commissioned by a Quebec grocer, Thomas Fraser, whose father was a prominent lumber man—it too shows an ambition equal to if not surpassing the earlier effort.[188] It is a remarkable image of an industrial landscape, the large cove covered with the booms and floating piles of huge squared timbers that represented what was historically one of the principal sources of wealth for the country. The composition, with its dramatic light and shadow effects, rich foliage treatments, and tiny pastoral figures, reflects the style of the great seventeenth-century French master Nicolas Poussin. This hint of the antique combines with the curious monumentality of the piled lumber to create a slightly elegiac air that, in spite of the evident intention of the organizers of the Canadian representation at Paris in 1867 to celebrate the old capital Quebec, suggests a passing glory.

Quebec remained Krieghoff's principal Canadian connection throughout the sixties. In April 1868 Maxham announced that a small but choice collection of new subjects by the artist was about to arrive by steamer from Portland, Maine, which means it was coming from overseas.[189] No date was mentioned for the sale, and no further notice has yet been found. Some eighteen months later Maxham announced another sale, to be held 11 November 1869, of a collection of "original paintings consigned from Paris" by Krieghoff.[190] Some were "from his own pencil," but the bulk of the sale was paintings by European and British artists like Jean-Léon Gérôme (1824–1904), Gilbert Stuart Newton (1794–1835), and Petrus van Schendel (1806–1870), and copies after Rosa Bonheur (1822–1899) and Paul Delaroche (1797–1856). Nine months later there was a short notice in one of the Quebec newspapers: "Mr. Krieghoff, the celebrated painter, and family are in town on a visit."[191]

RETURN TO QUEBEC

A month later Maxham announced a sale of modern oil paintings chosen by Krieghoff in Paris and Munich, along with some of the artist's Canadian and other subjects. Krieghoff had decided to live in Quebec again, he added.[192] The sale was held late in October, and among works listed in an advertisement at that time were sketches done in the Tyrol region of Bavaria by Anton Doll (1826–1887), two portraits by another Munich genre painter, Heinrich Bürkel (1802–1869), some interiors by French and German artists, a selection of copies, and Canadian, Russian, and English subjects by Krieghoff.[193] So he had definitely spent some time travelling in Europe. He had probably returned to Schweinfurt following the death of his mother in February 1867 and his father a little over a year later.[194] Either or both events might have offered the occasion to travel

on to Munich. The Russian subjects, however, are no reason to imagine he actually travelled farther east.[195] We have no idea where else he visited, other than very likely London and certainly Paris and Munich. That he arrived in August 1870 with "family" must have meant his wife and presumably his daughter, and it is clear he intended all to stay for some time, for at the end of the month he signed an eight-month lease for the two upper floors and garret of a house on Richelieu Street in St. John Ward.[196] Then in May 1871 he moved to the upper floor of a two-storey house he had leased for a year on Prevost Street.[197] He must have begun painting when still on Richelieu Street, for although we know of only one work dated 1869 and another 1870, there are at least eight paintings known of 1871.

Everything about the works completed following his return to Quebec suggests a desire to make his mark again. What must have been one of the first paintings completed is *The New Year's Day Parade*, showing revellers on their day-after rounds, converging on a seasonal "inn" that has been temporarily erected on the St. Lawrence ice downriver from the city (pl. 149). It is not *Breaking Up of a Country Ball...*, but it is a new subject, and it does project the particular ethos residents of Quebec had come to expect, the air of carefree bonhommie when the military, the bourgeoisie, and habitants mingled in the imaginary world of Krieghoff's Canada. *J.B. Jolifou, Aubergiste* (pl. 150) also can't help suffering in comparison with the great merrymaking scenes of the late fifties, but it still sent a message that Krieghoff wanted to pick up where he had left off. It is in many ways a truncated version of its wonderful predecessors, nonetheless, with a tighter, slightly cramped point of view, smaller tree, fewer figures, fewer incidents, and distinctly desultory air, as though it were depicting the scene in *Merrymaking* or *Breaking Up of a Country Ball...* a half-hour later. *Return from the Hunt*, on the other hand, is another new subject, showing two sportsmen and a Huron guide stopped at the cabin of a *colon* with a sledge laden with hunting trophies, the heads of caribou and moose (pl. 151). The conifer behind the cabin is beautifully described, open and full of articulating light, and the area within the driving shed to the left is remarkably well observed, the muted colours calibrated perfectly to create a sense of contained space. There are other new subjects that year, including *The Blacksmith's Shop*, a muted, gently comforting variation on the mid-winter stop at a country haven (pl. 152), but there is something static about them all, in spite of the evident action, a muffled, distant quality of something that has passed, or at least is slipping away.

Krieghoff participated in the Provincial Exhibition at Quebec in September 1871 showing "two of his famous paintings—'Quebec,' from New Liverpool, and 'Returning from Hunting,' a winter scene"; the former a painting we don't know today, the latter is the 1871 *Return from the Hunt*.[198] Critical response was reserved. The reviewer cited above opined that "all true lovers of the art of painting must hail" Krieghoff's return to Canada "with delight," but a writer in another English newspaper remarked, "A couple of Krieghoff's oil colours are worthy of admiration,

though his style is somewhat mannered and invariable."[199] The day after it was announced that Krieghoff had won the prize for "best landscape in oil," the same writer commented in his second look at the exhibition, with classic faint praise, "Krieghoff is too well known to most of our readers as a careful delineator of Canadian subjects to need further comment."[200] The two reviews of the exhibition in the French press that notice his contribution both also remark with pleasure his return, but neither makes more than brief general remarks about the paintings.[201] As it turns out, he would not be remaining much longer in the city. Maxham once again was called in to sell his household goods in mid-October, offering "nearly new" furniture and other effects, including paintings and prints, at the artist's residence, 6¾ Prevost. Krieghoff, it was noted in the advertisement, was about to leave for the United States.[202] His library was offered in a separate sale, 24 October, and since the furniture sale either had been postponed or was of limited success, at the end of November Maxham staged yet another auction at the artist's flat.[203] Krieghoff likely left Canada shortly afterward. News of his death in Chicago reached Quebec early in March.[204]

He had died 4 March at 721 West Jackson Street, where, Budden later reported, he was living with his wife.[205] The writer of an obituary in Quebec tried to capture the sense of loss felt there. "Who in Quebec has not been delighted and instructed in art by Krieghoff's beautiful and faithful pictures of Canadian scenery," he asked, adding, with some exaggeration, "a man whose name had become a household word both in Canada and the United States." Then regaining some perspective, he concluded, "Krieghoff's fame belongs peculiarly to Canada; it was the country of his adoption, and in depicting its scenes he has always stood without a rival. There is hardly a Canadian home without some memento of him. Canada will not easily replace his loss."[206] Krieghoff did not benefit from government or Church commissions during his lifetime, so did not enjoy the public profile such patronage usually brought, and his wife and daughter seem to have done little, if anything, to encourage the honouring of his memory in Quebec and Canada following his death.[207] It has been collectors—owners of one or two treasured pieces as well as the more fervent devotees, not uncommon in his lifetime and since, with thirty or forty or more—who have preserved the legacy, assuring its survival, while steadily enhancing its value. Krieghoff was an artist particularly attuned to his audience. That is perhaps the main reason his images of Canada fascinate us so much still.

41. Seigneury at Sainte-Anne-de-la-Pérade, 1846

oil on canvas, 29.9 × 40.5 cm

McCord Museum of Canadian History, Montreal, gift of David Campbell, 1992 (990.758.1.3)

42. KING'S WALDEN, HERTFORDSHIRE, 1846

oil on canvas, 31.0 × 41.2 cm

McCord Museum of Canadian History, Montreal, gift of David Campbell, 1992 (990.758.1.1)

43. Lt. Robert McClure, 1847

oil on canvas, 60.6 × 46.0 cm

The Thomson Collection (P-C-665)

44. CHARLES THEOPHILUS METCALFE, BARON METCALFE (AFTER ALVAH BRADISH), 1847

oil on canvas, 117.6 × 92.1 cm

Musée du Château Ramezay, Montreal, gift of W.B. Mathewson, 1899 (1998.1865)

45. Montmorency Falls, 1853

oil on canvas, 91.4 × 121.9 cm

The Thomson Collection (P-C-116)

46. Quebec Viewed from Pointe-Lévis, 1853

oil on canvas, 36.6 × 53.9 cm

Musée du Québec, Québec, purchased 1984, with the assistance of the government of Canada

through the Cultural Property Export and Import Act (84.18)

47. Quebec from Pointe-Lévis, 1853
oil on canvas, 36.0 × 53.5 cm
Royal Ontario Museum, Toronto, gift of Raymond A. Willis, Esq., 1955 (955.84)

48. Falls of Lorette, near Quebec, 1854

oil on canvas, 31.1 × 38.6 cm

Musée du Québec, Québec, purchased 1949 (49.101)

49. The Passing Storm, St. Féréol, 1854

oil on canvas, 39.0 × 50.2 cm

National Gallery of Canada, Ottawa, purchased 1963 (15190)

50. The St. Anne Falls near Quebec
from Above and Looking Upward, 1854–5

oil on canvas, 31.0 × 46.5 cm

National Gallery of Canada, Ottawa, purchased 1995 (37781)

51. The St. Anne Falls, 1855

oil on canvas, 40.0 × 48.6 cm

National Gallery of Canada, Ottawa, purchased 1995 (37780)

52. View of Quebec from the
Grand Trunk Railway Station at Pointe-Lévis, 1856
oil on canvas, 41.2 × 61.4 cm
Private collection

53. In the Jardin de Caribou, below Quebec, 1856

oil on canvas, 39.5 × 39.4 cm

McCord Museum of Canadian History, Montreal, bequest of Arnold Wainwright, Q.C., 1967 (M967.100.13)

54. THE ARTIST AT NIAGARA, 1858

oil on canvas, 38.2 × 51.5 cm

Art Gallery of Ontario, Toronto, gift of Charles and Lois Thomson, Milton, Ontario,

in memory of Mr. and Mrs. H. Dewar Thomson, 1998 (98/20)

55. The Chaudière, 1858

oil on canvas, mounted on plywood, 51.1 × 74.9 cm

National Gallery of Canada, Ottawa, gift of Edith Wilson, Ottawa, 1923, in memory of Senator and Mrs. W.C. Edwards (2037)

56. The Tubular Bridge at St. Henry's Falls, 1858

oil on canvas, 36.4 × 54.0 cm

McCord Museum of Canadian History, Montreal, bequest of Arnold Wainwright, Q.C., 1967 (M967.100.1)

57. Portage at Grand'Mère Falls, c. 1860
oil on panel set in top of table, 22.4 × 33.0 cm
Private collection, Guelph, Ontario

58. In the Jardin de Caribou, 50 Miles below Quebec, 1861

oil on canvas, 53.6 × 47.3 cm

The Thomson Collection (P-C-574)

59. JAM OF SAWLOGS, SHAWINIGAN FALLS, 1861

oil on canvas, 45.5 × 66.0 cm

The Thomson Collection (P-C-224)

60. Lac Laurent: Autumn, 1862

oil on canvas, 33.8 × 50.0 cm

The Thomson Collection (p-c-168)

61. Landscape with Deer and Doe, 1862

oil on canvas, 52.7 × 92.3 cm

The Thomson Collection (P-C-618)

62. Early Winter on the St. Anne's, below Quebec, 1863

oil on canvas, 51.2 × 51.8 cm

The Thomson Collection (P-C-531)

63. Dery's Bridge, Salmon Leap, Jacques Cartier River, 1863

oil on canvas, 33.3 × 49.1 cm

McCord Museum of Canadian History, Montreal, bequest of Arnold Wainwright, Q.C., 1967 (M967.100.6)

64. View of Quebec City from Pointe-Lévis, 1863

oil on canvas, 34.9 × 59.0 cm

Montreal Museum of Fine Arts, Miss Mary Fry Dawson Bequest, 1954 (1954.1103)

65. The Steamship Quebec, 1853

oil on canvas, 67.7 × 93.4 cm

The Thomson Collection (P-C-714)

66. Lt. Alfred Torrens and
His Wife in Front of the Citadel, c. 1854

oil on canvas, 29.3 × 46.3 cm

The Thomson Collection (P-C-715)

67. FRASER, WITH MR. MILLER UP, 1854

oil on canvas, 63.7 × 79.7 cm

National Gallery of Canada, Ottawa, purchased 1964 (14609)

68. Elizabeth Bickell, c. 1854

oil on canvas, 59.6 × 49.7 cm

National Gallery of Canada, Ottawa, purchased 1953 (6107)

69. John Palmer Bickell, 1854

oil on canvas, 61.2 × 51.1 cm

National Gallery of Canada, Ottawa, purchased 1953 (6106)

70. SELF-PORTRAIT, 1855

oil on canvas, 28.8 × 24.8 cm

National Gallery of Canada, Ottawa, purchased 1920 (1657)

71. ANDREW JOHN MAXHAM, 1856

oil on canvas, 35.8 × 29.0 cm

Musée du Québec, Québec, acquired before 1934 (34.268)

72. The Country House of Capt. John Walker, near Quebec, 1857

oil on canvas, 45.7 × 68.9 cm

Musée du Québec, Québec, gift of the Honourable Maurice Duplessis Estate, 1959 (59.584)

73. THE NARROWS ON LAKE ST. CHARLES, 1859

oil on canvas, 36.0 × 53.0 cm

The Thomson Collection (P-C-703)

74. Death of the Moose at Sunset. Lake Famine South of Quebec, 1859

oil on canvas, 36.0 × 53.0 cm

Glenbow Collection, Calgary, Alberta, anonymous donation, 1981 (81.7.1)

75. The Artist Painting, c. 1860

oil on canvas, 23.0 × 33.0 cm

The Thomson Collection (P-C-279)

76. THE PETS AND THE MATERIALS, 1860
oil on canvas, 26.8 × 31.8 cm
National Gallery of Canada, Ottawa, gift of Leanora D. McCarney, Ottawa, 1987,
in memory of her parents, Ethel and Frank De Rice (29,785)

77. Sportsmen at Jacques Cartier Falls, 1861

oil on canvas, 51.0 × 64.2 cm

The Thomson Collection (P-C-575)

78. (cat. 81) INDIAN CHIEFS, 1860, opposite page 9 in CONSTRUCTION
OF THE GREAT VICTORIA BRIDGE IN CANADA (London: J. Weale, 1860)
colour lithograph (Kell Brothers), 20.2 × 28.9 cm (image)

Edward P. Taylor Research Library & Archives, Art Gallery of Ontario, Toronto, purchased with the assistance of
the Walter and Duncan Gordon Charitable Foundation, 1997

79. (cat. 78) THE ICE CONE AT THE FALLS OF MONTMORENCY NEAR QUEBEC,
LOWER CANADA, IN 1853, 1853
colour lithograph on paper (Simpson), 40.0 × 58.8 cm (image)
National Archives of Canada, Ottawa, acquired from the W.H. Coverdale Collection of Canadiana, 1970 (c-041048)

80. (cat. 79) "Pour l'amour du Bon Dieu?", 1858

chromolithograph on paper, 26.8 × 27.0 cm (image)

Collection of Peter Winkworth, London

81. (cat. 80) "Va au Diable!", 1858

chromolithograph on paper, 26.8 × 22.8 cm (image)

Collection of Peter Winkworth, London

PASSENGERS AND MAIL, CROSSING THE RIVER.

C. Krieghoff, delt.   Published by John Weale, London 1860.   Kell Broᵗ lithᵈ Castle Sᵗ Holborn.

82. PASSENGERS AND MAIL, CROSSING THE RIVER, 1860
colour lithograph (Kell Brothers), 19.5 × 28.0 cm (image)
Royal Ontario Museum, Toronto, gift of Miss Mary B. Dickenson, 1962 (962.156.1)

83. View of Quebec, Canada:
From the Railway Station Opposite Quebec, the City, 1862

lithograph with watercolour on paper, 41.2 × 60.3 cm (image)

Collection of Peter Winkworth, London

THE OUTSIDER AS INSIDER:
Cornelius Krieghoff's Art of Describing

RAMSAY COOK

> By his toil, which ensured his family's livelihood, the habitant also ensured the survival of a people and its values. A brave woman by his side, settled in the shadow of the church steeple, he raised many children. Attached to the land and to the family, he ensured the continuity of his material and spiritual heritage by devoting himself to his children. His existence was a token of stability, respect and morality in keeping with a system of values he hoped to pass on to his descendants.
>
> —Jacques Mathieu and Jacques Lacoursière, *Les mémoires québécoises*

I

Krieghoff's two decades or so in Canada were a time of change for the country. Most obviously, the colony, which exercised only very limited powers of self-rule in 1841, became a largely autonomous federal dominion in 1867. Those constitutional changes were paralleled by the gradual spread of industry and urban settlement, though rural life and agriculture remained dominant until the beginning of the twentieth century. Evidence of this transformation occasionally appears in Krieghoff's paintings, but his eye was mainly trained on the French-speaking farmers and the Native people who lived at the margins. Yet it would be a serious mistake to interpret his canvases as mere exercises in

THE NARROWS ON LAKE ST. CHARLES, 1859 (detail of pl. 73)

nostalgia for a passing age. In fact, his work created an image of the lifestyle of the Quebec majority in his time, a lifestyle that would endure well beyond his death.

In emphasizing the rural life of French Canadians, Krieghoff was far from unique. Indeed, exhortations that life on the land was the essential French-Canadian vocation lay at the heart of the nationalism that developed in the nineteenth century. The challenge *Emparons-nous du sol* (We must seize the land) and other slogans romanticizing habitant life were commonplaces in the rhetoric of politicians, clerics, intellectuals, and artists. "Fellow French Canadians, remember that if we are to secure our national existence, we must cling to the land,"[1] the railway lawyer and politician George-Étienne Cartier declared in 1855. Forty years later, Bishop Louis-François Laflèche of Trois-Rivières seconded and significantly extended the preachment: "Agricultural work is the natural vocation of man on earth, the calling of the majority of the human race. It is also the one that most favours the development of man's moral, physical and intellectual qualities, and above all, that brings him closest to God."[2] On a superficial viewing, then, Krieghoff's paintings might be seen as part of this clerico-nationalist romance. But that too would be a mistake. What gives these paintings their continuing interest, both aesthetically and as a portrait of their time, is that Krieghoff drew on a different tradition. Ironically, that perspective may have helped the immigrant painter to see his subjects with a clearer eye and a sharper imagination than those who preached *la mission rurale.*

So what did Krieghoff choose to see in his new surroundings, and how did he present what he saw? Before I attempt to answer those questions by looking at the context of his art, one point needs emphasizing. Though Krieghoff is frequently described as a "documentary" artist who either succeeded or failed to capture accurately the world around him, that is not the only—or even the most important—test of his work. His paintings are not literal "documents" but rather imaginative reactions to the scenes that met his eye. As an outsider, he brought his own way of seeing; he was, as Simon Schama wrote of Benjamin West, "not a reporter in paint, a writer of historical prose. He was a poetic inventor."[3]

Exploring the context that inspired Krieghoff's poetic invention nevertheless remains essential. After that, it may be easier to understand, to assess, and even to see what he made of it. The outsider, paradoxically, became an insider.

II

The French-speaking community that Krieghoff joined in the 1840s was still recovering from the failed Rebellion of 1837–8 and struggling against the inequitable terms of the union of the Canadas that Lord Durham had imposed on it. The purpose of that union was to fulfil Durham's recommendation that the French Canadians be gradually assimilated; the new union recognized only English as the language of public affairs and gave each section of the colony equal representation, though Canada East had the larger population. French-Canadian leaders at first were angered and depressed by this situation, but they certainly did not accept it as unchangeable. Within a decade Louis-Hippolyte La Fontaine and his supporters had successfully asserted their right to speak French in the Legislative Assembly. In co-operation with Robert Baldwin and the Reform party of Canada West, they had also forced the imperial government to accept Durham's liberal recommendation: the governor should choose his advisers from the majority party in the assembly and in internal matters should accept the advice of those advisers. In 1849, when Lord Elgin accepted a bill reimbursing French Canadians, some of whom had been rebels, for losses during the rebellion, the practice of responsible government was dramatically confirmed. Angry English-speaking Tories rioted and pelted the governor's carriage with missiles and set fire to the parliament buildings. But these futile acts did little but emphasize La Fontaine's victory and Lord Elgin's good judgment. Krieghoff, doubtless seeking patronage, dedicated a series of prints to the governor in 1848; one of them, *Sledge Race near Montreal* (pl. 35), depicted Lord and Lady Elgin, together with two friends, seated in a curvaceous sleigh behind a driver and four spirited horses prancing out onto the frozen St. Lawrence.

Nor was it only at the level of organized politics that the Canadiens displayed their unwillingness to knuckle under the rule of their masters. The habitants had never in fact been the docile, uncomplaining, order-taking sheep that they are sometimes presented as, both by their own leaders and by foreign observers ("among the most harmless people in

the world," one wrote admiringly in the 1850s, "they are moral, sober and contented").[4] Even under the French regime, they had been known to erupt in protest over food shortages, high prices, and forced work.[5] So too in the years leading up to the rebellion, farmers made their complaints against landlords heard and protested local government and parish regulations, sometimes taking the law into their own hands. The raucous charivari, half celebration, half popular riot designed to enforce local customs in marital arrangements (protesting a widower's marrying a young girl, for example), often shattered the silent night in the countryside.[6] Census collection and school laws were also evaded or ignored.

Then there was the matter of winter roads and sleighs, and careless driving. The problem—or at least part of it—is set out in this detailed description: "The cariole ... is placed on low runners of wood, so that the front part of the body almost touches the ground; and when it meets with any slight impediment in the shape of a heap of snow, it drives it onward till a ridge is formed, over which it has to mount; when coming down on the other side it forms a corresponding hollow. Thus it progresses, covering the whole road with ridges and hollows like the waves of the sea, which gradually increase in size as the carioles pass them. These hollows are called *cahots*."[7]

Naturally, many travellers found these bumpy, rutted roads uncomfortably inconvenient, especially those whose sleighs sat high on narrow metal runners, these for the most part belonging to the British and the bourgeoisie. Something had to be done. Governor Sir Charles Metcalfe ordained that these flat-runnered sleighs, which the habitants favoured, should be replaced by ones with narrow metal runners, the passenger boxes sitting well above the snow. He also wanted roads cleared and horses hitched on the left side, again as measures to improve winter travel. The farmers declined to follow orders. Their work, and sometimes their play, demonstrated that their sleighs—*traînes à batons*—provided the strength and the stability required for heavy loads of logs, ice, and people. Close to the ground, as Krieghoff portrayed them in such works as *Habitants on a Trip to Town* (pl. 131), they did not subject their riders to such bone-rattling bumps. Pictures such as this one demonstrate that the independent, stubborn, and sensible habitant won the battle.[8]

If *cahots* left the habitants untroubled, their rugged sleds sometimes racing over them wildly, another obstacle to free travel was often greeted with defiance and scorn: the tollgate. Travel by water and later by railway always seems to have had a higher degree of government support than roads in Lower Canada and subsequently in Canada East. Much road building was left in the hands of property owners, and under a law passed in 1855, local roads were made the responsibility of local authorities. From the beginning of the nineteenth century, toll roads and turnpikes were built by private contractors and groups in order to provide access to the major centres of population.[9] The resulting tollgates, and the level of fees, were a constant source of irritation and controversy. The owners, naturally enough, appealed repeatedly for rate increases, while special-interest groups requested exemption from tolls; priests, lawyers, doctors, carters, and others probably received them.[10]

Among most regular road users and toll payers, farmers and their families doubtless felt the pinch most severely. One observer set out the problem this way: "The toll-gate on the St. Foy road was quite an important institution to the simple *habitans* [sic] who paid their shilling toll for the privilege of bringing to market a bunch or two of carrots and as many turnips, with a basket of eggs and some cabbages and onions in a little cart drawn by a little pony, with which surprising equipage they would stand patiently all morning in St. Anne's market, under the shadow of the old ruined Jesuit barracks, and return home contented with three or four shillings realized from their day's traffic."[11] If a third or a quarter of the day's earnings threatened to disappear at the tollgate, and especially if another portion had vanished at the tavern, the contented habitant can readily be imagined in another, more aggressive, mood. Krieghoff captured that mood several times: the nose-thumbing middle passenger standing on the typical country sleigh in *The Toll Gate* (fig. 16) is an example. If, as Dennis Reid's essay suggests, the tollgate and the tollgate keeper were identified with British authority and patronage, this visual anecdote becomes even more powerful. No wonder the assembly received petitions "to Prevent furious driving on certain Highways in Lower Canada"[12] (see pl. 128).

As the state found the habitant difficult to regulate, the Roman Catholic Church, that other source of power and discipline in *canadien*

society, also experienced problems in its sphere. The principal lesson that the Church hierarchy had learned from the abortive rebellion—a rebellion that might have led to a considerable diminution of ecclesiastical authority—was that reinforcements were essential. In the 1840s, recruitment to clerical orders, both at home and abroad, was intensified. Religious orders were founded and imported, new social activities were undertaken, and most important, control over education was reasserted as lay teachers were replaced by clerics.[13] Bishop Ignace Bourget of Montreal and later Bishop Laflèche of Trois-Rivières were new leaders determined that Catholic moral and political teachings should permeate every aspect of French-Canadian life. Their doctrine of ultramontanism taught that the Church should guide the state by ensuring that popularly elected politicians followed the precepts of their Church. Otherwise, immorality and secularism would sap the strength of Church and nation, leaving the Canadiens victims of such heresies as popular sovereignty and the separation of church and state.[14]

While the Church hierarchy dealt with the political leaders and issued pronouncements—*mandements*—to local clerics and the faithful, it was the parish priests who knew what rules were being broken, as Krieghoff showed in *Lent* (fig. 17). Enforcement of observations such as the Lenten fast, to say nothing of policing the myriad of venial sins, must often have been an infuriating challenge. The least sign of moral danger had to be checked. In 1877 one parish priest warned, "Ostentatious attire, the indecent manner in which women and young girls indulge are

Figure 16 *(top)*
THE TOLL GATE, 1863
oil on canvas, 45.0 × 64.8 cm
The Beaverbrook Art Gallery, Fredericton, N.B.,
gift of the Royal Securities Corp. Ltd., 1963
(1963.5)

Figure 17 *(bottom)*
LENT, 1848
oil on canvas, 31.3 × 40.0 cm
The Collection of Power Corporation of
Canada, Montreal

not the way to earn God's blessing…. Such attire has not escaped my notice, the so-called hats covered in flowers, those who wear neither collarets nor shawls."[15] The parish priest knew from the confessional that large gaps often existed between the Church's commands and his parishioners' behaviour in, for example, sexual matters. Even when the spirit was willing—and it wasn't always—the flesh was weak.[16] And if the rules of life were broken, the rules of death, which were also the priest's responsibility, could be a problem as well. Freethinkers and Protestants could readily be refused burial in consecrated ground, but what about adulterers, deserters, and drunkards? They too existed.[17]

The immoral behaviour that shocked the priest in the confessional or forced him to refuse a parishioner the last rites could best be eliminated, or at least minimized, by regulating those everyday activities that nurtured temptation. Leisure time was at least potentially the devil's time: festivals, charivaris, and carnivals encouraged singing, dancing, drinking, card playing, and lotteries. "The only way to impose high morals in a parish is to banish entertainment," a bishop advised a local *curé* (see pl. 13). Efforts to suppress these activities were made repeatedly, suggesting limited success. In 1870 an instruction stated, "Do not keep company with a woman who likes to dance… Dance hall: Devil's dwelling."[18]

No "Devil's dwelling" caused more clerical consternation than the tavern and the inn, or *auberge* —those "public houses of debauchery," those "sanctuaries of dissipation and idleness."[19] Repeated attempts to regulate the *auberges* failed; their popularity and their numbers grew. In the St. Anne quarter of Montreal alone, there were reported to be fifty-four unlicensed drinking spots.[20] The country *auberge* naturally became one of Krieghoff's favourite subjects (see pl. 150). He certainly displayed the merriment and inebriation that the Church and other leaders of society deplored.

Drinking and drunkenness, while hardly a new phenomenon in post-rebellion Canada, became a major cause of concern in the 1840s. Cheap liquor, rum in particular, had long been widely available in the countryside—consumed at celebrations and festivals, useful in trade, and sometimes added to polluted water as a purifier. By mid-century Bishop Bourget and others recognized the growing number of licensed and unlicensed outlets as a major social issue and also as an area in which the Church could assert its influence as part of the ultramontane religious revival. Initiated with the help of a well-known French temperance cleric, Msgr. Charles Forbin-Janson, bishop of Nancy, temperance campaigns were begun and temperance societies established in many parishes. One of the earliest converts to the new cause was Father Charles Chiniquy, the *curé* of Beauport, near Quebec City. He rapidly became the star—even the comet—of the temperance campaign. His rhetorical skills, earthy language, and ability to appeal to both religious and ethnic sentiments made him, by the late 1840s, a major figure in the life of Canada East.

Bourget recognized his talents and invited him to the campaign in the Montreal diocese, where Chiniquy had come to live at Longueuil with his mentor, Father L.-M. Brassard. Between 1847 and 1851 the temperance missionary toured the colony brandishing a gold crucifix, declaiming on the evils of drink, and thoroughly enjoying the adulation of the crowds. He was a great success. *Les Mélanges religieux*, a leading Catholic paper, reported that in one eighteen-month period he had preached five hundred sermons and signed 200,000 penitents to the pledge. By 1850, two years later, the figure had risen to 400,000, more than half the French-speaking population of Canada East.[21] Wherever he went, Chiniquy attracted followers, and his importance was quickly recognized. At Longueuil in July 1849 he was presented with a gold medal before a crowd of 12,000; a year later the Legislative Assembly of the Canadas voted five hundred pounds to support his endeavours.[22]

Chiniquy, like some other performers on the temperance-revivalist stage, proved a man capable of demagoguery and possessed of unbounded egoism and powerful appetites. Early in his campaign, Bourget rebuked him for using vulgar language, and the bishop later accused the temperance leader of eating meat on Friday. In 1851 Chiniquy was suddenly banished from the Montreal diocese—indeed, from the Canadian Church—for sexual misbehaviour, neither the first nor the last such infraction of priestly rules.[23] Exiled to Chicago, he was eventually excommunicated; following a short and disruptive period with the Presbyterian Church in the United States, he returned to Canada to work as a missionary among his former compatriots on behalf of the Canadian Presbyterians.[24]

During the Montreal-Longueuil years Chiniquy certainly enjoyed the company of a wide circle of people, apparently including the young Cornelius Krieghoff. The high-spirited Chiniquy would probably have been a figure of interest to the recently arrived artist, although Krieghoff was of Protestant background and was not, if his later paintings are evidence, a temperance supporter. Perhaps the relationship was a purely professional one: a story circulated in Longueuil that Krieghoff painted the temperance crusader's portrait, perhaps on commission. Isidore Hurteau, a Longueuil businessman and politician who was convinced by Chiniquy that he should close his brewery,[25] may have been the patron. It was from Hurteau's property that the portrait was taken and burned later in the nineteenth century, after the priest had defected to the Protestant cause.[26]

Chiniquy sat for two other portraits, both commissioned by admirers, one painted by Théophile Hamel and the other by Antoine Plamondon, the leading portrait artists of the time (see fig. 18, page 152). It is at least possible that Chiniquy makes an appearance in one Krieghoff painting that may be anti-clerical. *Breaking Lent* (or *A Friday's Surprise*) (pl. 11) is the first of two versions of this scene. Both paintings, made at Longueuil, sympathetically depict a family caught in the act of breaking Church rules. There is some variation in the number of sinners and in facial expressions, but the most striking change between the two versions is the priest. In *Lent*, the second painting, the priest is an elderly cleric dressed in a conventional manner: probably Father Brassard, the local priest and Chiniquy's mentor and defender. In *Breaking Lent* the

Figure 18
Francis Davignon (after Hamel)
Father Chiniquy, Advocate of
Temperance in Canada, 1848
lithograph, 48.3 × 35.4 cm
Musée du Québec, Québec, purchased 1978
(78.383)

priest is much younger, elegantly dressed, and sporting a handsome silver-headed cane. This obviously dramatic figure may have been modelled on Chiniquy, though there is no documentation to support the speculation. Too bad, for in their different fashions Chiniquy and Krieghoff were two of nineteenth-century Quebec's most intriguing outsiders: one a rebel priest, the other an immigrant painter.

III

The economic and social structure of Canada East between the rebellion and Confederation resembled the *ancien régime* in many respects. The presence of the British merchant and capitalist class, of course, marked one radical difference. With the Conquest had come a new language and religion and a flow of immigration, most of it English-speaking, that would alter the demographic structure of the colony significantly. But change was slow, especially in the rural areas. The seigneurial system of land tenure, in which habitants were granted strips of the seigneur's domain in return for specified duties and obligations, remained in force until 1854. Only after that did most farmers become landowners in their own right. But the shift did little to resolve the problem of the scarcity of land to meet the demands of a rapidly increasing rural population. For the French-speaking community the highest birth rate in the Western world during the nineteenth century was both a strength and a challenge: it ensured the culture's dominance in the face of immigration, but it also created a crisis of rural overpopulation.

A very large majority of Canadiens lived in the country, working in agriculture. In 1851 just under 15 per cent of the population inhabited urban areas, mainly Montreal and Quebec City; that proportion reached about 20 per cent in 1871. Over those same decades the total population of Canada East grew from 890,261 to 1,191,516, while the representation of francophones in the total increased from 75 to 78 per cent. Francophones dominated the countryside, except in the Eastern Townships and to a lesser degree in the Outaouais and south of Montreal. The anglophone presence was also important in the two major cities. In 1851, 54 per cent of Montrealers were English-speaking, as were 35 per cent of the inhabitants of Quebec City. By the 1871 census the percentages had been reversed in Montreal, 60 per cent now being French-speaking. The same trend was evident in Quebec City, where English speakers remained a strong, but declining, minority.[27] Obviously a very large proportion of francophones continued to be attached to the land during these years when Krieghoff was at work painting the French-Canadian farmer's way of life.

Rural life was certainly not an easy existence, yet it apparently was for the Canadiens the best available. In 1855 *Le Journal de Québec* remarked that the habitant

> knows no other love than the one he feels for his small farm. Of all places on earth, he cherishes the place where he was born, even if at times life is harsh... His longings never extend beyond his hearth; his imagination is restricted by the fences around his property. He asks nothing more than

to live and die where his forefathers lived and died.... No fellow is as cheerful, happy and satisfied with his lot.... As far as audacity and undertakings are concerned, the Canadian habitant falls behind the other populations in America, but his incapacity to look forward does not depend on his intelligence.... Everything that America could teach him in the way of business could not match what he could teach America in the way of kindness, courtesy, and know-how.[28]

Without doubt an idealized picture, though one often repeated by local and foreign observers alike. In fact, no matter how firmly attached to the acres of his ancestors, the farmer on the overpopulated St. Lawrence lowlands faced a different reality. The rapidly growing rural population, combined with agricultural methods that failed to improve productivity and often exhausted the soil, forced many young Canadiens to leave home. One option was emigration to the United States, where work in the cotton mills and other labour-intensive, and low-paid, employment beckoned. Between 1840 and 1870 more than 170,000 chose this alternative; the numbers would increase over the next twenty years.[29] Such figures suggest a less than contented, more mobile rural population than the literary evidence would indicate.

Nor did this unhappy state of things go unnoticed. "*La grande hémorragie*" revealed rural distress and poverty. It was also thought to threaten national survival and, not incidentally, to depopulate Catholic parishes. The colonization movement of the mid-nineteenth century was founded on the conviction that the Canadiens must be kept at home.

It sometimes united opposites—clerics such as Bishop Bourget, anti-clericals such as Louis-Joseph Papineau—in the common cause of national survival. The goal was to redirect the southern flow of emigrants toward the underdeveloped regions of Quebec north of Montreal, in the St-Maurice valley, in the Saguenay–Lac St-Jean region, later in Témiscamingue, and sometimes in western Canada. While many priests and laymen worked to establish colonization societies and to pressure politicians with the urgency of the crisis, Curé Antoine Labelle of St-Jérôme was the most energetic of them all. His motivation was both religious and national. The north became the promised land, colonization "a providential mission," which, Christian Morissonneau has written, "can be accomplished through the cross and the plow, the two symbols of French-Canadian values."[30]

Colonization proved considerably less than a complete solution to the "national hemorrhage," but it certainly drew tens of thousands of farmers into new territories. There, together with his family, the new settler cleared land, sowed crops, built a house, and in winter went to work in the woods cutting timber. For some the cold, isolation, and unproductive soil proved unbearable; partly cleared farms were abandoned in favour of the cotton mills of New England. For the ones who persevered, there were the comforts of the family and the *chantier* (shanty), which Krieghoff captured in many canvases. *Return from the Hunt* (pl. 151) sets out the main elements of the colonists' existence, including the house so carefully described by a contemporary:

It's a box consisting of twelve or twenty squares of unhewn timber, fir or pine, superposed one on top of the other, and whose ends are fitted together; this type of architecture is technically referred to as dovetail. The roof, which is 8 or 10 feet from the ground, with a slope of 2 to 3 feet, is generally made of birch, fir or ash bark, and sometimes of split cedar. As the camps were generally built before the establishment of a local sawmill, the doors and windows, if they were of polished wood, came from neighbouring parishes. We visited some camps where not one plank had been sawn and not one nail had been hammered in. Everything had been accomplished with an axe and dowels.[31]

For colonists and those who remained on the long, narrow lots along the St. Lawrence alike, rural life changed only slowly in the decades before Confederation. Daily life was focused on the home, the family, and the Church and often enough on the *auberges* and taverns, especially during shopping trips to the village (see fig. 19).

Occasionally this closed little world was disrupted by a dancing party, a festival, a charivari, a horse race, or even a travelling salesman (see fig. 20). Rail links, especially after 1850, began to draw communities together, but they touched mainly the larger centres: the St. Lawrence and Atlantic Railway between Longueuil and Sherbrooke, and the Grand Trunk, with five hundred miles of line in Canada East, running from Lévis to Montreal (see pl. 83). But most rural Canadiens—and they were the majority—would probably have recognized this solemn modern description of their lives: "Poor, uneducated if not illiterate—some

counties have more churches than schools—forced to slave away, this rural world has few openings on the outside world. It branches out into parishes where life revolves around the village inhabited by the priest, the blacksmith, the shoemaker, in most cases a notary and a shopkeeper, sometimes a bailiff, a doctor, an underpaid teacher, a few of independent means"[32] (see pl. 17).

That world fascinated Cornelius Krieghoff.

IV

So little is known with certainty about Krieghoff's educational background, formal or otherwise, that it is impossible to determine why he was so drawn to the lives of ordinary people in Canada East. Perhaps, like any immigrant, he was struck by what was distinctive about the country where he had chosen to settle. Or perhaps he discovered a market niche for pictures of rural life among the members of the English-speaking community, particularly those soldiers in the garrison at Quebec City who doubtless wanted to take home authentic souvenirs. But it also seems likely that his Dutch-German background gave him a familiarity with the genre painting that the Dutch since the seventeenth century had made their own.[33] By the nineteenth century many German, British, and American painters had taken up this style, and Krieghoff may have had an opportunity to view some of the American examples during his soldiering years in the United States.[34] But no concrete evidence exists to confirm any of these possibilities. What is certain is that genre painting

Figure 19 *(top)*
RETURN FROM THE VILLAGE, 1848
oil on canvas, 35.5 × 53.3 cm
The Thomson Collection (P-C-117)

Figure 20 *(bottom)*
THE PICTURE PEDDLER, 1846
oil on canvas, 31.8 × 41.9 cm
Private collection

was the style that Krieghoff introduced to Canada in the 1840s and would practise with such success throughout his career.

He was not, of course, exclusively a genre painter. Occasionally he tried his hand at portraits and often produced work featuring Native people, both individually and against a romantic wilderness. His *Steamship Quebec* (pl. 65) and the occasional railway or lumbering canvas, especially the series said to have been done for the Legislative Assembly in Quebec,[35] demonstrate his consciousness of commercial life.

Yet the scenes from habitant life—usually in isolation but occasionally in contrast with bourgeois activity—form a very special, even central, part of Krieghoff's oeuvre. Soon after he arrived in his new country, he began to record rural life, and he never lost interest in it. He did not stereotype the habitant, though he repeated certain formulaic elements—blue and red tuques, *ceintures fléchées*, sleighs, dogs, and children. But there is variety too, and attention to detail that becomes more impressive the more closely the work is examined. These people evidently had a strong appeal for Krieghoff. He presented them as self-assertive and proud, a people who often lived in harsh surroundings, but who did more than merely endure. His image, combining colourful dress, occasional defiance of law and convention, and enjoyment of life, might almost have been the habitant's view of himself.

At first, naturally, Krieghoff depicted farm life in the long-settled areas around Montreal, where his wife's family lived. *Habitant Sleigh, View near the Canada Line* (pl. 12) introduces many of the main elements.

Winter provides the backdrop for a family bundled up in heavy coats, tuques, and fur hats and loaded into a horse-drawn sleigh. A scrappy black-and-white dog teases the horse, while a few undernourished chickens peck at the frozen ground in search of food. As is so often the case, trees—sometimes barren of foliage, sometimes evergreens—dot the frozen landscape, here close to outbuildings and a square-timbered house. A similar habitation can be seen in the distance.

From his earliest genre paintings to some of his last works, Krieghoff attempted to portray what he thought was distinctive about habitant life. The family he recognized as central, and it almost always included several generations. Isolated and harsh though rural existence might seem, Krieghoff recognized that what made it acceptable and productive was that it was communal: people worked and played together whenever possible, whether in established villages such as Longueuil or on the colonizing frontier. Despite the isolation of *Habitant Home in Winter* (fig. 21), there is a sense of community, everyone involved in what appears to be a homecoming from market. Krieghoff took pains to include babies, wrapped in winter blankets, and children with toboggans or throwing snowballs. *Playtime, Village School* (pl. 124) captures the spirit of rural community effectively. Here, as so frequently, Krieghoff's affection for, even identification with, rural families is palpable.

Dress was also a distinctive feature of habitant life. Since so many of these paintings are winter scenes, the characteristic tuque is always present in its red, blue, and sometimes white variations. If these colours had

Figure 21
HABITANT HOME IN WINTER, 1855
oil on canvas, 42.5 × 59.7 cm
The Thomson Collection (P-C-111)

regional or political significance in real life—blue for Montreal, red for Quebec, and white for Trois-Rivières—Krieghoff varied them only for artistic reasons. Women wear bonnets, while fur hats usually adorn the heads of the more prosperous classes. White blanket coats, usually with two horizontal stripes and held tight with a colourful sash, the traditional *ceinture fléchée*, appear repeatedly. The women's attire is also colourful: full, floor-length skirts, often in red, combined with woollen jackets and scarves in contrasting hues. Children appear like small adults. Krieghoff's habitants are clothed in fashions that had scarcely changed since the days of New France, a fact that suggests stylization.[36]

Another constant in these scenes of everyday life is the horses; sleighs and horses together reveal Krieghoff's perception of class and ethnic differences in mid-century Canada. The horse that he obviously enjoyed painting was a distinctive breed known as the *canadien*. A rather small horse with powerful legs and shoulders, broad hooves, and a heavy mane and tail, this animal descended from the Norman and Breton horses introduced into New France in the seventeenth century. A mid-nineteenth-century description details the horse so often present in Krieghoff's work:

> The Canadian is generally small, rarely exceeding fifteen hands, and more often falling short of that....
>
> His characteristics are a broad forehead; ears somewhat wide apart, and not infrequently a basin face; the latter perhaps a trace of the far remote Spanish blood said to exist in his veins....

His crest is lofty and his demeanour proud and courageous. His breast is full and broad; his shoulder strong, though somewhat inclined to be heavy; his back broad and his croup round, fleshy and muscular.... His legs and feet are admirable; the bone large and flat, and the sinews big, and nervous as steel springs.... His fetlocks are shaggy; his mane voluminous and massive, not seldom, if untrained, falling on both sides of his neck, and his tail abundant, both having a peculiar *crimped* wave....

He cannot be called a speedy horse in his pure state; but he is emphatically a quick one, an indefatigable undaunted traveller, with the greatest endurance, day in and day out, allowing him to go at his own pace, say from six to eight miles the hour, with a horse's load behind him.... He is extremely hardy, will thrive on anything, or almost nothing; is docile, though high-spirited, remarkably sure-footed on the worst ground, and has a fine, high action, bending his knee roundly and setting his foot squarely on the ground.[37]

This is the horse that invariably appears, singly, in Krieghoff's habitant scenes, often decorated with a dangling red or blue ribbon and harnessed in the recognized rural fashion—*attelage à fetons*.[38] *Carting Ice* (fig. 22) shows the worthy animal in its many virtues: strength, sure-footedness, even docility under the driver's whip. Krieghoff captured it in many poses and in the variety of colours that characterized it. "The Canadians drive single, that is only one horse to a sleigh," one observer wrote in the early 1840s, "a mode which gives at once the most perfect control of the animal, and taxes his powers to the utmost."[39] And the large hooves ensured that this small horse "capable of pulling a sleigh

just as easily as a plough, getting over snowbanks without sinking in too deep, braving blizzards, managing winter with agility and relative ease."[40]

The *canadien* was not the only type of horse in Canada East or the only breed to appear in Krieghoff's pictures. The British introduced several new strains both for heavy work and for pleasure. Especially notable is the larger, elegant trotter. *Lady and Gentleman Driving Cariole Tandem with Two Bay Horses* (fig. 23) portrays people from a class clearly separated from the habitant farm. The passengers, almost certainly British, are stylishly dressed and warmly robed. The proud horses, trained to trot on their narrow hooves, are decorated with upright red plumes and move in tandem.

The sleigh, as much as the horses, distinguished the classes and often the ethnic groups. It oversimplifies matters only slightly to observe that the habitant sleighs were built for work, the bourgeois sleighs for personal transport and pleasure. Krieghoff recognized this distinction over and over again. For the British, and for the French-speaking middle class in the cities, who appear in *Place d'Armes à Montréal* (pl. 34), the sculpted, high sleigh with narrow metal runners was best suited to the city, where the snow was cleared. It slid easily along a smooth surface and created few, if any, *cahots*. In the country, where snow was abundant, deep, and long-lasting, the habitant favoured, and the city folk deplored, a quite different model. This one, with its wide wooden runners, sat nearly flat on the snow, pushing it aside as it moved along and creating bumps. At its most elementary, it was called un *traîne à batons* and was used for heavy loads of wood, ice, or game (see fig. 22). In *Habitants on a*

Figure 22
CARTING ICE, c. 1850
oil on board, 17.2 × 27.0 cm
The Thomson Collection (P-C-326)

Figure 23
LADY AND GENTLEMAN DRIVING
CARIOLE TANDEM WITH TWO BAY
HORSES, c. 1850
oil on canvas, 24.2 × 44.5 cm
The Thomson Collection (P-C-181)

Figure 24 (top)
THE BAKER'S MISHAP, c. 1854
oil on canvas, 20.2 × 28.2 cm
The Thomson Collection (P-C-330)

Figure 25 (bottom)
ON THE ST. LAWRENCE, 1858
oil on canvas, 33.6 × 45.7 cm
The Thomson Collection (P-C-670)

Trip to Town (pl. 131) Krieghoff catches it, and its impact on the roads, almost perfectly. A more sophisticated version, the *berline*, also sat close to the surface but had a box and seats built on top of the runners, making it more comfortable for family travel. A further modification in which the box sat slightly above the runners, such as the one that Krieghoff showed in *Habitant Sleigh, View near the Canada Line* (pl. 12), was known as a *berlot*. It could also be adapted to the needs of deliverymen bringing milk or bread (see fig. 24).

The *berline* appears in many of Krieghoff's scenes, not always easily distinguishable from the somewhat more shapely sleigh known as a cariole, whose low-slung box sat on runners that curved upward at both front and back. The mobile drinking party travelling *On the St. Lawrence* (fig. 25) is taking place in a vehicle of this variety. Almost any of Krieghoff's outdoor group scenes, whether merrymakers tumbling out of Jolifou's *auberge* (see pl. 123) or gathered on a Sunday afternoon at the frozen falls of Montmorency (see fig. 26), include most of these sleigh models except the habitant's obviously *déclassé traîne à batons*. On the other hand, revealingly, every version of toll evasion includes this model. Krieghoff had a very sharp eye for social gradations.[41]

While many of his habitant horse-and-sleigh pictures depict family travel or everyday tasks, some display hard-working people at play, often in a reckless posture. Driving carelessly in winter was obviously hazardous, as *Off the Road—The Upset Sleigh* (fig. 27) suggests. Here pigs and people are all in a heap, the *canadien* horse upended, tangled in its harness.

Figure 26
MONTMORENCY FALLS IN WINTER,
QUEBEC, 1852
oil on canvas, 67.0 × 96.8 cm
The Thomson Collection (P-C-239)

Figure 27
OFF THE ROAD—THE UPSET SLEIGH,
c. 1856
oil on canvas, 33.9 × 54.7 cm
The Thomson Collection (P-C-183)

Then there was racing. This was a pastime that since the eighteenth century the authorities had attempted to curb without much success. One writer in the 1840s remarked that with "a glorious little nag to convey him from the Church door on a cold winter's day, when speed is gain, the Canadian engages in racing even at the close of divine service. The practice has gone to such [an] extent as to endanger the safety of persons on foot, and the law now ordains that no fast driving shall be permitted within a certain short distance of the sacred edifice.... Prone to indulge in contests of speed on Sundays, and festivals, of which his calendar affords a goodly number, *Jean-Baptiste* is not less inclined to rejoice in swift riding on convenient occasions at other times."[42] *Sleigh Race on the St. Lawrence at Quebec* (pl. 21), set against the Citadel and the gathering winter storm, brilliantly recreates this exhilarating sport. Organized horse racing, which grew in popularity in the nineteenth century, came to Quebec with the British as a sport for the upper classes.[43] *Fraser, with Mr. Miller Up* (pl. 67) provides a nice contrast with the tough little *canadien* horse and adds yet another interesting social commentary.

There are many other examples of the sharpness of Krieghoff's powers of observation when it came to describing in paint the rural life. In many variations he captures the solitary life of the colonists opening up new farmlands. After 1854, when the seigneurial system was abolished, he turned more frequently to the new colonization areas. *Bringing in the Deer* (pl. 126) illustrates the stark existence that these families endured, their dependence on each other and on the fruits of the land for basic

subsistence. Not often prominent in Krieghoff's pictures, the rudimentary cross at the right edge of the painting symbolizes the faith that, together with so much work, went into the colonization venture. *Winter in Laval Mountains near Quebec (The Crack in the Ice)* (pl. 138), a painting of remarkable quality, tells a similar story in another way. This time the large dead tree at the centre of the canvas suggests a life so far out on the frontier that survival and failure weigh constantly in the balance. The lengthy crack in the ice only emphasizes the point. Those urban intellectuals and clerical leaders who preached the virtues of colonization might have found in Krieghoff's art some questions about the human costs of this nationalist enterprise.

If life was sometimes very hard, it could also be filled with exuberant pleasure. Krieghoff knew, as others knew before him, that the French Canadians liked to enjoy life, sometimes to excess. Early in the nineteenth century a traveller discovered what the Church had long known:

> They are fond of dancing and entertainments, at particular seasons and festivals, on which occasions they eat, drink, and dance in constant succession. When their long fast in Lent is concluded, they have their "jour gras," or days of feasting. Then it is that every production of the farm is presented for the gratification of their appetites: immense turkey pies, huge joints of pork, beef and mutton; spacious tureens of soup, or thick milk; besides fish, fowl and a plentiful supply of fruit pies decorate the board. Perhaps fifty or a hundred sit down to dine; rum is drunk by the half pint, often without water, ... and the room resounds with jollity and merriment. No sooner, however, does the clash of knives and forks cease, than the violin strikes up and the dances commence....[44]

Forty years later Krieghoff demonstrated that this joyful spirit was thriving in the *auberges* that dotted the countryside. Several times he reworked the well-known scene presented in his masterpiece, *Breaking Up of a Country Ball in Canada, Early Morning* (pl. 125). Here is a riot of tipsy action combining in Bruegelesque fashion many of the familiar elements found in other Krieghoff paintings: colourful dress adorning bourgeois and habitant alike, good *canadien* horses, *berlines* and carioles, snow-shoes, barking dogs, escaping pigs, the last few drinks for the road, and hints of hangovers to come. Here was life being enjoyed to the full, lacking, as Gérard Morisset would later complain, "the spiritual element of these countrymen,"[45] but no less convincing for that. Working, sleigh racing, colonizing, hunting, drinking, dancing, and shouting—this is a vital slice of life, set against the astonishing range of beautiful colours that nature wears in Canada.

V

Krieghoff, the outsider, painted central aspects of mid-nineteenth-century French-Canadian society that his best-known contemporaries—Joseph Légaré, Antoine Plamondon, Théophile Hamel—largely ignored. They made sacred art, historical art, and portraiture, work that found a growing market.[46] They painted in a tradition, Laurier Lacroix has argued, where "the purpose of art was to elevate people above the human condition; it had to obey certain rules and conventions governing the genre, structure and organization of the works; and to imitate specific models."[47]

With his background in Dutch and German genre painting, Krieghoff had a different goal: to portray the human condition, not to elevate his viewers above it. Indeed, his pictures often seem designed to make the viewer part of the incident depicted, to bring the viewer inside the picture. That, according to the nineteenth-century French critic Eugène Fromentin, was the great achievement of Dutch art and what distinguished it from the French academic tradition. "We live in the picture," he wrote in 1876, "we walk about in it, we look into its depths, we are tempted to raise our heads and look at the sky."[48] Krieghoff's most successful images evoke exactly that response (see pl. 60). The more closely these works are examined, the more convincingly they reveal this outsider's success in drawing his viewers inside part of the world that was nineteenth-century French Canada. Krieghoff saw what he painted; then he transformed it into art. "The eye," as Sir Kenneth Clark once remarked, "always knows more than it sees...."[49]

PLATES 84–122

84. A LORETTE INDIAN, c. 1855

oil on canvas, 28.3 × 23.2 cm

McCord Museum of Canadian History, Montreal, bequest of Arnold Wainwright, Q.C., 1967 (M967.100.9)

85. A CAUGHNAWAGA WOMAN, c. 1855

oil on canvas, 28.0 × 23.1 cm

McCord Museum of Canadian History, Montreal, bequest of Arnold Wainwright, Q.C., 1967 (M967.100.10)

86. INDIAN WOMAN, MOCCASIN SELLER, c. 1855

oil on canvas, 28.4 × 23.4 cm

The Thomson Collection (P-C-678)

87. The Trapper, c. 1855

oil on canvas, 28.5 × 23.5 cm

The Thomson Collection (P-C-499a)

88. Head of a Habitant, c. 1855

oil on canvas, 33.5 × 25.6 cm

Montreal Museum of Fine Arts, Mrs. J.H.R. Molson Bequest, 1910 (1910.307)

89. Head of a Habitant, c. 1855

oil on canvas, 30.5 × 25.4 cm

Montreal Museum of Fine Arts, Mrs. J.H.R. Molson Bequest, 1910 (1910.308)

90. The Indian Moccasin Seller, c. 1855
oil on canvas, 28.5 × 23.5 cm
The Thomson Collection (P-C-499b)

91. THE WOODCUTTER, 1857

oil on canvas, 28.2 × 23.3 cm

The Thomson Collection (P-C-727)

92. Hunter in a Blizzard, c. 1858

oil on canvas, 28.5 × 23.5 cm

The Thomson Collection (P-C-717)

93. Indian Trapper on Snowshoes, 1858

oil on canvas, 28.2 × 23.0 cm

The Thomson Collection (P-C-231)

94. "Pour le Bon Dieu?", 1859

oil on canvas, 26.7 × 21.6 cm

Kastel Gallery, Montreal

95. "Va au Diable!", 1859

oil on canvas, 26.7 × 21.6 cm

Kastel Gallery, Montreal

[177]

96. Calling the Moose, c. 1860

oil on canvas, 27.0 × 21.5 cm

The Thomson Collection (P-C-66)

97. Hunter Resting Gun on a Snowshoe, c. 1860

oil on canvas, 28.5 × 23.0 cm

The Thomson Collection (P-C-452)

98. GOING TO MARKET, c. 1860

oil on canvas, 28.2 × 23.0 cm

The Thomson Collection (P-C-675)

99. The Old Poacher, c. 1860

oil on canvas, 28.3 × 23.1 cm

The Thomson Collection (P-C-291)

100. The Berry Seller, 1860

oil on canvas, 28.8 × 23.6 cm

National Archives of Canada, Ottawa, acquired before 1922 (C-010698)

101. Lorette Caribou Hunter, 1862

oil on canvas, 28.4 × 23.2 cm

The Thomson Collection (P-C-677)

102. The Indian Hunter, 1866

oil on canvas, 28.3 × 23.5 cm

The Thomson Collection (P-C-175a)

103. Indian Encampment at Big Rock, c. 1853

oil on canvas, 32.4 × 55.5 cm

The Thomson Collection (KRT-C-5)

104. THE HUNTERS, 1854

oil on canvas, 38.4 × 50.2 cm

McCord Museum of Canadian History, Montreal, bequest of Arnold Wainwright, Q.C., 1967 (M967.100.3)

105. Portage near Falls of Grand'Mère, St. Maurice River, 1855

oil on canvas, 53.2 × 61.1 cm

The Collection of Power Corporation of Canada, Montreal

106. INDIANS DANCING, 1855

oil on academy board, 18.9 × 30.3 cm

National Archives of Canada, Ottawa, acquired before 1934 (C-146150)

107. The Indian Campsite, 1857

oil on canvas, 38.5 × 51.2 cm

The Thomson Collection (p-c-333)

108. Taking Shelter from the Storm, 1857

oil on canvas, 33.3 × 46.0 cm

The Thomson Collection (p-c-616)

109. In the Thousand Islands, c. 1858

oil on canvas, 34.0 × 50.8 cm

Art Gallery of Ontario, Toronto, bequest of Mrs. H. M. Mowat, Toronto, 1939 (2533)

110. INDIANS IN THE EMPLOY OF THE HUDSON'S BAY COMPANY AT A PORTAGE, 1858

oil on canvas, 40.6 × 50.8 cm

The Thomson Collection (P-C-656)

III. Indians Hunting a Caribou, c. 1860

oil on canvas, 45.7 × 38.0 cm

The Thomson Collection (P-C-244)

112. LAKE MEMPHREMAGOG, c. 1860

oil on canvas, 23.0 × 28.1 cm

The Thomson Collection (P-C-874)

113. Indian Hunters on the St. Maurice River, 1860

oil on canvas, 46.7 × 43.1 cm

The Collection of Power Corporation of Canada, Montreal

114. Chippewas on Lake Superior, 1860

oil on canvas, 40.6 × 61.3 cm

The Thomson Collection (P-C-314)

115. INDIAN HUNTERS, 1861

oil on canvas, 23.2 × 28.3 cm

The Thomson Collection (P-C-331)

116. After the Kill, 1861

oil on canvas, 20.5 × 34.5 cm

The Thomson Collection (P-C-69)

117. Shooting the Rapids, 1861

oil on canvas, 23.2 × 28.3 cm

National Archives of Canada, Ottawa, acquired before 1934 (C-146152)

118. Canadian Autumn, View on the Road to Lake St. John, 1862

oil on canvas, 56.8 × 88.4 cm

Private collection

119. On Lake Laurent, 1863

oil on canvas, 36.2 × 54.0 cm

The Thomson Collection (P-C-746)

120. (cat. 121) THE HABITANT FARM, 1856
oil on canvas, 61.0 × 91.5 cm
National Gallery of Canada, Ottawa, gift of Gordon C. Edwards, Ottawa, 1923,
in memory of Senator and Mrs. W. C. Edwards (2036)

121. (cat. 120) WINTER SCENE, BLIZZARD, 1856

oil on canvas, 33.6 × 46.1 cm

The Thomson Collection (P-C-632)

122. Settler's Log House, 1856

oil on canvas, 62.2 × 92.7 cm

Art Gallery of Ontario, Toronto, purchased with funds from the Reuben Wells Leonard Estate, Toronto, 1937 (2413)

Perceiving the Other:
French-Canadian and Indian Iconography in the Work of Cornelius Krieghoff

François-Marc Gagnon

Krieghoff's Place in Canadian Art

I would find it difficult to discuss Krieghoff, and particularly his French-Canadian iconography, without taking account of the writings of the great French-Canadian art historian Gérard Morisset. His approach was so deeply connected to his nationality that I feel a certain discomfort in distancing myself from it. Morisset's position within the historiography of his country's art was defined largely by his questioning of the place his English-speaking predecessors had assigned to Krieghoff—that of a pioneer of Canadian art.

> Not so long ago, art critics believed that Canadian painting began with Cornelius Krieghoff. In their minds, it was quite clear that Canadians before Krieghoff, poor, uncouth and narrow-minded, were capable of nothing but inadequately tilling their land, producing numerous children and indulging in various vulgar amusements. It was suggested that Canadians of the 1860s had failed to understand Krieghoff's art— the height of infamy!—and that their grandchildren had finally only been awakened to painting through contemplation of the works of the "Group of Seven." Needless to say, the history of Canadian painting was full of deficiencies.[1]

As far as Morisset was concerned, these "deficiencies" were in fact monumental omissions that amounted to virtually ignoring the art of New France and denying the French contribution to the development of Canadian art. Worse still, that perception constituted a major injustice to his people, his nation, represented as a "poor, uncouth and narrow-minded" rabble, incapable of appreciating the arts before Krieghoff's era.

Morisset mentioned no names. Which "art critics" was he talking about? First in line, most probably, was Newton MacTavish.

> The reasons for Krieghoff's popularity are rather odd. This painter is a merrymaker who is not above lifting a pint with his affluent clients; the painting he produces at an industrial rate—his depictions of drinking bouts and the drunken faces of his characters, the rather crude humour of his genre scenes, the violent and garish colours of his autumn landscapes—is accessible to everyone. Most important, he exploits the secret desires of his clientele.... This *amusing, anecdotal painting* is often nothing but a rehash of the most mediocre productions of the School of Düsseldorf. To think that McTavish [*sic*] saw Krieghoff as the "Father of Canadian painting"![2]

MacTavish had actually used the word "pioneer" rather than "father," but his book nevertheless contained plenty to anger Morisset, including the following blunt statement: "We must come down to the beginning of the nineteenth century before we can find the beginnings of art in Canada."[3] It was as if New France had never existed! MacTavish also affirmed that Krieghoff, on his arrival in Canada, had discovered a country "where the people were compelled, after settling questions of politics and religion, to think about the prime necessaries of life and to ignore the refining influences of painting and the high grades of literature."[4]

In MacTavish's view, genuinely Canadian art did not exist, although there were some manifestations of art in Canada. It was therefore not by chance that he titled his book *The Fine Arts in Canada* rather than *Canadian Art*, the title subsequently in general use. He explained his position on the subject clearly in his preface.

> Much conflicting opinion is expressed from time to time as to nationality in art.... For that reason the term "Art in Canada" is used purposely in this book, in contradistinction to the term "Canadian Art," and also for the reason that the writer is not convinced that there is anywhere any art that is peculiarly Canadian. Many pictures of Canadian landscape and other features of the country have been painted in Canada by Canadian painters, but it would be difficult to explain just how, as works of art, they differ from pictures painted in the United States by Americans, in England by Englishmen, in Russia by Russians or in France by Frenchmen. We ask, What is national art? ... We feel that a picture ... in order to be described as being national must possess some quality that elicits sympathy and receives the admiration of a great mass of the people of the country in which it was produced. And yet that picture ... might not be in any precise sense a work of art.... Nationality, therefore, becomes a riddle.[5]

Nothing could have been further from Morisset's position than this essentialist concept of art as being situated above, or at least on the fringes of, the society that had produced and supported it. For him, nationality was not an enigma, or a "riddle" as MacTavish termed it, but rather the ultimate explanation for the French-Canadian style that he prided himself on being able to define. It was all very well that MacTavish admitted that the arts had made progress in Canada, that certain Canadians had achieved considerable artistic success, that their contributions both at home and abroad were not negligible, but by denying the existence of a national art, he demonstrated a fundamentally defeatist attitude toward the task Morisset had set for himself. Although the definition of an English-Canadian style might have had to await the Group of Seven, the case of French Canada, with its three-hundred-year history and its French roots, was very different.

In spite of the reservations he had about Krieghoff, MacTavish's opinion was diametrically opposed to Morisset's. First of all, MacTavish had a tendency to conflate the painter's interest in Indians and in French Canadians. "There were also Indian and French-Canadian types, subjects that appealed greatly to Krieghoff.... The French Canadian and the Indian were his special subjects. Therefore the wigwam, the canoe and the mansard roof are important accessories to his compositions."[6]

This amounted to creating an undifferentiated category of the Other, which may have seemed valid from MacTavish's anglophone point of view but took no account of the tense relations between the Aboriginal and French-Canadian communities that were the inheritance of a long colonial past. Morisset could accept that Indians might be a subject of interest to Canada's painters, but he could not understand that they should be placed on the same footing as his compatriots. Moreover, he himself showed little interest in Indian people and even less in their art, which he never referred to in his books.

When MacTavish goes on to consider the role in Krieghoff's work of the specific Other represented by the French Canadian, while deploring certain "exaggerations," he stresses the type's "amusing" qualities.

> The breaking up of a dance at a French-Canadian farmstead and running the toll-gate were subjects that appealed to his sense of humour, and the results of his efforts to realize these events on canvas are amusing, even if exaggerated. His weakness for exaggeration ran to such lengths as that of having a rheumy old man running on crutches, after a horse that has passed, galloping, through the toll-gate, or that of sleighs upsetting, dogs fighting, horses bolting and persons looking on from upstairs windows during the leave-taking after the dance.[7]

We shall come back to Krieghoff's "exaggerations" later, which far from representing a defect of his style were actually one of its inevitable consequences.

Newton MacTavish was certainly not the only critic targeted by Morisset. He also took to task "one of the authors" of *Canada and Its Provinces: A History of the Canadian People and Their Institutions by One Hundred Associates*, a twenty-three-volume encyclopedia published between 1914 and 1917. "And yet, in 1898, Robert Harris had published, in *Canada, An Encyclopedia of the Country*, an incomplete but well documented study of Canadian painting. This long article apparently had little impact on commentators, for in 1914 one of the authors of *Canada and Its Provinces* ignored most of the facts Harris had brought to light. Sixteen years later, the knowledge had disappeared."[8]

Morisset was almost certainly alluding to a chapter on the arts written by a certain E.F.B. Johnston. The idea that Canadian art began with Krieghoff is not explicitly stated in the text, but several assertions would undoubtedly have shocked Morisset, including "… the birth and life of Canadian art are both within the memory of man."[9] While not actually naming them as the founders of the Canadian School, the author also presented Paul Kane, Cornelius Krieghoff, John Innes, and Edmund Morris as the first artists to have given their work a specifically Canadian character.

> Whilst there is not, strictly speaking, a national phase of art in Canada, it may be stated that a laudable attempt has been made at different times to render through the medium of the painter's vision some important features of national character.
>
> Among those who have in no small degree given a national cast to their work may be mentioned the names of Paul Kane, Cornelius Krieghoff, John Innes and Edmund Morris…. Krieghoff, the painter of the wilds of Canada, with the Indians and their camps and canoes, found many of his subjects in Quebec, then Lower Canada.[10]

Johnston did nevertheless mention a few painters from the French regime.

> The first painter in Quebec was Father André Pierron whose work was produced between the years 1660 and 1673, the time of his death. Another artist, François Luc, a Récollet, died in 1685. Hughes Pommier, who died in 1686 in France, painted many pictures in Canada. Crequi painted a number of pictures, but as they were principally for churches they are not known to the public. It is said that he was a man of considerable genius as an original painter. There were apparently no secular artists in New France during the seventeenth and eighteenth centuries if we except Beaucourt, who was born about 1735 and was the first native Canadian painter who studied art in France.[11]

If Johnston felt able to state simultaneously that Quebec's first painters lived during the seventeenth century and that the current generation had witnessed the origins of Canadian painting, it was because he drew a distinction between the early days of painting and the emergence of a truly Canadian painting style. And because he defined this national style by its themes—particularly landscapes and typically Canadian characters (including Indians)—he excluded all the early artists, who for the most part restricted themselves to religious paintings and portraits of leading figures.

The quoted paragraph from Johnston's essay is full of errors that Morisset would obviously have found extremely annoying. Pierron's first name was Jean, not André; he arrived in New France in 1667, not 1660, and nothing is known about his work as a painter prior to that date; François Luc was actually Claude François, called Frère Luc; Crequi was Abbé Jean-Antoine Aide-Créqui, and there is no evidence to support Johnston's view that he was an outstanding painter. In addition, of course, there were non-religious painters in New France, such as Michel Dessailliant and

Jean Berger. And finally, Beaucourt was not the first Canadian painter to have studied art in France, having been preceded by Abbé Jean Guyon.

We cannot begin to examine Krieghoff's work, then, without immediately encountering these fundamental problems. When Marius Barbeau later turned his attention to the subject, things only got worse. In one of his first texts on Krieghoff's career, he wrote: "Krieghoff's pictures of early Canadian life place him in the front rank of the pioneers of modern art on this continent. And he is more than a primitive. His work…is varied and resourceful, embracing as it does French Canadian and Indian folk life, river and forest lore, autumn and winter landscapes in a direct and inspired vein, and even at times, fiction, portraiture and still life."[12]

Krieghoff as a precursor of modernism? We shall return to this question. It is understandable, however, that such claims were a source of frustration to Morisset. He was right in maintaining that the country's art history was full of "deficiencies." Did he concur, on the other hand, with the following statement by Robert Harris? "Any attempt to deal with what has existed in the Art of Painting in the Province of Quebec and the Maritime Provinces resolves itself mainly into some record of the artists who have worked there…. Many of the names in the following notes, though as regards Art itself of little or no importance, are yet of interest because only through them can we get any light in tracing the beginning of artistic expression in our country."[13]

One could almost say that Morisset's entire work was dedicated not only to undermining the notion that Canadian art began with Krieghoff but also to showing that he had been preceded by more than a few unimportant painters whose only merit was to give us an idea of how painting developed in Canada under the French regime (whence the historian's emphasis on Frère Luc) and in the Province of Quebec. Each attribution to a francophone prior to Krieghoff served to advance Morisset's cause. For him, "Canadian painting began with our explorers. These universal men knew how to sketch the flora and fauna of the lands they described in such colourful and economical language."[14]

We must also recognize Morisset as the first to have understood that the definition of a specifically Canadian art could not be reduced to subject matter alone. As Meyer Schapiro has recently explained, the task of defining the characteristic style of a movement or an individual artist involves identifying all the expressive "constants" of the work in question: "… the style is, above all, a system of forms with a quality and a meaningful expression through which the personality of the artist and the broad outlook of a group are visible. It is also a vehicle of expression within the group, communicating and fixing certain values of religious, social, and moral life through the emotional suggestiveness of forms. It is, besides, a common ground against which innovations and the individuality of particular works may be measured."[15] In this passage, Schapiro coincidentally outlined the main elements of Morisset's intellectual project, which was the definition of a French-Canadian style. "We can defend the paradox that our most perfect monuments are those that revive not the spirit of certain forms but a certain form of spirit."[16]

It goes without saying that for him this "spirit" was a particular form of the French spirit—Cartesian, cherishing "clarity and distinction," but tempered by a generous measure of peasant "simplicity" and "geniality." This is why he laid such stress on the conditions surrounding artistic creation and considered it so important that the study of these conditions begin with the country's very earliest artistic manifestations, even if these were the "poor sketches" produced by Champlain himself.

MORISSET ON KRIEGHOFF

It seems evident, then, that Krieghoff's work represented the stumbling block of Morisset's art historical approach. If the principal criterion of a specifically "Canadian" form of painting was rooted not in the subjects portrayed but in the style of their portrayal, it was vital that the origins of this style be sought in the earliest examples of painting executed on Canadian soil. To assume that Canadian painting began with Krieghoff was to deny everything that had taken place in Canada before his time. This was tantamount to ignoring the existence of the French regime, or at least assuming that its contribution to the arts was insignificant or inconsistent. Morisset's indignation at this inevitable conclusion can be sensed each time he discusses Krieghoff.

> Krieghoff's huge popularity, spawned by Maxham and Company, has paralyzed genuine criticism; material success has eclipsed the intellect. Comparing Krieghoff to Ziem, as Canon Scott has done, is one thing; but linking his name to those of Courbet and Corot goes beyond the boundaries of good taste. Such excesses of praise do him no good.... Krieghoff is a popular illustrator. He has a fondness for "drinking parties, fairs and crude jokes." His heroes are not averse to "boozing" in the sleazy hotels around Quebec City, to dancing all night to the accompaniment of a tipsy fiddler, or to stretching out on the floor to sleep off a surfeit of white whisky or *Jean-Marie* (Jamaican rum). Such, typically, are Krieghoff's models. Even when he paints an honest *habitant*, he gives him the face of a reveller.[17]

The Canon Scott referred to was Abbé Henri-Arthur Scott, whose enthusiasm for Krieghoff was indeed virtually boundless.

> We have seen paintings by Krieghoff, sunsets of a brilliance that truly evokes the marvellous splendours of the setting sun and allows us to affirm that the richness of his palette was every bit as impressive as that of the very finest works of the kind to be seen in European museums. So why is this painter not known over there, recognized with Corot, Courbet, Ziem, Théodore Rousseau as one of the great landscapists? Because he painted our "few acres of snow," and this was not enough to excite interest in Europe.[18]

There were probably reasons other than that his content reflected Voltaire's famous epigram to explain Krieghoff's absence from the museums of Europe, alongside Corot and Courbet! He was not the only Canadian painter to be excluded, and German Romantic painters of the period were not receiving better treatment.

But Morisset, having described Krieghoff as an unrefined "popular illustrator" with a weakness for "drinking parties, fairs and crude jokes," takes umbrage at the way the artist represented our peasant forefathers.

Krieghoff's peasants are disconcertingly caricatural. The artist has no understanding of them, either because they are too different from those he has observed in Holland and elsewhere, or because his taste for humorous anecdote distorts his perception. He paints the outward appearance of what he sees quite effectively, but he does not capture the soul of his models. In his haste to produce … he spares little thought for the spiritual nature of these countrymen, simultaneously uncouth and resourceful, cheerful and mischievous, lovers of good food and racy stories, possessors of an indefinable refinement and a quintessentially French geniality…. In a single day, he dashes off quaint little pictures that are easy and full of imperfections; using Canadian subjects that he does not really *feel*, he makes the kind of German painting practised in Düsseldorf—in other words, ersatz Flemish painting.[19]

The problem is thus one of perception—*of* the Other (from Krieghoff's point of view) or *by* the Other (from Morisset's). According to Morisset, this particular perception disregards the soul or inner life of its models and fails to capture their "indefinable refinement" and "quintessentially French geniality." It remains superficial, and we French Canadians are unable to recognize ourselves in the image it projects. Krieghoff, felt the historian, shared the perception of his patrons and their view of French Canadians (of Indians too, but the representation of Indians was of very little interest to Morisset). Or, going further still, he saw Krieghoff's images of French Canadians as corresponding to the fantasies of his backers: the French Canadians who had seemed so dangerous during the Rebellion of 1837[20] were now concerned solely with having a good time.

Clearly there are difficulties in the transition from commission to execution, from patrons' needs to artist's intentions. What do we know of Krieghoff's real intentions? As far as Morisset was concerned, they boiled down to one thing: "In fact, his goal is money." His aim, according to the historian, was to "sell, either by mutual agreement, or by auction," and his success was based more "on speculation than on aesthetics." Anyone who naively expressed surprise that people were ready to pay as much as "a thousand dollars" for a Krieghoff landscape was sharply reminded that it did not do to confuse "the market value of paintings by the German artist" with "their artistic quality."[21] These insinuations about Krieghoff's venality are a little suspect, particularly since all Morisset's biographical profiles of the painter invariably begin with the information that he was the "son of a German working man of Polish-Jewish descent."[22] Is it possible that the father of Quebec art history, in relying so heavily on the stereotypical relationship between Jews and money, was succumbing to the temptations of anti-Semitism? In any case, it is an argument that works both ways. There are numerous examples of commercialism among French-Canadian artists, beginning with Antoine Plamondon, whose ferocious defence of his territory against invasion by foreign painters—Henry Thielke and James Bowman, for instance, as well as the Italian painters who were beginning to obtain church decoration contracts—is well known and was well documented by Morisset himself![23] The old painter from Neuville was evidently far from impervious to basely material considerations.

Such considerations explain little. Some painters have undeniably sought to make money. However, the opposite isn't true—the financially ambitious do not seek careers as painters! It is impossible to explain Krieghoff's intentions—or Plamondon's, for that matter—from a strictly materialist point of view.

Why, as Morisset seems to imply, would Krieghoff harbour a dislike for French Canadians? Why would he wish to tarnish their image? Did he not marry a French Canadian, Émilie Gauthier?[24] Did they not have two children—a son, Henry (or Ernest), who died in infancy, and a daughter, Emily? Did he not settle in Boucherville as early as 1840, moving later to Montreal and finally to Quebec City?

We can hardly blame his patrons for preferring to take back to their homes in England or elsewhere in Europe cheerful pictures full of details illustrating the country's costumes and customs and accurately portraying its seasons, particularly fall and winter, rather than austere portraits of local notables or religious paintings.

In fact, the main problem resides in the fact that we French Canadians, and Morisset in particular, fail to recognize ourselves in Krieghoff's pictures. We find it impossible to break with the image of our "peasant forefathers" imposed on us by our religious and secular elites, an image that is often fundamentally contradicted by the popular traditions brought to light by Marius Barbeau—Morisset's implacable enemy—and his collaborator, Carmen Roy. The thousands of folk tales gathered so tirelessly by these ethnologists revealed a totally different picture of Quebec's peasantry. The heroes of such stories were sometimes bawdy, sometimes noble-minded, but invariably capable of the wildest flights of imagination rooted in the ancient, pre-Christian past, explored in Europe by the French ethnographer Charles-Arnold Kurr van Gennep. It is certainly not without significance that Marius Barbeau wrote the first major book on Krieghoff. Nor is it surprising that his upbeat and spontaneous style should have grated so dreadfully on the nerves of Morisset, who wrote rather nastily:

> Cornelius Krieghoff now has his historian, Mr. Marius Barbeau, attached to the National Gallery in Ottawa. His book (*Cornelius Krieghoff, Pioneer Painter of North America*) is written simply, in a rather novelistic style—as is the fashion. It is packed with picturesque, slangy and popular expressions. No long discussions about the contentious points of Krieghoff's biography; no learned notes on the state of French-Canadian painting in the mid-nineteenth century. Specific facts, a few dates, anecdotes, dialogues that are lively, or at least clear, an unpretentious style; surprisingly, no romanticism. And, never a bad thing, a faultless and original typographical layout, with coloured pictures.[25]

The tone could hardly be more ungenerous. Naturally, the "slangy" language of Barbeau's peasants was not that of the notary Morisset. The ethnologists' eagerness to save this *argot* was unusual at the time, for it seemed to clash with the ideal of "good French," which was one of the hobby horses of contemporary ideologues.

Krieghoff's image of the French-Canadian peasant was nothing like

Morisset's. For Krieghoff, this man was successful in transforming harsh living conditions into something positive, even something pleasant and attractive. Although the artist was fully aware of the hard work integral to peasant life—witness his figures of land clearers and lumberjacks—he often preferred to show the peasantry at leisure, offering in contrast to his fellow painters' austere images of the bourgeoisie a picture of the French Canadian as happy and cheerful. Morisset saw things quite differently.

> Our ancestors were … simple, thoughtful, provident men.… We twentieth-century Canadians, complicated by education, thoughtless through fear of glimpsing the naked truth, profligate through vanity and indolence, no longer understand our ancestors and for over seventy-five years have been squandering our heritage.… I wish simply to encourage my readers to reflect on the profoundly human life of our forefathers, on the source of their moral strength, on the causes of our own decadence.

> Our ancestors … were simple, thoughtful, provident men. These qualities are inseparable from a family education that was a little rough, perhaps, but carefully conceived; inseparable, too, from peasant discipline … in short, inseparable from a healthily balanced social order, where each social class plays its role.… For as long as our forefathers kept to such a social order, they retained their ethnic characters, a powerfully intense inner life, a sense of economy. The day this social order allowed itself to be gradually penetrated (as in almost all the countries of the world) by the growing complexities of life, by unthinking behaviour and by lack of concern, it began to break down.… Certain great nations have resisted the rising wave of frenzied modernism. Small nations have become its innocent victims. This is what has happened to us.…[26]

This comparison of traditional French-Canadian society with modern "decadence" is difficult to assess fairly. It could be said that there is slight resemblance to what we know about society under the French regime—a society that was fundamentally mercantile, fiercely colonialist, and in constant competition with its Aboriginal and American neighbours. Moreover, the view could be labelled anachronistic, for "the squandering of our heritage" whose advent the text dates to the end of the nineteenth century, was in fact a much more recent phenomenon—also described by A.Y. Jackson—that was the unhappy result of the Depression of the 1930s and the extremely aggressive trade policies that were part of America's New Deal. It was Jackson, in fact, who deplored that "some of the villages where we painted are no longer of any interest for the artist. Now that the roads are cleared of snow, motorcars and trucks run all winter; the sleigh has disappeared. In the houses the shingle roof is now aluminium, asbestos sheeting covers the walls, and the oil furnace has done away with the woodpile."[27] That Jackson, a member of the despised Group of Seven, should make the same observations and express the same laments as Morisset must have been disconcerting, for Morisset could no longer claim his perception to be an exclusive one, peculiar to French Canadians; it was evidently shared by those whom Borduas called our "hereditary enemies"—not only Jackson but all the anglophone painters who worked in Charlevoix. It even reflected the views of Marius Barbeau, whose entire career was dedicated to "saving" an oral heritage that was even more fragile than old furniture and houses.

To what extent was Morisset's view of our peasant forefathers borrowed from Canon Lionel Groulx? Without question, certain characteristics resemble those attributed by the cleric to "the French-Canadian family" in a lecture given at the closing of the Semaine Sociale, in August 1923, and subsequently published as a chapter of *Notre maître, le passé*.[28] Groulx imagined the family of our ancestors as "the very opposite of the modern family, a family overrun by democratic ideas, where the children share the running of the household with the parents, and where authority, belonging to all, belongs to none. In our traditional family, there is a head, and this head is the natural head, the father, who embodies, as Frédéric Le Play would say, *the sole authority instituted by God through the eternal Decalogue*."[29] Like Morisset, Groulx believed that although "our earliest forefathers were often poor people, they were rarely sad people."[30] They were even acknowledged to have been fond of drink. On this subject, which so delighted Krieghoff, Groulx said "… the children are raised to revere sobriety. While the older French Canadian partakes of his shot of Jamaica rum often, perhaps too often, with his family and friends, there is a rule in the taverns that no drinks may be served to boys who are not of age…."[31] This, moreover, is the only concession he makes in his extremely austere (his word) portrait of the traditional French-Canadian family. "Our forefathers practised an austere chastity that did not always avoid falling into a certain excess of reserve."[32] This chastity evidently had its limits, however; in the same text Groulx extols the truly extraordinary fertility of French-Canadian families! "One need only … recall that the 65,000 French people of 1760, despite an excessive concentration in the towns and an absolutely inexcusable infant mortality rate, became in under two centuries a people of close to four million."[33] He goes on to mention families of ten to twelve children as being entirely commonplace.

Was Morisset's position, then, a reactionary one? We should be cautious about his view, shared by A.Y. Jackson, that the destruction of our heritage was a tragedy. Expressing regret at the disappearance of traces of the past does not necessarily involve fetishizing the past. Nostalgia for certain standards—simplicity, functional design, common materials—supports the modernist cause just as much as the affirmation of related values without any reference to the past. Modernism in art can be defined in a number of ways. Historiography in Quebec has laid considerable emphasis on the particular process that began with James W. Morrice and Ozias Leduc and led eventually to Paul-Émile Borduas and abstraction. But this type of modernism coexisted quite happily—for a time, at least—with another that looked to tradition, archaism, peasant art, and what used to be called "the domestic arts" for models of simplicity, authenticity and even primitivism that were no less "modern." Morisset was actually a defender of that current of modern thought known as "primitivism." Rereading the conclusion of his synoptic *Coups d'œil sur les arts en Nouvelle-France* reveals that in spite of the work's title, he used it to set out his opinion on the art of his own time. He clearly defends the work of Morrice, Marc-Aurèle Fortin and Alfred Pellan, stating that these artists "come together in the same undertaking: the quest for a modernity that is not arrogant, or brutal, or abstruse."[34] He rejected with equal force "sentimentality"—along with its attendant "squeamishness"—and "imitation," which he saw as the opposite of authenticity rather than of originality (the quest for newness for its own sake).[35] His position is congruent with that of Stanley Cosgrove, who proposed Mexico rather than the School of Paris as a model for the renewal of Canadian art; or of Jean-Marie Gauvreau, principal of the École du meuble, whose aim was to form an elite of skilled craftsmen capable of counteracting American mass production and at the same time meeting local needs; or of Jean-Paul Lemieux in his early period, who although treating traditional customs with a certain irony nevertheless made them the main subject of his paintings.

Krieghoff's perspective was entirely different, for he belonged to the Romantic branch of pre-modernism. Admittedly, we cannot accuse Krieghoff's painting of sentimentality, still less of squeamishness. However, it is a form of painting that operates on the emotions. To amuse or charm spectators, to liberate them from their inhibitions, is no less a matter of emotion than to make them weep or experience shame. Krieghoff can generally be situated on the positive side of the emotional spectrum, but not always. Some of his characters are comic, but some are serious, absorbed in an activity or a recollection, inspiring respect rather than derision—the *Self-Portrait* is a prime example (pl. 70). His main goal is to win the viewer's total acquiescence, a kind of surrender reflected as often in laughter as in tears.

Krieghoff was a product of the German Romantic School, which, more than any other artistic group, valued the joke (*Witz*). One of humour's functions is to act as a safety valve in repressive societies, a way of getting around the rules by means of transformations and evasions perceived as harmless. Within the French-Canadian Catholic society of Lower Canada, humour undoubtedly played this role in Krieghoff's work.

Romanticism cannot be reduced to pathos, as work by the eighteenth-century French artist Jean-Baptiste Siméon Chardin proved. The affective quality favoured by certain Romantics, which encompassed the erotic, does not exhaust the entire emotional range. Although he might seem light-years away from the dramatic Romantics, Krieghoff nevertheless shared with them not only the desire to touch and impress the spectator but also the means to achieve this. The American art historian Michael Fried has shown us how to look with a fresh eye at the paintings of this period, especially those of the French painter Jean-Baptiste Greuze. His pictures aim to capture the spectator's attention by portraying what Fried has described as "absorbed" figures: in both his genre scenes and his portraits, Greuze's characters appear completely engrossed in their own activities or thoughts. The result is an organization of figures, gestures, poses, and facial expressions that is distinctly theatrical.

Speaking of Greuze, Fried writes: "The primary emphasis is not on the variety and multiplicity of individual responses to a central event so much as on the merging of those responses in a single collective act of heightened attention."[36] In his discussion of *Filial Devotion* (fig. 28),

Figure 28
Jean-Baptiste Greuze (1725–1805)
FILIAL DEVOTION, 1763
oil on canvas, 115.5 × 146.0 cm
The State Hermitage Museum, St. Petersburg,
purchased 1766 (1168)

Diderot had shown himself very conscious of the painting's synergy of attention, firmly dismissing the usual criticisms.

> Some say too that this attention on the part of all characters is not natural; that a few of them should have been concerned with the old man and the others left to their own occupations; that the scene would have been simpler and truer, and that this is how the event actually happened—of that they are certain.... [But in fact:] The moment for which they ask is commonplace, uninteresting; whereas the one chosen by the artist is special. By chance it happened that, on that particular day, it was his son-in-law who brought the old man some food, and the latter, moved, showed his gratitude in such an animated and earnest way it interrupted the occupations and attracted the attention of the whole family.[37]

In *The Head of the Family* (1755), Greuze seems to have followed the advice of his detractors, for as well as the wife and older children who listen attentively to the father's Bible reading, he has portrayed a couple of youngsters, who, not understanding, have begun to play. Remarkably, though, the attention of the others is not distracted by these scamps. They do not destroy the painting's unity—on the contrary, discreetly restrained by the mother and grandmother, they reinforce it. Greuze, it is true, selected his subjects with care. He invariably chose unique situations, ones that were touching or highly emotionally charged—sometimes even with a sexual undercurrent.[38] Since the emotional content of the two artists' paintings is so entirely different, the relationship between Krieghoff and Greuze may not seem immediately obvious. Krieghoff's are often—though not always—comic rather than tragic, but the artists' works have a similarly forceful effect on viewers: Krieghoff's scenes are captivating in their humour, just as Greuze's are poignantly moving. The basic mechanism is the same, and viewers are absorbed effectively and totally. Moreover, looking at Krieghoff's pictures, we find ourselves carefully examining the individual characters, trying to imagine the words they speak, our own attention equalling the complete absorption of each painted figure.

In the events portrayed by Krieghoff, all the expressiveness of the characters is in their gestures, which strike us now as exaggerated and artificial. The gestures are theatrical, and theatre is by definition an imitation of nature. We sense a certain lack of sincerity and would prefer more genuine feelings, however clumsily expressed. Diderot gave some thought to this problem, comparing the style of English actors with French. Was it better for an actor to play with as much sincerity as possible and to invoke in each performance the full range of emotion and sensitivity (with the risk of being less successful on some nights than others), or to perfectly imitate nature and act with emotional detachment, relying on understanding states of mind and the way they are reflected in bodily positions and facial expressions? In *Paradoxe sur le comédien*, Diderot invites the reader to reflect on "what it means in theater *to be true*." "Is it to present things as they are in nature? Not at all. The true in this sense would be merely vulgar. What then is the truth of the stage? It is the conformity of actions, speeches, physique, voice, movement, and gesture imagined by the poet and often exaggerated by the actor."[39]

Diderot was not just unwilling to reject artifice, he advocated it, preferring it to the genuine emotion experienced in life but impossible to repeat and thus inimitable by art. It seemed to him, moreover, that the performance of an accomplished actor would not be subject to fluctuations of mood from one performance to the next but would improve with each presentation. Repetition would therefore not be a threat to quality but a guarantee of it. With each presentation, the actor could refine his interpretation and improve particular details and, as long as he managed to combat fatigue, would give a finer performance at the end of the play's run than at the beginning. It is simply too easy to attribute the thematic repetition of Krieghoff's work to commercial motives. The themes are repeated because they function like plays. They do not suffer from repeti-tion—it is their very essence. We could hardly be further from the values defended by Morisset. Apparently rejecting Krieghoff in the name of tradition, Morisset was actually rejecting a certain form of modernism, which amounted basically to a rejection of Romanticism.

The best way to illustrate this idea is to re-examine an example used by Morisset himself, *Breaking Lent* (at least two versions exist, pl. 11 and fig. 17, page 149). First, I shall quote Morisset's rather maliciously sarcastic description of the work.

> In the family room of a country house, a few young people are at table: a young man wearing an overcoat of hand-woven fabric, with cowhide boots on his feet and a blue tuque on his head; another, seen from the back, sporting a beige jacket and a red shirt; a young girl and a child. The young folk are busy stuffing themselves with slices of roast pork and *cretons*, when suddenly the parish priest bursts in without knocking, a hat on his head and a vicious expression on his face, intent on ensuring that his parishioners are respecting the harsh proscriptions of Lent. On seeing the priest, the grandmother stands dumbfounded; one of the children, caught red-handed in his greed, cringes as if anticipating a cuff on the head, while the mistress of the house peers through the half-open door to get a glimpse of the intruder's face. There are several variants of this scene; they are alike in that they all recall the long-outdated Flemish painting of the time of Teniers the Younger.[40]

By likening Krieghoff's art to that of the Flemish genre painter David Teniers II (1610–1690), Morisset was implying not only that the artist lacked originality but also that he had employed a formula developed in Europe a century earlier to represent a Quebec society to which it was totally unrelated. Morisset was obviously aware that breaches of Lent occurred among French-Canadian Catholics, but he saw little point in making them the subject of a painting. Did Krieghoff have nothing better to say about our ancestors?

It is interesting to compare Morisset's description with Russell Harper's account of the same picture, or at least a picture with the same title and the same theme.[41]

> On two occasions Krieghoff painted a family eating forbidden meat at Lent. Father Brassard, the local curé, has walked in unannounced and holds his silver-headed cane like a badge of authority. He dominates the room in his outrage. The housewife tries to hide her serving of meat by turning a plate over the offending food. One member of the family slips his steak to the dog; the animal, quite incredulous at the unexpected generosity, bolts it greedily but not fast enough to escape notice. A young and hungry lad continues his meal, blissfully unaware of the indiscretion. Brassard was no friend of Protestants; years later his assistant at Longueuil, Father Charles Chiniquy, wrote how the priest had spent evenings thinking up ways to harass them. Krieghoff, whose religious roots go back to one of the German Protestant Reformation groups, may have suffered at his hands, and his biting portrayal of the churchman's high-handed action is a measure of ironical retribution. Its satire must have been secretly appreciated by others who had been victims of Brassard's ways.[42]

There is appropriately no question of Teniers here. The names mentioned by Harper—Father Brassard and his protégé, Chiniquy, a well-known champion of temperance—are decisively local, with no links to "Old Europe." But is the work's context, as Harper suggests, that of the squabbles between Catholics and Protestants that Krieghoff had witnessed in Longueuil? In showing a scene of Catholics failing in the observance of their faith, was Krieghoff attempting to add fuel to the fire? It seems to me more likely that he was expressing sympathy for ordinary folk, victims of the censure of their overzealous religious leaders. The fact that there were rumours concerning Chiniquy's own behaviour makes this even more probable. Echoes even reached the ears of the celebrated Montreal Archbishop Bourget, who felt it his duty to inform his subordinate: "I forgot to bring to your attention that it has been repeated that you have eaten meat on Fridays, after you have been heard proclaiming from the pulpit that your health has been perfect since you have been practising temperance."[43]

Admittedly, there is no question in Bourget's letter of Lent, but the obligation to avoid the consumption of meat on Fridays, except in the case of illness or indisposition, certainly falls into the same category as the fasting recommended during Lent. Whether or not Krieghoff had heard the rumour, it certainly fitted in well with the subject of *Breaking Lent*.

Krieghoff is said to have executed a full-length portrait of Chiniquy, though the work unfortunately seems to have been destroyed by "the children of Ladislas Lasnier," who "found it in a shed belonging to Isidore Hurteau."[44] The portrait painted by Plamondon for the church of Beauport[45] has come down to us, however. It shows a young clergyman, rather haughty and self-assured, looking steadily ahead, but with sensual lips and a double chin—a detail of his anatomy that he claimed was attributable to nothing stronger than water![46]—and a paunch ill concealed beneath his surplice and stole. Théophile Hamel also made a portrait of Chiniquy, which we know only through a lithograph (see fig. 18, page 152). In this work, the subject holds a large crucifix in his left hand and makes a gesture with his right. As in Plamondon's picture, he is shown wearing a surplice, but minus the stole—thus in the role of preacher rather than confessor.

In presenting an image of French-Canadian society defying religious strictures, Krieghoff was illustrating the failure of Catholic moralism, which was obsessed at the time with the problem of alcohol. Chiniquy had begun his temperance campaigns while *curé* of Beauport, a parish apparently renowned for the number of its taverns and its rampant alcoholism. In 1846, the cleric was in Longueuil, having become a member of the Oblates and thus making clear his desire to become a missionary. It seems, however, that this move was merely designed to cover his sudden departure from Kamouraska, where he had been involved in a case of sexual misconduct. The Oblates quickly realized that he was not missionary material, and by the end of the following year he had been dismissed from the community. He then sought refuge with his protector, Father Brassard, although he never actually became Brassard's curate, as is sometimes claimed. Chiniquy's real talent was for missionary work at the local level. Using Longueuil as his home base, he began

preaching temperance in the region around Montreal, and it was about this time that Krieghoff may have encountered him. But Monseigneur Bourget, having initially shown faith in Chiniquy, was obliged to expel him from the diocese as a result of his "deplorable behaviour." Apparently Chiniquy—who eventually left the priesthood and married in Chicago—was personally less temperate than might have been expected of a man who so vehemently denounced alcohol!

While all this background information offers some insight into Krieghoff's milieu, it does not fully account for the style of his work, the focus of Morisset's harsh judgment. To compose his pictures, Krieghoff first of all definitely conceived a scene, in the theatrical sense. The spectator is kept at a distance, and the foreground is empty of distracting objects. In *Breaking Lent*, the background is flat, like a theatre backdrop, with a door opening onto the "backstage" area and a window looking onto the garden. An oval of light appears on the floor, and Father Brassard stands at one end of this ellipse. From the silver-topped cane he holds to his lips seem to emanate the words of reproach he addresses to his wayward flock. Each character reacts in a personal way, expressing variously remorse, shame, or feigned innocence. Even the woman concealed behind the door listens respectfully to the cleric's words. The dog alone reacts unselfconsciously. None of the characters betrays any awareness of being observed, and, as in Greuze's work, the gestures, poses, and expressions are exaggerated to emphasize individual feelings. The untidiness created by objects lying around here and there reinforces the mental turmoil caused by the *curé*'s irruption into the room. It was this theatricality, of course, this exaggeration of attitudes and expressions, that was unacceptable to Morisset, who championed simplicity, honesty of feeling, and authenticity.

Breaking rules was also the underlying theme of Krieghoff's numerous paintings illustrating tollgates. There are about thirty works devoted to this subject, bearing such titles as *Running the Toll*, *Bilking the Toll*, *The Toll Gate*, and *Cheating the Toll Man* (pl. 136). In the late 1830s there was a marked increase in traffic of all kinds on the roads around Quebec City and Montreal, and as a result the roads were deteriorating rapidly. Two decrees were therefore issued, in 1840 and 1841, requiring that all vehicles pay dues at tollgates situated along the main roads leading to the two cities. The aim was to generate sufficient revenue to ensure the ongoing maintenance and eventual tarmacking of the roads.

Responsibility for the tollgates and road maintenance fell to officials appointed by the governor. One of these gates, the St-Louis tollgate on Quebec City's Grande Allée, was located not far from Krieghoff's home, so he was familiar with the situation. The gate was manned by a gate-keeper, who received a small salary and a rent-free house nearby. Anyone attempting—as in Krieghoff's paintings—to get through the gate without paying was fined, and the system was consequently not very popular with country people, particularly as certain classes of citizen had managed to be exempted from the toll. The system was finally abolished in 1910.

In his frequent depictions of this humorous subject, Krieghoff once again pictured French Canadians as intrepid rule breakers, especially when, as in this case, the rules were applied according to a system of privilege. This was not a religious edict, like the proscriptions of Lent, that was being disobeyed but a civil decree that should have been imposed indiscriminately on all road users. It was no more acceptable for Chiniquy to eat meat on Fridays even as he boasted of his robust health, attributable to his temperate habits, than for the privileged classes to pass through tollgates without charge while poorer folk were obliged to pay up. It's also worth noting that the impotent indignation of the tollkeepers and the wild joy of the offenders are evidence of the complete involvement of the people in Krieghoff's extremely lively scenes.

We can also classify works like the famous *Merrymaking* of 1860 as explorations of this theme of transgression or infringement (fig. 29). What is most striking when this particular painting is examined closely is the very high degree of interaction between the various figures (human and animal), and their *projection*—in the most physical sense of the word— toward one another. People on the balcony call out to others below. Blankets are handed down over the railing to visitors preparing to set off in a sleigh. Someone climbs a ladder to fetch hay to feed the horses. At the bottom of the central staircase, two habitants exclaim at the fate of the passengers of an overturned sled in the foreground, while a water carrier without snowshoes sinks into the snow, and another man prepares to don these essential winter accessories. The interaction that links the people and animals in the picture, that causes them to be totally absorbed

Figure 29
MERRYMAKING, 1860
oil on canvas, 88.9 × 121.9 cm
The Beaverbrook Art Gallery, Fredericton, N.B.,
The Beaverbrook Canadian Foundation, 1959
(1959.120)

in their own activities and presents them to the spectator like actors in a play, available to contemplation, is remarkable, perhaps a strategy to attract viewers' attention. Like a theatre audience, viewers must be as engaged with the painting as the participants are in their endeavours. Viewers begin to relate to amusing persons, situations make them smile, but they soon realize that what they are observing is theatre, not life. They are entertained, but through the agency of a painting, a work of art. If Krieghoff can be seen as a precursor of modernism, it is not because of his subject matter—winter landscapes or harmless transgressions—but

for formal reasons, for this theatricality that gives a painting unprecedented autonomy as a picture—it creates a singular world of its own.

Even when transgression is not the central subject of the work, as in *The Horse Trader* of 1871 (fig. 30), for example, theatricality is the means for the painter to carry through his intentions. Each character plays a role. We can almost hear the men arguing about the price of the horse (who appears a little perplexed at being the focus of controversy), expressing indignation at the small sum being offered on the one hand and regret at being unable to pay more on the other. Once again the composition,

Figure 30
THE HORSE TRADER, 1871
oil on canvas, 35.6 × 50.8 cm
J. Blair MacAulay, Oakville, Ontario

with its unencumbered foreground and flattened backdrop, is decisively scenographic. This combination of the total involvement of the participants (including the animals) in their respective roles and the convincing theatricality of the whole image justifies, in my view, the application to Krieghoff's work of the categories defined so brilliantly by Fried, which reveals the artist as an unlikely emulator of Jean-Baptiste Greuze.

This, moreover, is what makes Krieghoff unique, the quality that distinguishes him from his contemporaries. He was by no means the only artist to have represented the French-Canadian habitant, as many have claimed, but he was the only one to have done it in precisely this way. We need only examine a few works by his immediate predecessors or his contemporaries to grasp the difference. As a first example, there is George Heriot's well-known watercolour titled *Dance in the Château St. Louis* of 1801 (fig. 31). Although admittedly this is hardly a country scene, it is interesting to note the way it has been composed. In the foreground, a mother with her children and a dog (one of the youngsters seems more interested in the dog than the dancers) form a small independent group. The grandmother on the left seems to be lost in thought, despite the surrounding racket. And if we look closely at the young men gathered in the background, we see that several are more concerned with the girl beside them than the dancers in the centre of the picture. This fragmentation of attention, even within a space that could be described as theatrical, is typical of Heriot's approach and contrasts sharply with the way Krieghoff would have portrayed the same subject.

William Henry Bartlett used an approach like Heriot's. His scenes are shown from a greater distance, but his figures are either in the foreground or placed farther in (encouraging us to enter the scene) or do not interact. This is very evident in the watercolour *Village of Cedars on the St. Lawrence River* of about 1838 (fig. 32), where the peasants praying at the roadside cross remain entirely unconnected to those making ready to embark on the St. Lawrence in their canoe. James Pattison Cockburn often used a similar strategy. He portrays one or two figures, sometimes a hunter and his dog, with whom spectators can identify and alongside whom they can contemplate the view presented, whether *Cape Diamond from below No. 1 Tower* of 1828, *The Natural Steps of Montmorency River* of 1828 or *Quebec City, from Beauport, Lower Canada* (fig. 33).[47] Instead of being kept far away, viewers are encouraged to step into the scene, persuaded by the perspectival treatment of a road, a diminishing line of trees, or the distance from the horizon. The resulting impression of deep space is the exact opposite of Krieghoff's technique: he compresses his figures into a space with practically no depth.

Occasionally a painter will depict himself in the foreground, in the process of sketching the scene he invites us to observe, as *A South View of the Great Falls of the Genesee River on Lake Ontario* of 1761 by Thomas Davies (fig. 34). The viewer is shown what is virtually a painting within a painting, becoming witness to the artist's own involvement. However, such figures are exceptional and do not convey the theatricality sought by Krieghoff.

Figure 31 *(top)*
George Heriot (1766–1844)
DANCE IN THE CHÂTEAU ST. LOUIS, 1801
watercolour over pencil on laid paper,
24.9 × 36.6 cm
National Archives of Canada, Ottawa,
purchased 1921 (C-000040)

Figure 32 *(bottom)*
William Henry Bartlett (1809–1854)
VILLAGE OF CEDARS ON THE ST.
LAWRENCE RIVER, c. 1838
brown wash heightened with opaque white on
wove paper, 11.9 × 18.1 cm
National Archives of Canada, Ottawa, acquired
from the W.H. Coverdale Collection of
Canadiana, 1970 (C -040325)

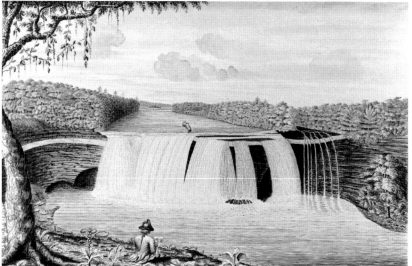

Figure 33 *(top)*
James Pattison Cockburn (1778/79–1847)
QUEBEC CITY FROM BEAUPORT, LOWER
CANADA, 1829
watercolour, pen and ink, 26.0 × 48.9 cm
National Archives of Canada, Ottawa, acquired
from the W.H. Coverdale Collection of
Canadiana, 1970 (C-040023)

Figure 34 *(bottom)*
Thomas Davies (1737–1812)
A SOUTH VIEW OF THE GREAT FALLS
OF THE GENESEE RIVER ON LAKE
ONTARIO, 1761
pen and ink, grey and brown wash over pencil
on laid paper, 37.7 × 55.3 cm
National Archives of Canada, Ottawa,
acquired from the W.H. Coverdale Collection
of Canadiana, 1970 (C-036648)

Further examples are unnecessary. Krieghoff's work can be distinguished from other Canadian painting of the period by its subject matter, but above all by the way that subject matter is treated.

THE IMAGE OF THE INDIAN

It is now time to turn to the second part of our study, the image of the "Indian" in Krieghoff's work. First of all, however, we must clarify a linguistic issue. I am aware that it is no longer acceptable to speak of "Indians" when referring to Canada's First Nations. This label is merely a reflection of the mistaken belief held by Columbus and his successors that they had reached India—or at least Asia—and that the people they encountered were therefore "Indians." But it would be just as anachronistic to describe Aboriginal people of the nineteenth century as anything other than Indians, just as it would be to refer to French Canadians of the same period as Québécois. For the purposes of this study, we will therefore maintain this erroneous designation, in the interests of historical accuracy and on the grounds that striving to understand the past is more worthwhile than modifying it to suit current tastes. Such adjustments seem to me dangerous, for if we are to judge history—and we must, if we wish to avoid repeating its mistakes—it is vital that we reconstruct it as accurately as possible.

Although Morisset showed little interest in the theme of the Indian in Krieghoff's painting, Russell Harper assiduously explored the meaning. Harper was initially struck by the large number of Krieghoff paintings devoted to the subject: 450, or about a third of the entire known oeuvre. The theme of Indians seems, moreover, to have fascinated Krieghoff from his earliest days in North America. Before settling in Canada, he had enlisted in the American army and taken part in the war against the Seminoles of Florida. One presumes that during this period he made a number of sketches that he developed into large oil paintings, which have not survived. As soon as he moved to the Montreal region, his interest in Indians resurfaced, and he began painting, as Harper writes, "the solitary moccasin or basket sellers who wandered in the streets of Montreal and Quebec City in all seasons."[48] The Indians he encountered in the Montreal area were almost certainly descendants of the Mohawks who had been converted to Christianity by the Jesuits and relocated close to the city, notably in Kahnawake (or Caughnawaga, as it used to be called).

Krieghoff did not lose interest in the theme after moving to Quebec City—indeed, he returned to it with growing frequency—but his treatment altered quite dramatically. As Harper noted, "Increasingly he viewed them [Native people] romantically and at the same time he shrank them into large landscapes."[49]

Curiously, the image of the Indian in Krieghoff's work seems to have developed inversely to that of the French Canadian. Initially, he painted isolated individuals (never real portraits—except for *Red Jacket*,[50] if this is indeed who it is, which is no longer certain—but rather types) based on his observation of Indians encountered in the streets of Montreal. Only after his move to Quebec City did he paint genre scenes that included Indian figures. However, establishing a French-Canadian stereotype came after the genre scenes rather than before. A fundamental difference in the treatment of the two themes is thus apparent.

How can this difference be explained? Not easily, if we accept Morisset's analysis, for according to him the representation of French Canadians is equivalent to the representation of Indians—resulting, in both cases, in relatively unsympathetic superficial depictions. There is no explanation why Krieghoff did not adopt the same strategy in both cases, but as already indicated, to me Morisset's opinion seems unfounded. Krieghoff's French-Canadian images take on new meaning if the painter's strong empathy for his subjects is considered. He did not feel detached from French Canadians but was on the contrary sensitive to their resistance to religious and governmental authority, and much of his work illustrated their worthy attempts to settle new territory.

Although Krieghoff identified with and felt close to French Canadians, he was, at least initially, intimidated by Indians. Struggling with his approach to the subject, he was not immediately successful, and humour was notably absent in the early efforts. At first his treatment was from the outside; he used a realistic style and concentrated on details of costume rather than on faces, so these are invariably expressionless. The figures are simply there, like *A Red Indian Woman...* shown standing outside the door of his studio (fig. 5, page 59). Unlike most of his habitants who are frequently depicted in profile, she is looking directly at the viewer, and yet we cannot guess what she is thinking, for she seems lost in a world that we have no access to. Our only link with her is a commercial one, symbolized by the moccasins she carries under one arm. Martin Somerville, a lesser-known contemporary of Krieghoff's, produced works almost identical to these early attempts (see fig. 35).

But Krieghoff persevered in trying to penetrate a world he found foreign but irresistible. He explored the works of his predecessors for models. In a lithograph by Coke Smyth, Harper has noted the profile of a crouching Indian borrowed by Krieghoff, an image popular long before Smyth, used most notably in *The Death of Wolfe* of 1770 by Benjamin West, though there exist even earlier examples. The figure—whom I have described elsewhere as "melancholy"[51]—first appears in the mediocre illustrations that accompany Samuel de Champlain's *Brief discours*, where, seated on a rock, he stares out to sea. It was long thought that Indians had a tendency to melancholia. According to Jules Ballet, the missionary Father Raymond Breton had earlier observed the trait among the Caribs: "[They] would stand at the summit of a rock or on the shore, and, hands cupping their cheeks, remain entirely silent for hours at a time, for they are, says Père Breton, strangely melancholy, thoughtful and taciturn. Perched immobile on their rocks, whose colour blended with their reddish bodies, they seemed like statues of melancholia."[52]

Krieghoff's attempts to draw inspiration from his predecessors are, however, less than convincing. When we examine these works closely, we have the impression of a kind of collage with each figure isolated from the others. What is lacking is indeed a connection between the various characters within the pictorial space—in short, the theatricality that so remarkably characterizes his French-Canadian genre scenes. More interesting are the "collages" based on his own observation. Some of Krieghoff's Montreal works depicting meetings between Indians seem more successful than Coke Smyth's images. It is perhaps significant that the central theme of these paintings is interaction between Native people—as in *Indians in a Snowy Landscape* (fig. 36)—from which a white spectator is excluded; this sense of exclusion is in contrast to earlier paintings, especially of summer subjects, that seem more directed at the viewer. The figures in the foreground have their backs to the viewer, and the concentration of those whose faces can be seen is fully focused on their fellow Indians. At most, it might be said that one of these forward-facing characters occasionally casts a somewhat reproachful eye toward the spectator, imbuing the scene with an unexplained seriousness.

This theme of meeting, suggestive of social cohesiveness—a language, after all, is being spoken during these encounters, and these winter exchanges have a purpose—counterbalances the theme of defying social codes that is typical of one group of Krieghoff's French-Canadian subjects. The real "savage" is not who we might imagine. In adopting this view, Krieghoff was aligning himself with a traditionally Romantic position. "Good savages"—better yet, "noble savages"—are more "civilized" than whites, and if they are reduced to selling moccasins and basketware to survive, it is not because they lack intelligence but because

Figure 35
Martin Somerville
MOCCASIN VENDOR, 1852
oil on canvas, 30.6 × 25.7 cm
Musée du Québec, Québec, gift of the Honourable Maurice Duplessis Estate, 1959
(59.611)

our avaricious society has destroyed other options in the name of progress. This was the viewpoint of Krieghoff's contemporary, the American George Catlin, painter of Indians par excellence, who began his *Letters and Notes* with a sad account of genocide and isolation, going on to state that he had devoted all his energy to representing an "interesting race of people, who are rapidly passing away from the face of the earth—lending a hand to a dying nation."[53] Catlin was direct about what he saw as the causes of this disappearance. "Of the two millions remaining alive at this time, about 1,400,000 are already the miserable living victims and dupes of white man's cupidity, degraded, discouraged and lost in the bewildering maze that is produced by the use of whiskey and its concomitant vices; and the remaining number are yet unroused and unenticed from their wild haunts or their primitive modes, by the dread or love of white man and his allurements."[54]

Of course the only Indians he was interested in—those who remained untainted by contact with civilization—were also the most inaccessible. It is interesting to note, since Catlin himself mentions the subject, that this artist did not hesitate to portray Chief Wi-jun-jon on his return from Washington, dressed in a frock coat and a beaver hat, with a bottle of whisky sticking out of his pocket. Although Krieghoff made many references to drinking in his portrayals of French Canadians, there is not a single example in his work of an association between alcohol and Indians.

As Krieghoff's Indian iconography developed, the pathetic image of the Indian as a seller of moccasins or baskets or as a member of a small

Figure 36
INDIANS IN A SNOWY LANDSCAPE,
c. 1848
oil on canvas, mounted on board,
36.5 × 54.0 cm
National Gallery of Canada, Ottawa, gift from
the Robert Lindsay Estate, 1990 (35535)

group lost in a wintry landscape would not be the final incarnation. The concept of the "good savage," which owed much to both Montaigne and Rousseau, was associated with a long tradition of thinkers who focused on the simplicity of "primitive" peoples to illustrate what had been lost in the process of civilization. Montaigne's important essay on cannibals is well known.

> This a nation, I should say to Plato, in which there is no kind of commerce, no knowledge of letters, no science of numbers, no title of magistrate or of political superior; no habit of service [in the sense of *servitude*], riches or poverty, no contracts, no inheritance, no division of properties, only leisurely occupations, no respect for any kinship, but common ties, no clothes, no agriculture, no metals, no use of corn or wine. The very words denoting lying, treason, deceit, greed, envy, slander, and forgiveness have never been heard. How far from such perfection would he find the republic he imagined?[55]

It hardly matters whether this description accurately reflects the ethnographical reality of the Tupinambas of Brazil, a people Montaigne had heard about in Rouen. What is significant is that it sketches the portrait of an ideal "Republic" in order to denounce the shortcomings of contemporary society. It depicts Indians not for their own sake but to initiate a contemplation on the ills of civilization.

Jean-Jacques Rousseau had this to say on the subject:

> [B]ecause so many writers have not sufficiently distinguished between ideas and seen how far those peoples [the "savages" just mentioned]

already are from the first state of nature, these thinkers have hastened to conclude that man is naturally cruel and needs civil government to make him gentler [Hobbes's position], although in truth nothing is gentler than man in his primitive state where, placed by nature midway between the stupidity of brutes [animals] and the fatal enlightenment of civilized man and limited equally by reason and instinct to ward off the evils threatening him, his natural pity deters him from doing harm to anyone, even when he has encountered harm himself.[56]

In other words, man, born good, is corrupted by society. The study of "savages" is therefore not interesting in itself but for what it reveals about what we have lost and what we hope to regain.

Is it within this French tradition of social criticism—itself based on the classical view that led Herodotus to define the Scythians simply as non-Greeks—that we should seek the source of the fundamental change in Krieghoff's Indian iconography after his move to Quebec City? There is little doubt that eighteenth-century French ideas contributed in a major way to the reassessment by nineteenth-century thinkers and artists of the Native people they encountered. In Krieghoff's case, however, it seems to me that there was another operative factor. As the result of his German ancestry, the artist was linked to a tradition entirely different from this rather abstract questioning of the ill effects of civilization— whose incongruities Voltaire, with his usual wit, had pointed out in a letter to Rousseau: "After reading your book, one feels like walking on all fours."[57] Krieghoff had a greater affinity with Conrad Celtis, humanist of

Figure 37
Anonymous, German
THE TRIBES AND ISLAND DISCOVERED
BY THE KING OF PORTUGAL, c. 1505
coloured woodcut, 22.3 × 33.6 cm
Spencer Collection, The New York Public
Library, Astor, Lenox and Tilden Foundations

the German Renaissance, who, while recommending to his contemporaries that they cultivate the arts and scholarship, also preached revolt against Italian culture and Roman decadence.

It is probably no accident, then, that the most convincing portrayals of the Indians of the American West, and in particular of the proud Mandan nation, were executed by the Swiss artist Karl Bodmer, who accompanied the remarkable German naturalist Maximilian, Prince zu Wied-Neuwied, when he travelled up the Missouri River in 1833 and spent a full winter at Fort Clark. There are also the extraordinary Indian figures created by the Swiss artist Peter Rindisbacher during his Canadian travels. And who could forget the famous *Joseph Brant*, painted about 1807 by the German-born artist William Berczy?

Not enough, perhaps, has been made of the fact that the very first image of Indians was created not by a Portuguese illuminator or an Italian draughtsman or a Spanish painter but a German engraver. The wood engraving titled *The Tribes and Island Discovered by the King of Portugal* (about 1505), generally attributed to the German School (Augsburg or Nuremberg), features Aboriginal Brazilians (fig. 37). Were it not for the cannibalistic feast taking part in the left-hand part of the picture, we might almost be looking at an everyday hunting feast among the uncivilized people inhabiting the most isolated regions of the vast Hercynian forest, the *Sylva Hercynia*, the ultimate *Urwald*.[58] Counterbalancing the rather troubling meal are a young girl, a mother with her children, and three warriors chatting genially among themselves. Another engraving by Hans Leonhart Schaüfelein of a primitive family shows a woman holding a vine branch, symbol of fertility, and, like her husband, ruffling the hair of a chubby child.[59] "Primitive man," no longer displaying the fearsome qualities assigned him during the Middle Ages, has become a friendly *Homo sylvestris*, a *Waldmann*.

It had long been the German habit to search for national roots among the early Teutons described by Tacitus, the famous Semnones, the most ancient and prestigious of the Suebi tribes, *initia gens* of the German people. For Tacitus, they were intractable barbarians, eventually suppressed by the forces of Rome. But he nonetheless acknowledged among them certain admirable habits, including extreme frugality, sharing material goods, and hospitality—all qualities whose absence among his compatriots he deplored. In fact, Tacitus recognized in the Suebi people sufficient positive traits to justify their status as fathers of a nation, even going so far as to emphasize their racial purity—a dangerous observation that would reverberate down history to Nazi Germany.

The representation of primitive man was thus not unknown in Germany; indeed, it was the European country where this iconographical tradition had the deepest roots. When Krieghoff arrived at what was for him the definitive image of the Indian, two things occurred: all his Indians were henceforth set against the backdrop of a forest, and the scale of his figures changed, becoming much smaller, sometimes even difficult to distinguish from the environment that they were a human component of. As the American historian Simon Schama has pointed out, the picturing of such a union between primitive man and the forest, coming from a man moulded by German culture, was hardly an example of ethnographic detachment. From the Renaissance on, the battles described by Tacitus between the German hero Arminius and the Roman legions led by Varus (later replaced by Germanicus, Tiberius's nephew) were cited by religious reformers and thinkers as a model of German resistance against all subsequent ideologies coming from outside, such as French rationalism and Roman Catholic corruption. Not only was such "uncivilized" behaviour not sneered at or treated as a subject of scandal but it was lauded as a return to racial purity, to the simplicity of ancient ways and the special character of a way of life that was a compromise

between "barbarism" and the sophistications of so-called civilization— the hard-to-attain ideal of the *Deutsch Volk*.

It is possible to see a contrast of this link between primitive man and the forest in the many views of isolated farms painted by Krieghoff. Their practically treeless landscapes are generally seen as evidence of his interest in the settlement of the distant areas of the country. The resemblance observed between these works by Krieghoff and other artists—Petter Gabriel Wickenberg, for example (see fig. 4, page 57)— is undeniable. But for Krieghoff, an inevitable result of colonization was the pushing-back of the forest, a sort of "desertification," and the subsequent autonomy (or even complete self-sufficiency) of the small communities responsible. What results is something like the Swiss system of cantons, in which each valley jealously defends its independence, and which still today stands as a model of democracy, with major questions being settled in endless referendums.

Once this link between Aboriginal people and German nationalism was clear in Krieghoff's mind, the Indian became one of his favoured subjects. Just as Flaubert remarked about his identification with Madame Bovary, Krieghoff might have said, "*L'Indien, c'est moi!*" We thus arrive at a paradox: only by remaining true to his own tradition was Krieghoff able to create a convincing image of the Indian. For this reason his Indian image remains unique, quite distinct from that of his French-Canadian contemporaries—particularly Joseph Légaré (*Landscape with a Monument to Wolfe*, about 1840) (fig. 38) and Plamondon (*Portrait of Zacharie Vincent*

[*The Last of the Hurons*], 1838) (fig. 39).⁶⁰ These painters, shocked by the revelations of the Durham Report (which, along with its advocacy of responsible government, recommended that the French be assimilated), portrayed Indians simply as symbols of their own destiny as part of a "vanquished race," almost certainly fated—like the "race of primitives"— for swift disappearance "under waves of immigration," as Plamondon put it. Krieghoff did not share this depressing view, nor did he indulge in similar meditations on the ephemerality of ethnicity and the inevitable crushing of the weak under the weight of the strong. On the contrary, his image of the Indian conveyed a harmonious vitality, communicated with verve in the purposeful activity of the people against, for instance, the rich colours of his autumn scenes. Who can remain untouched by this affirmation of life and freedom in nature's wilderness? Krieghoff felt an affinity with these forest people, who had often acted as his guides on hunting expeditions. For him, at least, the Other had become the Subject.

Figure 38 *(top)*
Joseph Légaré
LANDSCAPE WITH A MONUMENT
TO WOLFE, c. 1840
oil on canvas, 131.3 × 174.6 cm
Musée du Québec, Québec, purchased 1955
(55.109)

Figure 39 *(bottom)*
Antoine-Sébastien Plamondon
PORTRAIT OF ZACHARIE VINCENT
(THE LAST OF THE HURONS), 1838
oil on canvas, 114.3 × 96.5 cm
Private collection, Toronto

123. After the Ball, Chez Jolifou, 1856

oil on canvas, 61.0 × 91.5 cm

The Thomson Collection (P-C-671)

124. (cat. 125) Playtime, Village School, c. 1857

oil on canvas, 63.5 × 91.5 cm

The Thomson Collection (P-C-174)

125. (cat. 124) Breaking Up of a Country Ball in Canada,
Early Morning, 1857
oil on canvas, 61.2 × 91.4 cm
The Thomson Collection (P-C-304)

126. Bringing in the Deer, c. 1859

oil on canvas, 52.0 × 84.5 cm

The Thomson Collection (P-C-413)

127. Habitants Returning from Town, c. 1860

oil on canvas, 33.0 × 45.8 cm

The Thomson Collection (P-C-234)

128. A WINTER INCIDENT, c. 1860

oil on canvas, 33.0 × 45.8 cm

The Thomson Collection (P-C-933)

129. Bargaining for a Load of Wood, 1860

oil on canvas, 36.2 × 47.7 cm

The Thomson Collection (P-C-242)

130. Clearing Land near the St. Maurice River, 1860

oil on canvas, 61.3 × 82.0 cm

The Thomson Collection (P-C-270)

131. Habitants on a Trip to Town, 1861

oil on canvas, 32.3 × 45.9 cm

The Thomson Collection (P-C-64)

132. Sleigh Race across the Ice, 1861

oil on canvas, 36.2 × 53.6 cm

Montreal Museum of Fine Arts, Lady Allan Bequest, 1958 (1958.1177)

133. LOG CABIN, WINTER SCENE, LAKE ST. CHARLES, C. 1862

oil on canvas, 45.7 × 63.5 cm

The Thomson Collection (P-C-235)

134. Crossing Cattle for Lumbering Purposes, 1862

oil on canvas, 28.2 × 46.7 cm

McCord Museum of Canadian History, Montreal, bequest of Arnold Wainwright, Q.C., 1967 (M967.100.2)

135. Log Hut on the St. Maurice, 1862

oil on canvas, 33.4 × 46.5 cm

McCord Museum of Canadian History, Montreal, bequest of Arnold Wainwright, Q.C., 1967 (M967.100.15)

136. CHEATING THE TOLL MAN, c. 1863

oil on canvas, 30.1 × 52.8 cm

Montreal Museum of Fine Arts, George B. Cramp Bequest, 1914 (1914.94)

137. (cat. 138) Habitant Returning from Market, 1863

oil on canvas, 44.2 × 64.6 cm

The Thomson Collection (P-C-450)

138. (cat. 137) Winter in Laval Mountains near Quebec
(The Crack in the Ice), 1863
oil on canvas, 61.5 × 92.0 cm
The Thomson Collection (P-C-633)

139. SETTLER'S HOUSE, LAVAL, 1863

oil on canvas, 33.0 × 45.6 cm

The Thomson Collection (P-C-673)

140. Sillery Cove, Quebec, c. 1864

oil on canvas, 93.2 × 116.0 cm

The Thomson Collection (P-C-585)

141. CHIPPEWA INDIANS AT LAKE HURON, 1864

oil on canvas, 64.6 × 90.3 cm

The Collection of Power Corporation of Canada, Montreal

142. Spill My Milk, 1865

oil on canvas, 35.5 × 55.0 cm

The Thomson Collection (P-C-115)

143. Cornelius Krieghoff's Death of the Moose at Sunset. Lake Famine
South of Quebec, plate 31, Notman's Photographic Selections, second series, 1865
albumen print, 14.1 × 21.3 cm (image)
Art Gallery of Ontario, Toronto, purchased 1983 (83/315)

144. THE CARIBOU HUNTERS, 1866

oil on canvas laid on board, 33.0 × 45.7 cm

The Thomson Collection (P-C-745)

145. WINTER SCENE IN THE LAURENTIANS—THE LAVAL RIVER, 1867

oil on canvas, 68.6 × 91.5 cm

The Thomson Collection (P-C-108)

146. Calling Moose, "Huron" Indian, c. 1868

chromolithograph and varnish on board, 27.6 × 22.7 cm (image)

McCord Museum of Canadian History, Montreal, purchased 1977 (M977.90.1)

147. In Doubt of Track, "Iroquois" Indian, c. 1868
chromolithograph and varnish on board, 27.4 × 22.7 cm (image)
McCord Museum of Canadian History, Montreal, purchased 1977 (M977.90.2)

148. Cornelius Krieghoff's Lake St. Charles: Two Canoes Tied Together (p. 19, Moulin)
and Viewing from Stone Block, Lake Memphremagog (p. 20, photographer unknown)
in Album of Carte-de-Visite Photos, c. 1870
hand-coloured albumen print, p. 19: 5.7 × 9.2 cm, p. 20: 5.6 × 8.8 cm
The Thomson Collection (P-C-680)

149. THE NEW YEAR'S DAY PARADE, 1871

oil on canvas, 64.3 × 109.2 cm

The Collection of Power Corporation of Canada, Montreal

150. J.B. Jolifou, Aubergiste, 1871

oil on canvas, 55.9 × 92.1 cm

The Thomson Collection (P-C-431)

151. Return from the Hunt, 1871

oil on canvas, 57.2 × 94.0 cm

The Thomson Collection (P-C-316)

152. THE BLACKSMITH'S SHOP, 1871
oil on canvas, 56.5 × 92.1 cm
Art Gallery of Ontario, Toronto, gift of Mrs. J. H. Mitchell, Toronto, in memory
of her mother, Margaret Lewis Gooderham, 1951 (50/13)

NOTES

**Notes to *Cornelius Krieghoff:*
The Development of a Canadian Artist
by Dennis Reid**

1 Register of birth of Cornelius David Krieghoff, dated 21 June 1815, city archives of Amsterdam, 1815, vol. 3, folio 202. The document is reproduced in Raymond Vézina, *Cornelius Krieghoff, Peintre de mœurs (1815–1872)* (Ottawa: Éditions du Pélican, 1972), 27, with transcriptions in the original Dutch and in French, 26–27.

2 Register of marriage of Johann Ernst Krieghoff and Isabella Ludovica Wouters, 12 May 1811, city archives of Amsterdam, transcribed in the original Dutch and in French in Vézina 1972, 23–24. It is noted that a copy of Johann Ernst's register of baptism, dated 1 May 1786, was forwarded by a Lutheran pastor from Ufhoven. Isabella Ludovica's record of baptism, dated 28 March 1783, was confirmed by the mayor of Ghent. Records of their first two children follow: register of birth 29 October 1811 of Frederika Louisa Krieghoff, dated 1 November, city archives of Amsterdam, 1811, vol. 6, folio 126, transcribed in the original Dutch and in French in Vézina 1972, 25–26. The mother's name was recorded as Charlotta, which she would retain in all subsequent documents. Register of birth 13 September 1813 of Charlotta Sophia Krieghoff, dated 17 September, city archives of Amsterdam, 1813, vol. 6, folio 79, transcribed in the original Dutch and in French in Vézina 1972, 26.

3 Register of birth 20 August 1820 of Johann Ernst Krieghoff, dated 25 August, city archives of Düsseldorf, birth record no. 554/1820, transcribed in the original German and in French in Vézina 1972, 28.

4 Wilhelm Sattler, *Das alte Schloss Mainberg bei Schweinfurt und seine frühern Bewohner* (n.p., 1836), 47.

5 Johann and his wife left Mainberg for Nürnberg in May 1850. *Intelligenz-Blatt der Stadt Schweinfurt* 19 (12 May 1850): 195.

6 G.M. Fairchild, Jr., *From My Quebec Scrap-Book* (Quebec: Frank Carrel, 1907), 122.

7 Budden letter to Robert Harris, c. 1897, Harris Papers, Confederation Centre Art Gallery and Museum, Charlottetown, Prince Edward Island, misplaced; cited in J. Russell Harper, *Krieghoff* (Toronto: University of Toronto Press, 1979), 7.

8 G.M. Fairchild, Jr., *Gleanings from Quebec* (Quebec: Frank Carrel, 1908), 68.

9 Harper 1979, 6.

10 See letter from Dr. Dawn M. Leach, Head of Archives and Collections, Kunst Akademie Düsseldorf, to Arlene Gehmacher, Art Gallery of Ontario, Toronto, 22 March 1999.

11 Catharina and Margaret were the daughters of Conrad Geiger (1751–1808), an artist active in Schweinfurt at the turn of the century. See Paul Ultsch, "Willhelm Sattler (1784–1859)—Der fränkische Farbenpionier," in Rainer A. Müller, ed., *Unternehmer—Arbeitnehmer Lebensbilderr aus der Frühzeit der Industrialisierung in Bayern* (Munich: R. Oldenbourg Verlag, 1985), 319. Harper 1979, 5, confuses Margaret with Catharina.

12 Letter of John S. Schofield, War Office Department, Washington, D.C., to Ethel Pinkerton, Art Association of Montreal, 1 December 1928, whereabouts unknown; cited in Marius Barbeau, *Cornelius Krieghoff: Pioneer Painter of North America* (Toronto: Macmillan Company of Canada Limited, 1934), 88.

13 Ibid.

14 Fairchild, *Scrap-Book*, 123.

15 Fairchild, *Gleanings*, 68–69.

16 See Harper 1979, 8.

17 See Raymond Vézina, "Krieghoff (Kreighoff), Cornelius," *Dictionary of Canadian Biography* vol. X (Toronto: University of Toronto Press, 1972), 29, for the misinterpretation of the term. *Oxford English Dictionary* gives the military usage as "a soldier mechanic attached to the...artillery... to be employed in the construction and repair of military materials."

18 Schofield to Pinkerton, cited in Barbeau 1934, 88. Vézina 1972, 28–29, cites National Archives, Washington, Record Group no. 93. Harper 1979, 182, fn. 19, correctly cites National Archives, Washington, Adjutant General's Office, Enlistment Papers, Record Group 94. Vézina finds no evidence of desertion in the records.

19 Register of birth of Henry Krieghoff, dated 18 June 1840, parish of Ste-Famille de Boucherville, the original French transcribed in Vézina 1972, 29.

20 Register of burial of Ernest Krieghoff, dated 14 June 1841, parish of Notre-Dame de Montréal, 1841 no. 499, transcribed in Vézina 1972, 31.

21 Register of marriage of Emily Krieghoff and Hamilton Burnett, 18 March 1862, Archives judiciaires de Québec. The document is reproduced in Vézina 1972, 34, with transcription in French, 35.

22 He is not listed in the Buffalo city directories of 1841, '42 or '44. None was published in 1843. Nor is he listed in the Rochester city directories of 1841 and '44, the only two apparently published during those years.

23 See Clifford McCormick Ulp, "Art and Artists in Rochester," *Rochester Historical Society Publication Fund Series* XIV (Rochester, New York: The Society, 1936): 32; William H. Gerdts, *Art Across America: Two Centuries of Regional Painting 1710–1920* (New York: Abbeville Press, 1990) I, 195.

24 *Daily Advertiser* (Rochester), 30 May 1843.

25 See Yves Lacasse, "La contribution du peintre américain James Bowman (1793–1842) au premier décor intérieur de l'église Notre-Dame de Montréal," *Journal of Canadian Art History/Annales d'histoire de l'art canadien* VII–1 (1983):74–91. Bowman, before travelling through British North America, had spent eight years in Europe (he was born in Alleghany County, Pennsylvania) and worked in Pittsburgh, Philadelphia, Washington, Charleston, and Boston. After Toronto he briefly settled in Detroit, then moved on to Green Bay, Wisconsin Territory, before landing in Rochester.

26 Krieghoff's copy was offered at Parke-Bernet, New York, 14 March 1968, lot no. 40, repr. p. 16 in the catalogue. Present whereabouts unknown.

27 *Portrait of a Notary*, now in the Beaverbrook Art Gallery, is repr. in Edwy Cooke, *Cornelius Krieghoff ca. 1815–1872* (Fredericton, N.B.: Beaverbrook Art Gallery, [1961]), n.p., where it is incorrectly described as dated 1848 (cat. 4). See also Harper 1979, 10. The other painting is repr. in Marius Barbeau, *Cornelius Krieghoff* ([Toronto]: Society for Art Publications/McClelland and Stewart Limited, 1962), pl. 6, as "Louise and Emilie, c. 1846." A photo of the work in the Marius Barbeau Papers, Canadian Museum of Civilization, Hull, Quebec, box (temp.) 294, file 5, is inscribed verso "signed and dated 1843." The photograph and note are from the Montreal dealer William Watson, who discovered the painting.

28 The letter, from Ernst Krieghoff, Mainberg, to Wilhelm Sattler, Schweinfurt, 5 May 1843, is known from a translation in a letter from Katherine Krieghoff Lewis, Grosse Pointe Farms, Michigan, to Russell Harper, 22 February 1980, Harper Papers, National Archives of Canada, Ottawa (MG 30, D 352, vol. 50, file 14).

29 Fairchild, *Gleanings*, 69.

30 Bradish is reported passing through Kingston with the portrait on his way to Montreal, *Chronicle and Gazette* (Kingston), 27 April 1844.

31 Laurier Lacroix, "Les artistes canadiens copistes au Louvre (1838–1908)," *Journal of Canadian Art History/Annales d'histoire de l'art canadien* II–1 (summer 1975): 64.

32 Barbeau 1934, 4–6.

33 His name was spelled Kreighoff in nineteenth-century Canada more often than the proper Krieghoff. We correct all but unusually aberrant forms in citations.

34 See Jean Trudel, "The Montreal Society of Artists, une galerie d'art contemporain à Montréal en 1847," *Journal of Canadian Art History/Annales d'histoire de l'art canadien* XIII–1 (1990): 61–87.

35 See Mario Béland, ed., *Painting in Quebec 1820–1850: New Views, New Perspectives* (Québec: Musée du Québec, [1992]), 250, for Duncan. The president of the society was Andrew Morris (active 1844–52), for whom see ibid., 388. The secretary was Robert T. Howden (active 1839–47); see J. Russell Harper, *Early Painters and Engravers in Canada* (Toronto: University of Toronto Press, 1970), 165.

36 See Béland, *Painting in Quebec*, 502, for Wilson, and see Michael Bell, *W. Sawyer, Portrait Painter* (Kingston, Ontario: Agnes Etherington Art Centre, Queen's University, 1978).

37 Béland, *Painting in Quebec*, 467; see also "Raffle of Paintings," *Gazette* (Montreal), 30 January 1846.

38 Harper 1979, 20, for Staunton; Harper, *Early Painters*, 85, for Davis.

39 A fourth, so far unlocated, is mentioned in the *Pilot* (Montreal), 29 January 1847, which notes that the editor of the *Morning Courier* was made an honorary member of the society in gratitude for a "correct and impartial review." Trudel, "The Montreal Society of Artists," 63, identifies him as Thomas Finney.

40 *Gazette* (Montreal), 15 January 1847.

41 H.N., M.D., "Montreal Gallery of Paintings," *Pilot* (Montreal), 29 January 1847. One of the scenes from Scott was offered at Sotheby Parke Bernet (Canada), Toronto, 18–19 October 1976, lot 119, repr. in cat. p. 63; and at Waddington's, Toronto, 27–30 October 1980, lot 865A, repr. in cat. p. 137. The location of *View near Boulogne* is unknown.

42 *Catalogue for the Montreal Gallery of Pictures. 1847. Exhibition the First* (Montreal: Lovell and Gibson, 1847). The catalogue is reproduced in its entirety in Trudel, "The Montreal Society of Artists," 78–87.

43 While *Sketches in the Canadas* is believed to have been published as early as 1840 (it is dedicated "with permission" to Lord Durham, who died in July that year), Krieghoff likely acquired his copy when it was offered by a Montreal bookseller in August 1846: see R. & C. Chalmers advertisement, "just received from London...," *Gazette* (Montreal), 3 August 1846.

44 Harper 1979, 21.

45 See Harper 1979, 20–21, and Laurier Lacroix's entry for the painting in Béland, *Painting in Quebec*, 339–41.

46 By Harper 1979, 21, fn. 7. R.H. Hubbard, *Painting in Quebec: Maurice*

and *Andrée Corbeil Collection* (Ottawa: National Gallery of Canada, 1973), 88, repr. 89, argues that it is closer to the style of Duncan. Unsigned (although Harper claims it bears a false Duncan signature), it is much more crude than would be expected of Krieghoff around 1846.

47 For a discussion of how physiognomy was perceived in the mid-nineteenth century to be profoundly revealing both of character and status, as well as of class and race, see Mary Cowling, *The Artist as Anthropologist: The Representation of Type and Character in Victorian Art* (Cambridge: Cambridge University Press, 1989).

48 Elizabeth Johns, *American Genre Painting: The Politics of Everyday Life* (New Haven and London: Yale University Press, 1991), 2.

49 Krieghoff also copied Wilkie's *Blind Fiddler*. Dated 1847, his version was offered at Waddington's, Toronto, 22–24 November 1996, lot 1414 (repr. p. 102). The original Wilkies are repr. in William J. Chiego, ed., *Sir David Wilkie of Scotland (1785–1841)* (Raleigh: North Carolina Museum of Art, 1987), 117, 137. Krieghoff would have worked from engravings, however.

50 Harper 1979, 29.

51 *Longue-Pointe, Canada East, 1860*, by W.H.E. Napier, National Archives of Canada (C35271), *Annual Report, 1974–5*, 79, repr.; Lucie Dorais of the National Archives first made the identification in a letter to Greg Spurgeon, National Gallery of Canada, 4 July 1983, letter in registration records, National Gallery of Canada. D.C. Smith, *The Seigneury of Longueuil* (Toronto: Ginn and Company, 1971), 171, repr., without explanation identifies the scene in the Krieghoff painting as at La Prairie.

52 A.Y. Jackson's description of his grandfather's relationship to Krieghoff is in Barbeau 1934, 89–90. Barbeau builds much of his narrative around the idea that every attractive young woman in a Krieghoff painting is the artist's wife, Louise, as he believed her name to be. That this was not a matter of utter conviction to him, however, is suggested by a letter he wrote the Montreal dealer William Watson about the 1843 portrait of a young woman and girl he believed depicted Krieghoff's wife and daughter (see fn. 27 above). He said, in part: "This is an exciting find. We are gradually finding out that our fictions on Krieghoff are becoming true! In the end we will believe it ourselves." Barbeau to Watson, 24 March 1938, copy in Barbeau Papers, box (temp.) 295, file 10. Harper 1979, 28, qualifies his own identification of the figures in *The Ice Bridge...* as the Krieghoff family with "possibly."

53 Lacroix in Béland, *Painting in Quebec*, 340. Krieghoff's copy was last seen in 1859 in Portland, Maine. See *Catalogue of the Gallery of Paintings at the Fourth Exhibition of the M.C.M. Association,... Tuesday, October 4th, 1859* (Portland: James S. Staples, 1859), cat. no. 65, "Winter, Krieghoff, after Wickenberg," lent by J.B. Brown.

54 Barbeau 1934, 104, notes an obscure inscription verso that he reads as 1846. The painting has since been lined.

55 The painting shows business signs of Somerville, Krieghoff, Dr. Elliot, dentist, and a Dr. Cyr[...], Dagu[erreotypist], around the entrance. We know from a newspaper advertisement that Somerville's studio was at 25 Great St. James Street by at least January 1846 (fn. 37), and remained there until at least May or June 1854 when the Montreal city directory for that year was corrected. Krieghoff probably had his studio there from 1847 to 1853. A Dr. W.H. Elliot, dentist, is there from 1848 (the directory corrected May that year) until at least 1853, when we stopped checking. A Dr. L.M. Cyrus offered "Daguerreotype Painting" at Rasco's Hotel, as advertised from 9 December 1845 until at least 17 March 1846 in the *Pilot* (Montreal), but there is no record of when he, presumably briefly, was installed at 25 Great St. James. It's interesting to note in addition that the main-floor tenant of the address from 1845 to 1847 was Joseph Fraser's furniture warehouse and upholstery business, possibly an attraction for Krieghoff, and certainly for his brother. The Montreal Gallery of Pictures was installed upstairs early in 1847.

56 "Les Sauvages du Saguenay," *L'Avenir* (Montreal), 18 March 1848. See also M. de LaTerrière, MPP, "Députation des sauvages au Saguenay," *La Minerve* (Montreal), 13 March 1848; reprinted in a shorter version that omits the text of the petition in *Le Journal de Québec*, 18 March 1848.

57 Raymond Vézina, *Théophile Hamel, Peintre national (1817–1870)* (Montreal: Éditions Élysée, 1975), 149–53, identifies the fourth person in the portrait as Peter McLeod, one of the interpreters. This figure earlier had been believed to be variously Lord Durham, Lord Elgin, or Elgin's brother, Robert Bruce, who was superintendent of Indian Affairs. See Roy Strong, *A Pageant of Canada: The European Contribution to the Iconography of Canadian History* (Ottawa: The National Gallery of Canada, 1967), 212. The painting was offered for sale by the descendants of Lord Elgin at Sotheby's, London, 4 November 1987, lot 33. Present whereabouts unknown. For discussion of the distinct views of Natives established within the anglophone and francophone communities in the previous generation, see Gillian Poulter, "Representation as Colonial Rhetoric: The Image of the Native and 'the Habitant' in the formation of colonial identities in early nineteenth-century Lower Canada," *Journal of Canadian Art History/Annales d'histoire de l'art canadien* 16, no. 1 (1994): 10–25.

58 An advertisement that ran in the *Gazette* (Montreal), 15 July–28 August 1848 is worded "now publishing."

59 "Canada's Artists," *Pilot* (Montreal), 11 July 1848.

60 "The Chippewa Indians and the Mining Companies," *Illustrated London News*, 15 September 1849, 179–80.

61 "Iroquois Chief," *Illustrated London News*, 7 July 1855, 27–28.

62 Coke Smyth, *Sketches in the Canadas* (London: Thos. McLean, n.d.), facsimile edition (Toronto: Charles J. Musson Limited, 1968), pls. xviii and ix.

63 "Moos Hunter" is pl. xxii in the portfolio; "Indians of Lorethe" is pl. iii. Krieghoff's copy was at Joyner Fine Art, Toronto, 20–21 May 1987, lot 132, repr. in the catalogue.

64 Barbeau 1934, 8, 9, 56, 90.

65 "Krieghoff's Scenes in Canada," *Morning Courier* (Montreal), 16 October 1848. A similar advertisement ran in the *Pilot* (Montreal), 16–31 October 1848.

66 "Krieghoff's Scenes in Canada," *Morning Chronicle* (Montreal), 15–21 November 1848. Although a comparative study of existing impressions has not been made, there are variants. Some have been printed on *papier chine*, which was then laid down on heavier paper; others were printed directly onto heavy stock. There seems to be some variation in

the application of a tint stone border, and at least one instance of tint stone highlights. Some impressions do not have all the letterpress.

67 It sold for £1 10s. a set plain and £2 10s. coloured to subscribers, £2 and £3 to non-subscribers, and by the end of the year Krieghoff's bank account is purported to have swelled to more than £66 8s. 9d. Hugues de Jouvancourt, *Cornelius Krieghoff* (Toronto: Musson, 1973), 41, refers to Krieghoff's opening an account with the Montreal City and District Savings Bank with £6 5s. in September 1846, and in the following pages periodically notes balances of 30s. (end of 1846), £66 8s. 9d. (end of 1848) and £5 1s. 3d. (end of 1850), without, however, citing a source. Harper 1979, 25, appears to misinterpret the jump in income to occur in the fall of 1846. These sums are a far cry from the £500 to £600 Fairchild believed Krieghoff made from the 1848 prints (*Gleanings*, 69).

68 Harper 1979, 43.

69 Peter Winkworth, *Exhibition of Prints in Honour of C. Krieghoff 1815–1872* (Montreal: McCord Museum, [1972]), n.p.

70 *L'Église de Notre Dame de Montréal*, drawn by John Murray, lithographed by G. Matthews in Montreal 1847; see Mary Allodi, *Printmaking in Canada: The Earliest Views and Portraits/Les débuts de l'estampe imprimée au Canada vues et portraits* (Toronto: Royal Ontario Museum, 1980), 215, repr. 214.

71 "The Fine Arts," *Gazette* (Montreal), 22 December 1847. The dimensions given here are the same as those of the Thomson canvas (pl. 7). There is also an editorial reference to the painting on another page, "The Wine Tasters."

72 *Toronto Society of Arts: First Exhibition, 1847* (Toronto: n.p., 1847) no. 7,

"The Confession (copy)"; no. 59, "Portrait of a Gentleman"; no. 61, "The Gentleman and Beggar." The latter is noticed in the *British Colonist* (Toronto), 20 April 1847. Works by both Krieghoff and Somerville were available at Scobie and Balfour. See *British Colonist*, 3 September 1847.

73 "Sales by Auction by John Leeming," *Gazette* (Montreal), 18–25 February 1848. The sale was 25 February.

74 "Sales by Auction by John Leeming," *Montreal Transcript*, 13 November 1849; "Vente par Encan. Par John Leeming," *L'Avenir* (Montreal), 13, 15 November 1849. The sale was 16 November.

75 "Sales by Auction by John Leeming, 40 Valuable Oil Paintings by 'Krieghoff,'" *Morning Courier* (Montreal), 18 February 1850. The advertisement is reproduced in Winkworth, *Exhibition of Prints*, n.p. Some seventeen of the offered works are listed. For the Mechanics' Institute Festival see "Catalogue of Articles at the Eighth Annual Festival, February 5, 1850," *Pilot* (Montreal), 12 February 1850. This catalogue also appears in the *Montreal Transcript*, 12 February 1850.

76 "The Provincial Exhibition," *Montreal Witness*, 28 October 1850.

77 "Industrial Exhibition," *Montreal Transcript*, 24 October 1850. The prize was worth £3. The table is briefly noticed in the same newspaper for 22 October. See Barbeau 1934, 149. It was on the art market as recently as 1982. See David Mitchell, Toronto, to Russell Harper 10 February 1982, Harper Papers, vol. 49, loose correspondence, 1982 (2d file).

78 This was *Interior—Card Playing*, listed in *Record of the Western Art-Union...* (Cincinnati, Ohio) 1–5 (October 1849), no. 87. When it subsequently was listed as purchased for distribution in *Record of the Western Art-*

Union... 1–7 (December 1849), p. 5, it was described as "Interior of a Dutch building—a party at cards and supper...."

79 "Sale by Auction by Scott & Glassford," *Daily Transcript* (Montreal), 8 September 1851. The sale was 10 September.

80 "Sales by Auction by Fisher & Armour," *Gazette* (Montreal), 1 October 1851; also "Ventes à l'Encan. Par Fisher & Armour," *La Minerve* (Montreal), 2 October 1851. The sale was that day.

81 "Great Variety of Oil Paintings Including a Splendid Collection of Mr. Krieghoff's," *Gazette* (Montreal), 29 May 1852. The sale was 4 June.

82 See *Catalogue of Paintings, Watercolours and Engravings, Exhibited in the Assembly Chamber, Parliament Buildings, Toronto, C.W. September, 1852* (Toronto: Henry Rowsell, 1852), no. 162, "The Wind Mill ... Krieghoff ... Mrs Boulton." The painting is now in the collection of the Art Gallery of Ontario (GS60).

83 See W.A. Craick, "Letters, Cornelius Krieghoff," *Atlantic Advocate* 53, no. 5 (January 1963): 11. The writer's mother took classes with Somerville and Krieghoff in a studio on St. James Street, 1847–50, arranged through the Misses Plimsoll school.

84 Bell, *W. Sawyer*, 9–11.

85 See *Pilot* (Montreal), 12 February 1850. For more on Lock, see Harper, *Early Painters*, 199.

86 "Panorama du Canada," *La Minerve* (Montreal), 17 July 1851; also "Panorama du Canada," *La Minerve*, 31 July 1851.

87 These panoramas received blanket coverage in the newspapers. The visits mentioned can be documented by the following sampling from *La Minerve* (Montreal): "Panorama de Brewer," 20 June 1850; "Panorama Colossal du Mississippi par Lewis,"

1 May 1851; "Salle St. André ... Panorama Gigantesque de Bayne," 13 September 1851; "Panorama de Craven," 12 August 1852. For more on Lewis and the international dimension of the phenomenon see Stephan Oettermann, *The Panorama: History of a Mass Medium* (New York: Zone Books, 1997).

88 "Oh Yes! Oh Yes!," *Gazette* (Montreal), 8 July 1851.

89 For Elizabeth Hale see Béland, *Painting in Quebec*, 277. Also in the same volume, the entry by Gilbert Gignac on a Hale sketchbook in the National Archives of Canada containing drawings of the Seigneury at Sainte-Anne-de-la-Pérade, Sleepy Hollow, and the Plantation, 278–82. It was Conrad Graham, "'House Portraits' Four Krieghoff Oil Paintings at the McCord Collection," *Fontanus* 7 (1994): 168–69, who first suggested Krieghoff had based the paintings in part on drawings in the Hale sketchbook. For a fascinating account of the broader implications of the Hale's aesthetic engagement with Sainte-Anne-de-la-Pérade, see Colin M. Coates, "Like 'The Thames towards Putney': The Appropriation of Landscape in Lower Canada," *Canadian Historical Review* 74, no. 3 (1993): 317–43.

90 Harper 1979, 43.

91 See Béland, *Painting in Quebec*, repr. p. 344.

92 Harper 1979, 23.

93 For the Fletchers, see Harper 1979, 23. For the Leemings, see letter of James S. Walker to Harper, 16 December 1979, Harper papers, vol. 49, loose correspondence 1979, file 3. Their current location is unknown.

94 H.N., M.D., "Montreal Gallery of Paintings," *Pilot* (Montreal), 29 January 1847.

95 "Correspondance éditoriale," *Le Journal de Québec*, 1 July 1847.

96 Harper 1979, 23. He gives no source for this information.

97 Krieghoff to the Hon. H. Pinhey, Bytown, 26 October 1849, Hamnett Kirkes Pinhey and Family Papers, National Archives of Canada, Ottawa (MG 24, I 14; vol. 1, file 4).

98 Angela Carr, "George Theodore Berthon (1806–92), Portraiture, Patronage, and Criticism in Nineteenth Century Toronto," *Journal of Canadian Art History/Annales d'histoire de l'art canadien* 12, nos. 1 & 2 (n.d.): 39–40.

99 The other is a painting of two women, probably a copy of a European picture, now in a Toronto private collection.

100 Harper 1979, 55. He gives no source for this, but it probably is Paul Ultsch, who in a letter to Harper 26 May 1977, quotes from his history of the Sattler family that the elder Krieghoffs arrived back in Schweinfurt in May 1852 after a stay in Montreal and New York. The journey from New York to Schweinfurt, via Bremen, took 2½ weeks, but he does not mention when they left for America. He also enclosed a photocopy of *Intelligenz-Blatt der Stadt Schweinfurt*, 19 (12 May 1850): 195, in which the Krieghoffs announce they are moving to Nürnberg (Harper Papers, vol. 50, file 16). Harper assumes this is the first leg of the trip to Canada.

101 Cited in Barbeau 1934, 149.

102 The painting since has been lined, so the inscription cannot be corroborated. It is recorded in Joyner Fine Art, Toronto, sale of 20–1 November 1990, lot 100; and Sotheby's, Toronto, 12–13 May 1987, lot 193.

103 Fairchild, *Scrap-Book*, 125, relates that Krieghoff visited Paris during the Quebec period for "two years," copying at the Louvre to improve his figure painting. Barbeau 1934,

21–29, faced with the lack of any corroborating evidence, determined the trip was in the spring of 1854 and for only six months. Harper 1979 does not even mention the possibility of a trip to Paris between the mid-forties and mid-sixties. It is likely that Fairchild's source, John Budden, somehow pulled the 1844–5 trip up a decade, although we might speculate that Krieghoff did return to Europe at some point during that time of low production in 1851–2, perhaps with his parents the summer of 1852, returning to settle in Quebec.

104 Fairchild, *Scrap-Book*, 123. The next year's version has the artist definitely in Quebec "in 1853," and there is no mention of shared residence at Mount Pleasant, Fairchild instead noting the city directory of 1854–5 gives 25 St. John Street as Krieghoff's town address, Cap Rouge Road as his country residence. See *Gleanings*, 69. Krieghoff did establish a studio at Mount Pleasant, a small new terrace development at the far north end of St. John Street (city directories 1855–6 and 1857), but resided during these years at 153 St. John Street, closer to the centre of town. Budden is listed as resident at Mount Pleasant in 1857. The terrace was later demolished to provide space for the residence of John Ritchie, 573 St. John Street.

105 Barbeau, *Cornelius Krieghoff*, 9. The word "gay" would not likely then have carried for Barbeau the sexual connotation it does for us today.

106 See *Quebec Mercury*, 31 August 1852, for a detailed description of the furnishings; reprinted in French in *Le Journal de Québec*, 9 September 1852.

107 "Panorama of Canada," *Morning Chronicle* (Quebec), 12 December 1855.

108 Petition of C. Krieghoff of Quebec,

Artist,... 22 February 1856, Legislative Council Papers, National Archives of Canada, Ottawa (RG 14, CI, vol. 23; petition 193 of 1856). Krieghoff addressed a second copy to the governor general, Sir Edmund Walker Head (RG 4, CI, vol. 389, file PSO/CW 573 of 1856). The complete text of the petition is given in Marius Barbeau, "Cornelius Krieghoff (1815–1871 [sic])," *The Educational Record* 70, no. 3: 156.

109 See Alfred Todd, *General Index to the Journals of the Legislative Assembly of Canada; in the 1st, 2nd, and 3rd Parliaments. 1841–1851* (Montreal: John Lovell, 1855), 281 for Hamel, 423 for Légaré, 303 for Kane. Hamel and Légaré appear to have been rejected. It was agreed to advance Kane "£500 for the purchase of some of his paintings." There was assistance as well for literary endeavours, including £250 to Major Richardson in 1842 in aid of his "War of 1812" (126), and the same amount to F.-X. Garneau in 1849 to continue his "History of Canada" (167).

110 See Alfred Todd, *General Index to the Journals of the Legislative Assembly of Canada; in the 4th, 5th, 6th, 7th and 8th Parliaments. 1852–1866* (Ottawa: Hunter, Rose & Company, 1867), 476 for Krieghoff; 473 for Kane; 427 for Hunter. Krieghoff, on the advice of the clerk of the Legislative Assembly, petitioned in triplicate. The copy addressed to the Assembly cannot be located and presumably has been lost to fire. William S. Hunter, Jr. (1823–94) was born and raised and worked most of his life in the Eastern Townships, principally at Stanstead. *Hunter's Ottawa Scenery* was published in 1855, and although the St. Maurice publication never appeared, a series of views in the Eastern Townships came out in

1860. A small travel book, *Hunter's Panoramic Guide from Niagara Falls to Quebec* (Boston and Cleveland, Ohio: John P. Jewett & Co. and Henry P.B. Jewett, 1857), has a long fold-out map that is like a pocket panorama. For Hunter, see Harper, *Early Painters*, 167.

111 Mrs. James Geggie reports in Barbeau 1934, 92, that her husband bought at an auction "a large wooden box which was full of sketches and wastepaper which had belonged to Krieghoff; these were little scratchings on coarse brown paper. They were thrown away." Could these have been preparatory drawings for the panorama?

112 It may have been finished as early as May 1853 when an "Ice Cone at the Falls of Montmorency" was put on view at the piano store of Messrs. Owen, St. John St. See *Morning Chronicle* (Quebec), 12 May–17 August 1853. For Todd, see Béland, *Painting in Quebec*, 480. Todd, who was born in northern England and practiced in Edinburgh before immigrating to Quebec in 1834, left the city in 1853. He presumably saw Krieghoff's painting before departing.

113 There is an excellent description of the Musée du Québec painting by Didier Prioul and Paul Bourassa in Béland, *Painting in Quebec*, 556–57.

114 Samuel McLaughlin (1826–1914), who published the Quebec City directory in the fifties and would later be an important photographer, in 1854 advertised a volume, *Quebec & Environs Illustrated*, that he proposed to publish with steel engravings of all the sights. His list of eight waterfalls and nearby recreational lakes reads like a catalogue of Krieghoff paintings. See "Prospectus. 'Quebec & Environs Illustrated,'" *Le Journal de Québec*, 2 November 1854.

115 The table has been attributed to

Krieghoff's brother, Ernst, who is described in the 1850 Montreal city directory as a cabinetmaker. He worked as an upholsterer earlier in Rochester, and a daughter of his second marriage, Natalie (Mrs. George E. Forsythe of London, Ontario), reported to Barbeau in an undated interview: "My father was interior decorator, but not cabinet making. He was the first to invent the coiled spring bed and patent sold." Transcription by Barbeau, Barbeau Papers, box (temp.) 295, file 8. Ernst settled in Toronto in 1863, and is listed in the 1866 city directory as "Foreman upholsterer" at Jacques & Hay.

116 Again see Prioul and Bourassa in Béland, *Painting in Quebec*, 557–58.

117 The owner of the ship is given in George Gale, *Quebec 'Twixt Old and New* (Quebec: Telegraph Printing Co., 1915), 39. Harper 1979, 60, states that the painting was commissioned by the ship's master, Capt. A.M. Raddall, but gives no source for the information.

118 See Paul Bourassa's entry on the painting in Béland, *Painting in Quebec*, 347.

119 Harper 1979, 18, 20, says "it seems he did not buy the house," but gives no source for the information.

120 O'Connor to Robert Harris, c. 1897, Harris Papers, Confederation Centre Art Gallery and Museum, Charlottetown, Prince Edward Island, misplaced; cited in Harper 1979, 60.

121 Barbeau 1934, 92.

122 Gale, *'Twixt Old and New*, 137.

123 George Gale, *Historic Tales of Old Quebec* (Quebec: Telegraph Printing Company, revised and enlarged edition, 1923), 265.

124 Ibid., 235–37.

125 Harper 1979, 113. Miss Minnie Shaw, who was interviewed by Barbeau before 1934, believed one of the figures was her father, who was a

partner of Campbell's, and that another figure was Budden. See Barbeau Papers, box (temp.) 294, file 6, transcriptions of interviews, p. 21. The figure to the right definitely is Gibb, as he is shown in another painting (*The Falls of the Little Shawinigan*, c. 1858, Thomson Collection, repr. in Harper 1979, 114), with a large food hamper or salmon creel bearing the initials J.G. Gabriel Teoriolen is identified in Barbeau 1934, 70–71.

126 Harper 1979, 108, suggests the location may be Lake St. Charles, while acknowledging that it was identified as Lake Famine as early as 1865 (f.n. 46, p. 185). Barbeau 1934, 129, locates it at Laval on the Montmorency River, and says the guides were "two Siouis of Lorette," and that an inscription on the back of the canvas records the names. The now partly obscure inscription is on the stretcher.

127 See Dianne Sachko Macleod, *Art and the Victorian Middle Class: Money and the Making of Cultural Identity* (Cambridge: Cambridge University Press, 1996). Her discussion of the new market demand for variants and copies is particularly interesting, 70–71.

128 For Légaré, see John R. Porter, *The Works of Joseph Légaré 1795–1855* (Ottawa: National Gallery of Canada, 1978); for Plamondon, see Béland, *Painting in Quebec*, 406; for Hamel, see Vézina, *Théophile Hamel*.

129 Raymond Vézina, "Trente-cinq tableaux inédits de Théophile Hamel," *RACAR* 9, nos. 1–2 (1982): 47–56.

130 Raymond Vézina, "Attitude esthéthique de Cornelius Krieghoff au sein de la tradition picturale canadienne-française," in *RACAR* 1, no. 1 (1974): 49. In the 1854 Quebec City directory, Krieghoff is listed at 25 St. John Street, Hamel at 48.

131 See the notice in *Morning Chronicle*

(Quebec), 2 June 1856. Somerville may have lived only at Mount Pleasant, as his studio address is given as 4 St. John Street in the 1854 and 1855 city directories.

132 For Murray, see Didier Prioul's entry in Béland, *Painting in Quebec*, 391–92; for Hawksett, see Joanne Chagnon's entry in Béland, *Painting in Quebec*, 547–51; for Dynes, see Harper, *Early Painters*, 100.

133 See the 1853 prize list in *Pilot* (Montreal), 12 October 1853; for 1854 in *Quebec Mercury*, 30 September 1854. Plamondon's painting is now in the collection of the Art Gallery of Ontario, Toronto, acc. no. 2601.

134 Fairchild, *Scrap-Book*, 124; *Gleanings*, 70.

135 See Anna Wells Rutledge, ed., *Cumulative Record of Exhibition Catalogues The Pennsylvania Academy of the Fine Arts 1807–1870* (Philadelphia: The American Philosophical Society, 1955), 116. Thomas F. Bell contributed two works in 1854, both "Winter Scene," and four in 1858: "Autumn—Group of Chippewas," "Little Dorritt—Portrait of a Favorite Spaniel," "Breaking up of a Country Ball in Canada, Early Morning," and "Snow Scene (School breaking up)." C.G. Presbury lent two in 1858: "Indians, Autumn" and "Snow Scene." W.H. Stewart lent two in 1860: "Canada Mail-Boat crossing the St. Lawrence on the Ice," and "French Canadians clearing Land and burning Stumps near the St. Maurice, Lower Canada." Thomas Bell lent one again in 1861, "Snow Storm in Canada," and George Whitney lent two in 1862: "Indian Squaw, with Moccasins," and "Indian Hunter on Snow Shoes." Thomas F. Bell is listed as an auctioneer in the Philadelphia city directories for 1858 and 1861, and C.G. Presbury was the proprietor of the

Girard House, located on Chestnut Street at the centre of the blocks containing many of the city's art dealers and artists' studios (directories for 1858 and 1861). Barbeau 1934, 43–44, discusses some of the more important of the paintings that since have been repatriated from Philadelphia.

136 The letter (21 June 1861) and invoice (12 July 1860) are reproduced in Barbeau 1934, facing p. 88, and transcribed pp. 88–89. Their current location is not known. John Young was a prominent lumber merchant and "a collector of everything," according to one Barbeau informant. He acquired many paintings and portions of Krieghoff's library. Barbeau 1934, 92, 99. James S. Earle & Son is listed as a purveyor of looking glasses in the 1861 Philadelphia city directory, and as an importer and manufacturer of paintings and looking glasses in 1858.

137 The note, now in a private collection, Toronto, is transcribed in Barbeau 1934, 88; reproduced in *Cornelius Krieghoff 1815–1872* (Toronto: privately printed, 1976), n.p. For the Lyceum Gallery, see *Catalogue of the American and Foreign Paintings, Now on Exhibition at 548 Broadway* (New York: n.p., 1860), no. 46, "Breaking up of a French Canadian Merry Making at Sunrise in Winter."

138 See "Great Exhibition," *Daily Witness* (Montreal), 1 September 1860.

139 See *Young Men's Association: A Catalogue of the First Exhibition of Paintings and Statuary,…Opened December 24th,…1861* (Buffalo: Joseph Warren & Co.,1861), no. 199, "View in Canada," contributed by Sherman S. Rogers; *Buffalo Fine Arts Academy Catalogue of Paintings and Sculpture on Exhibition at the Academy's Gallery. Third Season of Exhibition* (Buffalo: Joseph Warren & Co., 1863), no. 6,

"Winter Scene," contributed by Geo. Howard; *Report of the Christmas Bazaar, Held Under the Auspices of the Ladies' Hospital Relief Association, From December 14 to December 22, inclusive...* (Rochester: Benton & Andrews, 1863), 20: "Among those from the German school.... Three beautiful little pictures, 'Indians on a Rock,' 'The Russ Sleigh,' and 'Salmon Spearing by Torchlight,' by Krieshoff [sic]," contributed by James M. Whitney.

140 See "Oil Paintings by Mr. Krieghoff," *Morning Chronicle* (Quebec), 29 December 1854 and 5 January 1855; also "The excellent collection ...," *Morning Chronicle*, 29 December 1854.

141 At least 350 have been brought back from England. William R. Watson purchased "over a hundred" on the London market, as reported in his *Retrospective: Recollections of a Montreal Art Dealer* (Toronto: University of Toronto Press, 1974), 24. Leslie W. Lewis, who maintained art businesses in both London and Toronto, had brought back "over thirty" Krieghoffs by 19 February 1940, when he sent a list to Barbeau (Barbeau Papers, box [temp.] 294, file 3), and told Harper in a letter of 24 June 1972 he had handled nearly 200 altogether over the years, which must have included some more from London (Harper Papers, vol. 48, correspondence binders, file N-Z [8 of 10] 1964–77). G. Blair Laing, a Toronto dealer, repatriated "nearly 200." See his *Memoirs of an Art Dealer* (Toronto: McClelland and Stewart, 1979), 240.

142 The only advertisement located so far is Dawson's, "Canadian Pictures after Krieghoff," *Pilot* (Montreal), 29 October–10 December 1859.

143 James Hodges, *Construction of the Great Victoria Bridge in Canada* (London: John Weale, 1860), *Indian*

Chiefs opp. p. 9, *Passengers and Mail* opp. p. 78.

144 See Barbeau 1934, 100. Ross is reported to have taken "40 or 50 altogether" back to England with him when he returned about 1860.

145 Letter of 6 March 1859, Galt Papers, National Archives of Canada, Ottawa (RG 19, E 1(a), vol. 3368). The letter is reproduced in Vézina 1972, 56–67.

146 Gale, *'Twixt Old and New*, 192; *Historic Tales*, 157.

147 Harper 1979, repr. p. 110. Harper misread the name, which is inscribed lower right on the canvas, to be Thomas Sewell, who he says owned a hunting lodge on the lake, and for whom Harper assumed this guide worked.

148 See William H. Truettner, "Ideology and Image, Justifying Westward Expansion," in William H. Truettner, ed., *The West as America: Reinterpreting Images of the Frontier, 1820–1920* (Washington, D.C.: Smithsonian Institution Press for the National Museum of American Art, 1991), particularly 29–30. For examples of Bavarian paintings that similarly idealize Tyrolean peasant life, see Siegfried Wichmann, *Münchner Landschaftsmaler in 19. Jahrhundert* (Munich: Seehamer Verlag, n.d.), particularly 51–57, 88–95.

149 "Beaux-Arts," *Le Courrier du Canada* (Quebec), 1 February 1858.

150 Another version, dated 1857, is titled *Lorette in Winter*. See *Les Maîtres canadiens de la collection Power Corporation du Canada* (Quebec: Musée du Séminaire de Québec, 1989), 57, repr. Harper 1979, 117, explains the distinction between the two communities.

151 Harper 1979, 70.

152 See, for instance, Wilkie's *Pitlessie Fair* of 1804, repr. in Chiego, *Sir David Wilkie*, 111; or *The Country Election of 1851–2*, by the American

George Caleb Bingham (1811–1879), repr. in E. Maurice Bloch, *George Caleb Bringham: The Evolution of an Artist* (Berkeley and Los Angeles: University of California Press, 1967), pl. 94. The most modern and monumental example of the type in Krieghoff's day was the famous *Derby Day* of 1858 by the English painter W.P. Frith (1819–1909), repr. in Cowling, *Artist as Anthropologist*, 234–45.

153 See Barbeau 1934, 43.

154 "Important Sale of First Class Engravings, Chromo-Lithographs, Belonging to C. Krieghoff, Esquire," *Morning Chronicle* (Quebec), 1–6 August 1861; and "Vente Importante de gravures...," *Le Journal de Québec*, 1–6 August 1861. The sale was 7 August.

155 "Attractive Sale of a Large Valuable Collection of Oil Paintings," *Morning Chronicle* (Quebec), 14–19 November 1861; and "Vente attrayante...," *Le Journal de Québec*, 16 November 1861. The sale was 19 November, continuing 30 November (*Morning Chronicle*, 20 November 1861).

156 "A.J. Maxham & Cie.,.. L'Enchère publique," *Le Journal de Québec*, 21 December 1861, also 2 January 1862.

157 "Sale of Paintings, This Day," *Morning Chronicle* (Quebec), 9 April 1862.

158 "Auction Sale by A.J. Maxham & Co....," *Morning Chronicle* (Quebec), 25 March–9 April 1862; also "Vente importante," *Le Journal de Québec*, 27 March–8 April 1862.

159 See copy of the lease for one year from 1 May 1862 with the Quebec Permanent Building Society for half of a double house on Grande Allée (no number), Archives judiciaires de Québec, registry of the notary Alexander Charles Lindsay, no. 397; transcribed in Vézina 1972, 206–207. Harper 1979, 154, says the address

was no. 42, but an advertisement for Krieghoff's household sale a year later gives no. 44. His previous house is advertised in *Morning Chronicle* (Quebec), 22 March 1862, described as on St. Louis Street, near Spencer Wood. That was probably 11 Grande Allée, which is an extension of St. Louis outside the wall.

160 See fn. 21. Hamilton Burnett (b. 1840) joined the 17th Regiment of Foot (Leicestershire) in June 1858, was promoted through the ranks to lieutenant by July 1859 without purchase, exchanged rank with another lieutenant November 1860, and was posted to Quebec June 1861. This from the Public Records Office, London, notes in the Harper Papers, vol. 50, file 16.

161 "Attractive and Important Sale of Oil Paintings...," *Morning Chronicle* (Quebec), 12–23 December 1862; also *Quebec Mercury*, 19 December 1862; and "Vente importante de peintures à l'huile...," *Le Journal de Québec*, 13 December 1862. Fairchild, *Gleanings*, 72–73, gives the full text of the catalogue of the sale, listing 31 works. Barbeau 1934, 72–73, reprints it. Harper 1979, 151, lists the 31 works.

162 Lease for one year from 1 May 1863 with the Ladies' Protestant Home, Grande Allée, Archives judiciaires de Québec, registry of the notary Noël Hill Bowen, no. 2360. Vézina 1972, 218, fn. 24, remarks that the Ladies' Protestant Home was erecting a care residence at 95 Grande Allée 1862-3. The rented house doubtless was the "Krieghoff cottage," still today on Grande Allée in front of the former Ladies' Protestant Home. See Sylvain Laperrière and Rosemary Minnich, "La Maison Krieghoff, Histoire d'une résurrection," *Continuité* 78 (autumn 1978): 41–43. The sublet, 2 May 1863, with a Mr. De Courtenay,

is recorded in Archives judiciaires de Québec, registry of notary Edward George Cannon, no. 4962.

163 For the furniture sale, by Maxham of course, see "Sale of Household Furniture...," *Morning Chronicle* (Quebec), 20–29 April 1863; *Quebec Mercury*, 20–29 April 1863; and "Ventes de meubles de ménage...," *Le Journal de Québec*, 21 April 1863. The record of the power of attorney is in Archives judiciaires de Québec, registry of notary Fisher Langlois, no. 2498. Transcribed in Vézina 1972, 207–208. The only explicit instruction in the document is that Maxham sell Krieghoff's shares amounting to "one eighth in the Upton Mine in the eastern townships of Lower Canada." On 26 January 1861 he had bought 30 shares in the Colonial Mining Co. through Peter Arnold Shaw; see Archives judiciaires de Québec, registry of notary W. Bignell, no. 3369, transcribed in Vézina 1972, 206. For Krieghoff's departure see "Mr. Krieghoff...," *Globe* (Toronto), 28 August 1863.

164 Fairchild, *Scrap-Book*, 120; *Gleanings*, 74.

165 For the report of the summer at Lac Larron, and a second, German wife, see Barbeau 1934, 69, 78, 90. Although all the evidence points to Krieghoff's spending the next seven years mainly in Europe, there is an E. Burnett listed in the Chicago city directory for 1865, at 62 W. Randolph St. We have no reason to believe it is Emily.

166 *Second Conversazione Art Association of Montreal, Held February 11, 1864* (Montreal: Herald Steam Press, 1864), no. 60, "Winter Scene"; no. 61, "Falls of St. Ferreol"; no. 62, "Woodland Scene."

167 See W. Martha E. Cooke, *W.H. Coverdale Collection of Canadiana:*

Paintings, Water-colours and Drawings (Ottawa: Public Archives of Canada, 1983), 90–93; also Harper 1979, 186, fn. 46 and 47.

168 For the Toronto Mechanics' Institute exhibition, see reports in "The Mechanics' Institute Exhibition," *Globe* (Toronto), 23 March 1865; "The Mechanics' Institute Exhibition, The Arts," *Leader* (Toronto), 24 March 1865. *Hamilton and Gore Mechanics Institute Exhibition of Fine Arts,... opened 24 May 1865* (Hamilton: The "Spectator" Steam Press, 1865), no. 33, "Landscape, Fort Chambly," lent by Judge Logie; no. 34, "Landscape, Split Rock," lent by Judge Logie; no. 123, "Habitant, Lower Canada," lent by Judge Logie; no. 207, "Habitant," lent by Robert McKay.

169 "Exhibition of Paintings," *Citizen* (Halifax), 29 August 1865.

170 Harper 1979, 185, fn. 13, lists the subjects. Nine of the actual photographs deposited at the time are now in National Archives of Canada, Ottawa, Visual and Sound Archives, misc. Krieghoff photographs. Five are large size, four carte de visite, and one subject, "Canadians in Sleigh, Winter Scene," is in both formats.

171 See *Catalogue of the Canadian Contributions to the Dublin Exhibition, 1865* (n.p., 1865), 36–39.

172 Barbeau 1934, 151–52, lists nine Krieghoffs in this volume, but he mistakenly counted two photographs "from nature."

173 Barbeau 1934, 152.

174 Ibid., 151.

175 Harper 1979, 153, claims he received payments from both Notman and Ellison, but gives no evidence. Large coloured photographs occasionally are found with the Krieghoff blind-stamp, but most of the best are signed "Notman and Sandham,"

which means they date from 1877–82, after Krieghoff's death.

176 *Catalogue of Works of Art on Exhibition at the Gallery of the Buffalo Fine Arts Academy,...First Season of 1865* (Buffalo: Franklin Printing Press, 1865), no. 102, "Lake St. Charles, 12 miles North of Quebec"; no. 103, "Shooting Rapids, River Jaque Carten [sic]"; no. 104, "Devil's Bridge [sic], Jaque Carten [sic], The Salmon-leap on that River"; no. 105, "Lake St. Joseph, 30 Miles from Quebec"; no. 106, "Drawing Ice on the St. Lawrence, before Quebec." *Works of Art on Exhibition at the Gallery of the Buffalo Fine Arts Academy...* (Buffalo: Thomas, Howard & Johnson, 1867), no. 122, "Indian Camp," lent by C.F.S. Thomas, life member BFAA. *Catalogue of Works of Art on Exhibition at the Gallery of the Buffalo Fine Arts Academy,...* (Buffalo: Thomas, Howard & Johnson, 1867), no. 65, "Canadian Hunter in a Snow Storm," lent by Daniel Brown, life member BFAA. *Catalogue of the Paintings and Sculpture, Now Open for Exhibition by the Utica Art Association, 1867* (Utica, N.Y.: Evening Telegraph Steam Printing House, 1867), no. 218, "Indian Squaw"; no. 219, "Indian Hunter." Utica is on the Mohawk River, on the route of the Erie Canal between Rochester and Albany.

177 *Catalogue of an Important Collection of High Class, Original American and Foreign Oil Paintings,... May 10th and 11th* (Cincinnati, Ohio: Jacob Graff & Co., 1866). The collection was from the Pennsylvania Gallery of Art, 322 Chestnut Street, Philadelphia.

178 See Montreal city directory for 1866–7, when Scott is listed as carver and gilder at 4 Victoria Square, and 1867–8 when he is at 363 Notre-Dame with a new description. *Art Association of Montreal: Fourth*

Exhibition 1867. Catalogue of...works of Art...5th February, 1867 (Montreal: Louis Perrault & Co., 1867), no. 69, "Chippawa Indians," no. 81, "Crossing Mail at Quebec," for sale; no. 82, "Spill my milk."

179 *Canadian Contributions to the Dublin Exhibition*, 39.

180 "Le 'Sport' Canadien," *Le Canadien* (Montreal), 16 April 1866.

181 "Quebec and the Paris Exhibition," *Quebec Mercury*, 18 December 1866; and "Exposition de Paris," *Le Canadien* (Montreal), 19 December 1866. The fine art catalogue lists the Krieghoff simply as "Scène des forêts"; *Catalogue Général... Première Partie (Groupes i à v) contenant les Œuvres d'art* (Paris: E. Dentu, 1867), 238, cat. 5. The other Canadian contributors to the fine arts display were Théophile Hamel (two religious paintings, a group of portrait studies, and a group of portraits), Antoine Plamondon (a genre painting), Napoléon Bourassa (two cartoons for his "Apotheosis of Christopher Columbus," and Eugène Taché (three groups of drawings). The photographs must have been in the general Canadian display.

182 The photograph was first described by Abbé H.-A. Scott, *Grands anniversaires. Souvenirs historiques et pensées utiles* (Quebec: L'Action Sociale Ltée., 1919), 297–99. It was rediscovered in the Archives du Séminaire de Québec by Michel Doyon in 1985.

183 *Le Journal de Québec*, 21 May 1867.

184 There may not even have been room above the speaker's chair, as the women's public gallery was situated there. See Marcel Hamelin, *Les Premières Années du parlementarisme québécois (1867–1878)* (Quebec: Les Presses de l'Université Laval, 1974), 315. The building burned in April 1883 and there was looting during the fire. See "Les voleurs pendant

l'incendie," *L'Événement* (Quebec), 20 April 1883. Michel Doyon, who generously shared his research on this lumber industry grouping with me, believed the paper on which the photograph is printed dates from about 1880, and that the even lighting suggests an electrical source, which apparently was installed in the legislature that year. How the central painting came on the market about 1950 remains a mystery. William Watson, the dealer who discovered it, believed there was provenance directly back to its purchase from the artist by John Ogilvy of Montreal, although there is a period of unidentified ownership that casts this hearsay into doubt (see catalogue entry 140 elsewhere in this volume). Barbeau 1934, 116, relates Canon Scott's story of the grouping in the Quebec legislature, but remained convinced, without evidence of the photograph, that the paintings were destroyed by fire. Harper 1979, 92–96, also with only Canon Scott's description as an aid, attempts to reconstruct what he calls "an elaborate reredos" he mistakenly surmised was commissioned by the Legislative Assembly about 1858.

185 Printed in Montreal by the firm Burland & Lafricain, they must date from between 1867 and 1875. See Mary Allodi, "Focus," *Rotunda* 6, no. 3 (summer 1973): 2. The titles were revealed in Rosemarie L. Tovell, *A New Class of Art: The Artist's Print in Canadian Art, 1877–1920* (Ottawa: National Gallery of Canada, 1996), 153, fn. 5. Another set of chromolithographs, one of the head of an habitant of unknown title, the other the head of an old imbiber labelled *The First Commissioner of Excise*, are known only by single impressions in a Toronto private collection. Published in Buffalo by Clay

Cosack & Co., with A.J. Maerz as lithographer, they date from between 1871 and 1874 when Maerz is listed as a lithographer in the Buffalo city directory. That Krieghoff never knew them is further suggested by a credit on the label: "Copied from the original by permission of Mr. J.N. Matthews." Matthews was associated with the firm and owned other Buffalo businesses, including the *Express* newspaper, and later the art printing company Matthews, Northrup & Co. Barbeau 1934, 122, records what is likely another impression of the habitant head as though it were a painting.

186 See Stanley G. Triggs, *William Notman: The Stamp of a Studio* (Toronto: Art Gallery of Ontario/The Coach House Press, 1985), 150–51.

187 See Fairchild, *Gleanings*, 22, for Budden in the Notman photographs. For Rhodes's role and François Gros-Louis, see Joan M. Schwartz, "William Notman's hunting photographs, 1866," *The Archivist* 117 (1998): 20–29. The 1853 painting, *Sportsmen in Winter Camp*, is repr. in Harper 1979, 106.

188 Barbeau 1934, 100, for the Fraser commission. Harper 1979, 93, reproduces the 1862 version, *Log Rafts in Sillery Cove*.

189 "Vente par encan de peintures originales finies avec soin par C. Krieghoff, écuyer," *Le Journal de Québec*, 25 April 1868.

190 "A Collection of Original Oil Paintings, consigned from Paris by C. Krieghoff, Esquire," *Quebec Mercury*, 3–11 November 1869; also *Morning Chronicle* (Quebec), 3–11 November 1869; and "Vente par encan d'une collection de peintures originales consignée de Paris par C. Krieghoff, écuyer," *Le Journal de Québec*, 6, 8 November 1869.

191 "Very latest," *Quebec Mercury*, 5

August 1870.

192 See "Fine Arts," *Morning Chronicle* (Quebec), 16 September 1870; and "Beaux Arts," *Le Journal de Québec*, 17, 19 September 1870.

193 "Collection of Original Oil Paintings, selected by C. Krieghoff, Esq.," *Morning Chronicle* (Quebec), 15–26 October 1870; and "Vente par encan d'une collection de peintures à l'huile," *Le Journal de Québec*, 17–19 October 1870. Originally scheduled 20 October, then rescheduled for the 24th, the sale was finally held on 26 October.

194 The deaths are recorded in the archives of St. Johannis Church in Schweinfurt. She died 9 February 1867, he 28 May 1868. Reported by Paul Ultsch with a photocopy from the original documents in a letter to Russell Harper, 14 July 1977, Harper Papers, vol. 50, file 16.

195 A "Russ Sleigh" was exhibited in Rochester in 1863 (see fn. 139, above). Two Russian subjects are now in a Toronto private collection; see Sotheby Parke Bernet (Canada), Toronto, sale 15–16 May 1978, lots 71, 72, repr. pp. 36–37.

196 Lease for eight months from 30 August 1870 with Mme Germain Saint-Pierre, Archives judiciaires de Québec, registry of the notary Cyrille Tessier, no. 3542; transcribed in Vézina 1972, 209–10.

197 He refused to renew the lease with Mme Saint-Pierre. See document relating to the proposed lease, Archives judiciaires de Québec, registry of notary Cyrille Tessier, no. 3627; transcribed in Vézina 1972, 211. Earlier that day he had signed a lease for one year commencing 1 May 1871 with Bertha Martin, Archives judiciaires de Québec, registry of notary Cyrille Tessier, no. 3626; transcribed in Vézina 1972, 210–11.

198 "The Fine Arts," *Quebec Gazette*, 13

September 1871.

199 "The Exhibition," *Quebec Mercury*, 14 September 1871.

200 "The Provincial Exhibition. Prize List—Industrial Department. Class V," *Quebec Mercury*, 15 September 1871. The second review is "The Provincial Exhibition. The Fine Arts," *Quebec Mercury*, 16 September 1871. The two works are described here simply as "A view in the neighbourhood of Quebec," and "A Canadian Winter Scene."

201 See "L'exposition," *Le Journal de Québec*, 15 September 1871, which mentions that "the crowd stopped to admire the strikingly realistic Canadian scenes" by Krieghoff. In "Exposition Provinciale de 1871," *Journal de l'instruction publique* 15, no. 9 (September 1871): 120, we find nothing but "Canadian landscapes and genre scenes painted by Krieghoff that we are happy to welcome back among us."

202 "Auction Sale of Household Furniture, Carpets, Stoves, Paintings, etc.," *Morning Chronicle* (Quebec), 7–20 October 1871; and "Vente par encan de Meubles et effets d'ameublement," *Le Journal de Québec*, 7–13 October 1871. The sale was to be 16 October, but was postponed, or broken into portions.

203 "Auction Sale. Valuable Books, Oil Paintings, Water Colours, Chromos, etc.," *Quebec Mercury*, 14 October 1871. There is a long list of the books being offered. "Auction Sale of Household Furniture," *Quebec Mercury*, 25–27 November 1871; and "Vente par encan de meubles et effets d'ameublement," *Le Journal de Québec*, 25–27 November 1871. The sale was 28 November.

204 "Death of Mr. Krieghoff, Artist," *Morning Chronicle* (Quebec), 7 March 1872; also "Nouvelles du Jour," *L'Événement* (Quebec), 7 March 1872.

205 The address comes from the death certificate as recorded in a Report of Death issued 11 August 1972, Bureau of Vital Statistics, Chicago, registration no. 87–1. Krieghoff was buried at Graceland Cemetery. Budden wrote to Robert Harris, c. 1897, "I have a letter of his addressed to me about Eleven o'clock at Night, and within ten minutes his wife found him dead on his bed"; Harris Papers, cited above; quoted in Harper 1979, 163. *Morning Chronicle*, 7 March 1872, reported his death to have occurred at 11:10 p.m., 4 March.

206 *Morning Chronicle* (Quebec), 7 March 1872.

207 They seem to have remained in the United States, although not in Chicago, where Émilie Krieghoff is recorded in the city directory only in 1872. They appear in the Denver, Colorado, city directory beginning in 1888, living together at 2255 Stout Street. Émilie Krieghoff died in that city 2 September 1906. The death certificate is dated 3 September, Colorado Department of Health, Denver, no. 6768. Emily Burnett died there 29 December 1929, certificate dated 31 December, no. 11,849. There is no evidence that they had contact with Canada following the artist's death, although some books and engravings from Krieghoff's estate offered by Maxham in 1877 may have come from them. See "Vente de livres, gravures, etc. appartenant à la Succession de feu C. Krieghoff, écuyer," *Le Journal de Québec*, 19 May 1877. The sale was 21 May.

Notes to *The Outsider as Insider: Cornelius Krieghoff's Art of Describing* by Ramsay Cook

Dennis Reid, Allan Greer, and Tim Zuck generously read an earlier version of this essay and suggested improvements.

1 Fernand Ouellet, *Histoire économique et sociale du Québec, 1760–1850* (Montréal et Paris: Fides, 1966), cited 595.

2 Michel Brunet, *La présence anglaise et les Canadiens* (Montréal: Beauchemin, 1958), cited 126.

3 Simon Shama, *Dead Certainties* (Boston and Toronto: Knopf, 1991), 27–28; Francis Haskell, *History and Its Images: Art and the Interpretation of the Past* (New Haven and London: Yale University Press, 1993).

4 Isabella Lucy Bird, *The Englishwoman in America* (1856; reprint, Toronto: University of Toronto Press, 1966), 283.

5 Terence Crowley, "'Thunder Gusts': Popular Disturbances in Early French Canada," *Historical Papers*, 1979, 11–31.

6 Allan Greer, *The Patriots and the People: The Rebellion of 1837 in Rural Lower Canada* (Toronto: University of Toronto Press, 1993), 64–86; René Hardy, "Le charivari dans la sociabilité rurale québécoise au XIXᵉ siècle," in *De la sociabilité : Spécificité et mutations*, ed. Roger Levasseur (Montréal: Boréal, 1990), 59–72.

7 William Kingston, *Western Wanderings; or, A Pleasure Tour of the Canadas* (London: Chapman and Hall, 1856), 2: 163.

8 Stephen Kenny, "'Cahots' and Catcalls: An Episode of Popular Resistance in Lower Canada at the Outset of the Union," *Canadian Historical Review* 65 (1984): 184–208.

9 Jean Hamelin and Yves Roby, *Histoire économique du Québec, 1851–1896* (Montréal: Fides, 1971), 63–64, 154–56.

10 Alfred Todd, *General Index to the Journals of the Legislative Assembly of Canada; in the 1st, 2nd, and 3rd Parliaments, 1841–1851* (Montreal: John Lovell, 1855), and *General Index to the Journals of the Legislative Assembly of Canada; in the 4th, 5th, 6th, 7th and 8th Parliaments, 1852–1866* (Toronto: Hunter, Rose & Company, 1867), 737, 747, 748, 750, 751, 756.

11 Samuel Thompson, *Reminiscences of a Canadian Pioneer for the Last Fifty Years, 1833–1883: An Autobiography* (1884; reprint, Toronto: McClelland and Stewart, 1968), 221.

12 Todd, *General Index ..., 1852–1866*, 737.

13 Philippe Sylvain and Nive Voisine, *Histoire du catholicisme québécois. Réveil et consolidation*, t. 2, (1840–1898) (Montréal: Boréal, 1991), 13–93; Fernand Ouellet, "Nationalisme canadien-français et le laïcisme au XIXᵉ siècle," *Recherches sociographiques* 4 (1963): 47–70.

14 Louis LaFlèche, *Quelques considérations sur les rapports de la société civile avec la religion et la famille* (Montréal: Eusèbe Senécal, 1866).

15 Guy Trépanier, "Contrôle social et vécu religieux dans la paroisse de Champlain, 1850–1900," in *L'église et le village au Québec, 1850–1930*, ed. Serge Gagnon and René Hardy (Montréal: Leméac, 1979), cited 95.

16 Serge Gagnon, *Plaisir d'amour et crainte de Dieu : sexualité et confession au Bas-Canada* (Sainte-Foy: Presses de l'Université Laval, 1990).

17 Serge Gagnon, *Mourir hier et aujourd'hui* (Québec: Presses de l'Université Laval, 1987).

18 Gagnon and Hardy, *L'église et le village au Québec, 1850–1930*, cited 26, 62.

19 Jean-Marie Fecteau, *Un nouvel ordre des choses : la pauvreté, le crime et l'État au Québec, de la fin du XVIIIᵉ siècle à 1840* (Montréal: VLB, 1989), cited 175.

20 Hamelin and Roby, *Histoire économique du Québec, 1851–1896*, 25.

21 Sylvain and Voisine, *Histoire du catholicisme québécois*, cited 121.

22 Jan Noel, *Canada Dry: Temperance Crusades before Confederation* (Toronto: University of Toronto Press, 1995), 152–82; Nive Voisine, "Mouvements de tempérance et religion populaire," in *Religion populaire, religion de clercs?* ed. Benoît Lacroix and Jean Simard (Québec: Institut québécois de recherche sur la culture, 1984), 66–77.

23 Marcel Trudel, *Chiniquy* (Éditions du bien public, 1955), 126–27.

24 Yves Roby, "Chiniquy, Charles," in *Dictionary of Canadian Biography*, vol. 12 (Toronto: University of Toronto Press, 1990), 189–93.

25 Jean-Jacques Lefebvre, "Hurteau, Isidore," in *Dictionary of Canadian Biography*, vol. 10 (Toronto: University of Toronto Press, 1972), 373–74.

26 Robert Rumilly, *Histoire de Longueuil* (Longueuil: Société d'histoire de Longueuil, 1974), 283.

27 Hubert Charbonneau, *La population du Québec : études rétrospectives* (Montréal: Les Éditions du Boréal Express, 1973).

28 *Le Journal de Québec*, 12 juillet 1855, cited in Hamelin and Roby, *Histoire économique du Québec, 1851–1896*, 5.

29 Yolande Lavoie, *L'émigration des Québécois aux États-Unis de 1840 à 1930* (Québec: Éditeur officiel, 1979), 45.

30 Christian Morissonneau, *La terre promise : Le mythe du Nord québécois* (Montréal: Hurtubise HMH, 1978), 134.

31 Testard de Montigny, *La colonisation : Le nord de Montréal ou la région Labelle* (Montréal: Beauchemin, 1895), 168–69.

32 Hamelin and Roby, *Histoire économique du Québec, 1851–1896*, 22.

33 R.H. Fuchs, *Dutch Painting* (London: Thames and Hudson, 1978), 36–61.

34 Elizabeth Johns, *American Genre Painting: The Politics of Everyday Life* (New Haven and London: Yale University Press, 1991); David M. Lubin, *Picturing a Nation: Art and Social Change in Nineteenth Century America* (New Haven and London: Yale University Press, 1994).

35 H.A. Scott, *Grands anniversaires : souvenirs historiques et pensées utiles* (Québec: Action sociale, 1919), 297–99; J. Russell Harper, *Krieghoff* (Toronto and Buffalo: University of Toronto Press, 1979), 93–94. But also see Dennis Reid's essay, this volume, 92–93.

36 Robert-Lionel Séguin, *La civilisation traditionnelle de l'habitant aux 17e et 18e siècles. Fonds matériel* (Montréal: Fides, 1973).

37 Robert Leslie Jones, "The Old French Canadian Horse: Its History in Canada and the United States," *Canadian Historical Review* 28 (1947), cited 130–31.

38 Raymond Vezina, "Attitude esthétique de Cornelius Krieghoff au sein de la tradition picturiale canadienne-française," *RACAR* 1, no. 1 (1974): 53.

39 Jones, "The Old French Canadian Horse," cited 134–35.

40 Paul Bernier, *Le cheval canadien* (Québec: Septentrion, 1992), cited 76.

41 Paul-André Leclerc, *Les voitures à chevaux à la campagne* (La Pocatière: Musée François-Pilote, 1978), 7–42.

42 Jones, "The Old French Canadian Horse," cited 134–35.

43 Donald Guay, *Histoire des courses de chevaux au Québec* (Montréal: VLB, 1985), 11–135.

44 John Lambert, *Travels through Lower Canada, and the United States of North America, in the Years 1806, 1807, and 1809* (London: Richard Phillips, 1810), 1: 174–75.

45 Gérard Morisset, *Peintres et tableaux*, vol. 1 (Québec: Éditions du Chevalet, 1936), 215.

46 John R. Porter, "The Market for Painting: Basic Needs versus Artistic Taste," in *Painting in Quebec, 1820–1850: New Views, New Perspectives*, ed. Mario Béland (Québec: Musée du Québec, 1992), 11–35.

47 Laurier Lacroix, "Yesterday's Standards, Today's Fragments: Elements of Esthetics in Quebec, 1820–1850," in Béland, *Painting in Quebec, 1820–1850*, 60.

48 Eugène Fromentin, *The Masters of Past Time: Dutch and Flemish Painting from Van Eyck to Rembrandt*, trans. Andrew Boyle, ed. Horst Gerson (London: Phaidon Press; New York: Oxford University Press, 1948), 103; also quoted in Svetlana Alpers, *The Art of Describing: Dutch Art in the Seventeenth Century* (Chicago: University of Chicago Press, 1983), xviii. Alpers's distinction between Dutch genre painting as "description" and French academic art as "narration" (see xvii–xxvii and 109), though perhaps too sharply drawn, has greatly helped me to understand Krieghoff's place in nineteenth-century Canadian art.

49 Kenneth Clark, *The Nude: A Study of Ideal Art* (London: John Murray, 1956), 183.

Notes to *Perceiving the Other: French-Canadian and Indian Iconography in the Work of Cornelius Krieghoff* by François-Marc Gagnon

1 Gérard Morisset, *La peinture traditionnelle au Canada français* (Ottawa: Le Cercle du Livre de France, 1960), 7.

2 Gérard Morisset, *Coup d'œil sur les arts en Nouvelle-France* (Quebec City: Presses de Charrier et Dugal, 1941), 86–87.

3 Newton MacTavish, *The Fine Arts in Canada* (Toronto: The MacMillan Company of Canada Ltd., 1925), 8.

4 Ibid., 17.

5 Ibid., v.

6 Ibid., 16.

7 Ibid., 16–17.

8 Gérard Morisset, *La peinture traditionnelle au Canada français*, 7.

9 E.F.B. Johnston, in *Canada and Its Provinces: A History of the Canadian People and Their Institutions by One Hundred Associates* (Toronto, Glasgow: Brook & Company, 1914), vol. XII, 598.

10 Ibid., 596.

11 Ibid., 601.

12 Marius Barbeau, "Cornelius Krieghoff (1815–1872)," *Catalogue of Toronto Centennial Historical Exhibition*, January 1934, Art Gallery of Toronto, 15.

13 Robert Harris, "Art in Quebec and the Maritime Provinces," *Canada: An Encyclopedia of the Country* (Toronto: J. Castell Hopkins, 1898), vol. IV, 356.

14 Morisset, *Coup d'œil sur les arts en Nouvelle-France*, 49.

15 Meyer Schapiro, *Theory and Philosophy of Art: Style, Artist, and Society*, selected papers (New York: George Braziller, 1994), 51.

16 Morisset, *Coup d'œil sur les arts en Nouvelle-France*, 137.

17 Morisset, *La peinture traditionnelle au Canada français*, 142–43.

18 Quoted in Gérard Morisset, *Peintres et tableaux* (Quebec City: Les Éditions du Chevalet, 1936), vol. 1, 212. Other critics have compared Krieghoff to Hogarth. See M. O. Hammond, *Painting and Sculpture in Canada* (Toronto: The Ryerson Press, 1930), 10: "His pictures are enhanced in interest and value by the rich humour he displayed in recording the habitant life. For this Krieghoff has been called the Canadian Hogarth."

19 Morisset, *La peinture traditionnelle au Canada français*, 143.

20 For an English-Canadian view of the Rebels, see *The Rebels at Beauharnois, Lower Canada, 1838*, a watercolour by Katherine Jane Ellice, reproduced in Michael Bell, *Painters in a New Land* (Toronto: McClelland & Stewart Ltd., 1973), 96, which also quotes a passage from Katherine Jane Ellice's journal: "Wednesday, November 7, 1838. The whole house is surrounded by *Guards*—I sketched some of them from the window—picturesque ruffians."

21 Morisset, *Peintres et tableaux*, vol. 1, 211–13.

22 This false statement, corrected by Raymond Vézina in *Cornelius Krieghoff: Peintre de mœurs (1815–1872)* (Ottawa: Éditions du Pélican, 1972), appeared in *Peintres et tableaux*, vol. 1, 210, and was reprinted word for word in *La peinture traditionnelle au Canada français*, 141. Krieghoff's parents were Lutherans, and his grandparents lived in Germany during the eighteenth century.

23 On James Bowman and Henry Thielke, see Morisset, *La peinture traditionnelle au Canada français*, 104; on the Italian painters, see Morisset *Peintres et tableaux*, vol. 1, 227–30.

24 On Émilie Gauthier, see Hugues de Jouvancourt, *Cornelius Krieghoff* (Toronto: Musson Book Company, 1973), 22–23.

25 Morisset, *Peintres et tableaux*, vol. 1, 209. Admittedly, Vézina, *Cornelius Krieghoff*, 15, was scarcely more enthusiastic about Barbeau's book: "The fashion for the historical novel encouraged Marius Barbeau to regale us with the artist's personal adventures and even his conversations with his beloved, without taking the trouble to differentiate between these charming fantasies and duly proven facts."

26 Morisset, *Coup d'œil sur les arts en Nouvelle-France*, IX, X.

27 A.Y. Jackson, *A Painter's Country: The Autobiography of A.Y. Jackson*, (Toronto: Clarke, Irwin & Company Limited, Centennial Edition, 1967), 69.

28 Lionel Groulx, *Notre maître, le passé* (Montreal: Bibliothèque de l'Action française, 1924).

29 Ibid., 115. Groulx was referring to Frédéric Le Play (1806–1882), one of the leading proponents of the conservative and traditionalist social Catholic movement that aimed to reform society by reestablishing the authority of landlords, employers, and fathers.

30 Ibid., 105.

31 Ibid., 119.

32 Ibid., 125.

33 Ibid., 109–10.

34 Morisset, *Coup d'œil sur les arts en Nouvelle-France*, 141.

35 Ibid., 133.

36 Michael Fried, *Absorption and Theatricality: Painting and Beholder in the Age of Diderot* (Chicago and London: The University of Chicago Press, 1980), 55, in the commentary concerning *La Piété filiale* (Filial Devotion), 1763, by J.-B. Greuze.

37 Quoted by Fried, 55.

38 See *Une jeune fille qui envoie un baiser par la fenêtre, appuyée sur des fleurs, qu'elle brise* (Young Woman Blowing a Kiss through a Window, Crushing Flowers Under Her Arm), 1769, repr. in Fried,

60. An "absorbed" figure if ever there was one, the girl fails to notice she is crushing the flowers. *The Head of the Family* is also repr. in Fried, 9.

39 Quoted in Fried, 220.

40 Morisset, *La peinture traditionnelle au Canada français*, 144.

41 This is why the two descriptions do not entirely coincide.

42 J. Russell Harper, *Krieghoff* (Toronto: University of Toronto Press, 1979), 29. Harper directs his readers to C.T.P. Chiniquy, *Forty Years in the Church of Christ* (Chicago: F. H. Revell, 1900), 41–42, for more about Catholic harassment of the Protestants of Longueuil.

43 Letter from Monseigneur Bourget to Chiniquy, October 28, 1848, quoted in Marcel Trudel, *Chiniquy* (Éditions du Bien Public, 1955), 126.

44 Robert Rumilly, *Histoire de Longueuil* (Ottawa: Société d'histoire de Longueuil, 1974), 283. A reproduction of Plamondon's painting appears in this work opposite page 142. A letter from Michel Cartier to Marius Barbeau, dated 24 October 1956, now at the Canadian Museum of Civilization, Hull, Quebec (Marius Barbeau Papers, box (temp.) 295, file 1), states that "this portrait was the size of a door and framed with 3 inches of carved oak." When Chiniquy's popularity waned, the owner of the painting, Mr. Chénier, put it in his shed, where it was found by members of the Lasnier family when they bought his house in 1886. Not knowing what to do with it, they decided to destroy it. "These details were given [to me] by his son, who witnessed the scene," concludes Michel Cartier. The son referred to was probably Yves Lasnier, a well-known Montreal art dealer who died recently. We know that the Lasnier family owned a liturgical candle factory in Longueuil. I am grateful to

Professor Ramsay Cook for having brought this document to my attention.

45 Morisset, *Peintres et tableaux*, vol. 1, 164–66, describes Plamondon's painting as a full-length portrait. Had Morisset seen the work? He seems not have known its whereabouts when he wrote: "This painting was apparently formerly in Beauport; I assume it has been preserved."

46 Marcel Trudel, 127, which refers to his lecture of October 5, 1848, reproduced in *Mélanges religieux*, XII (October 10, 1848): 30.

47 W. Martha E. Cooke, *W. H. Coverdale Collection of Canadiana: Paintings, Water-colours and Drawings (Manoir Richelieu Collection)* (Ottawa: Public Archives Canada, 1983), 44 and figs. 83–84.

48 Harper, 44.

49 Harper, 129.

49 Harper, 129.

50 Repr. in Harper, 53.

51 F.M. Gagnon, *Ces hommes dits sauvages* (Montréal: Libre Expression, 1984), 145.

52 Jules Ballet, *La Guadeloupe. Renseignements sur l'histoire, la flore, la faune, la géologie, la minéralogie, l'agriculture, le commerce, l'industrie, la législation, l'administration, Basse Terre* (1894), 356. Raymond Breton, *Dictionnaire caraïbe*, 1765.

53 George Catlin, *Letters and Notes on the Manners, Customs, and Conditions of the North American Indians* (New York: Dover Publications, Inc., [1844], 1973), 3.

54 Ibid., 6.

55 Michel de Montaigne, *Essays* (London: Penguin Books Limited, 1958), 110.

56 Jean-Jacques Rousseau, *Discourse on the Origin of Equality*, trans. Franklin Philip (Oxford, New York: Oxford University Press, 1994), 61.

57 Letter from Voltaire to J.-J. Rousseau, dated August 30, 1755; in Jacques Roger, *Jean-Jacques Rousseau. Discours sur les sciences et les arts. Discours sur l'origine de l'inégalité* (Paris: Garnier-Flammarion, 1971), 237.

58 See Larry Silver, "Forest Primeval: Albrecht Altdorfer and the German Wilderness Landscape," *Simiolus* 13, no. 1 (1983): 4–43.

59 Repr. in Simon Schama, *Landscape and Memory* (Toronto: Vintage Canada, 1995), 97.

60 For more on this painting by Plamondon, see Yves Lacasse and François-Marc Gagnon, "Antoine Plamondon. Le Dernier des Hurons (1838)," *The Journal of Canadian Art History* XII, no. 1, (1989): 68–77; and François-Marc Gagnon, "Le dernier des Hurons: L'image de l'autre comme image de soi," *Où va l'histoire de l'art contemporain?* (Paris: École nationale supérieure des Beaux-Arts, 1997), 177–89.

CHRONOLOGY

RAYMOND VÉZINA

Documented events in
Cornelius Krieghoff's life and career

Social and political events
of importance

1783

25 March: birth of Isabella Ludovica
Wouters, mother of Cornelius, in Ghent,
Flanders

20 September: Treaty of Versailles establishes the independence of the United
States of America

1786

30 April: birth of Johann Ernst Krieghoff,
father of Cornelius, in Ufhoven,
Thüringen

1789

14 July: the French Revolution begins

1791

10 June: Canada Constitution Act is
passed in the British Parliament establishing two provinces, Upper and Lower
Canada

1793

21 January: King Louis XVI of France is
executed

August: foundation of the town of York
(Toronto)

16 October: Queen Marie Antoinette of
France is executed

1799

9 November: Napoleon becomes Consul
of France

1800

5 February: Act of Union of Great Britain
and Ireland comes into force

1803

Britain declares war on France

1804

18 May: Napoleon proclaimed Emperor of
France

1806

5 June: Louis Bonaparte becomes King of
Holland

1810

9 July: France annexes Holland

1811

12 May: marriage of Johann Ernst
Krieghoff and Isabella Ludovica Wouters
in Amsterdam

29 October: birth of Frederika Louisa,
sister of Cornelius, in Amsterdam

1812

19 June: United States declares war on
Britain

12 July: United States forces invade Upper
Canada

1813

27 April: United States forces burn Fort York (Toronto)

13 September: birth of Charlotta Sophia, sister of Cornelius, in Amsterdam

29 November: French expelled from Holland

1814

25 August: British forces burn principal buildings in Washington, D.C.

24 December: Treaty of Ghent ends British-American war

1815

18 June: Napoleon defeated at the Battle of Waterloo

19 June: birth of Cornelius David Krieghoff in Amsterdam

1820

20 August: birth of Johann Ernst, brother of Cornelius, in Düsseldorf

1822

February: family moves to Mainberg, near Schweinfurt, Bavaria, where Johann Ernst becomes the director of a wallpaper-manufacturing company

1837

20 June: Queen Victoria accedes to British throne

5 July: Krieghoff enlists in the United States Army in New York, assigned to Battery I, 1st United States Artillery, fighting in the Seminole Wars in Florida

November-December: rebellions in Upper and Lower Canada

1840

5 May: Krieghoff is discharged from the army at Burlington, Vermont, re-enlists for five-year term, then appears to have deserted

Around 15 May: birth of Henry, son of Krieghoff

18 June: baptism of Henry, in Boucherville, Lower Canada

23 July: Act of Union is passed in the British Parliament, joining Upper and Lower Canada, henceforth called Canada West and Canada East, into the Province of Canada

1841

birth of Emily, Krieghoff's daughter, by 1841, since she is "of major age" in 1862

14 June: the first Parliament of the Province of Canada opens in Kingston, Canada West

14 June: burial of Henry Krieghoff in Montreal

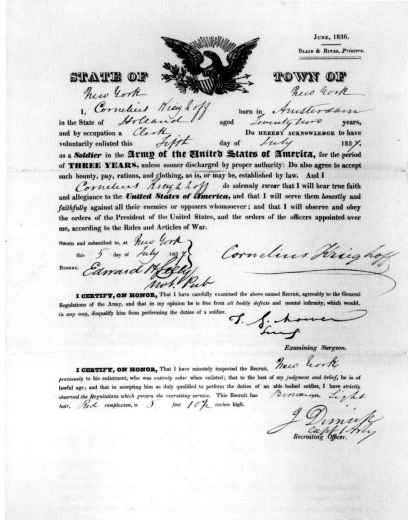

Figure 40 *(left)*
Ludwig Richter (1803–1884)
CASTLE AT MAINBERG, c. 1830
engraving with watercolour

Figure 41 *(above)*
RECORD OF ENROLMENT OF CORNELIUS KRIEGHOFF IN THE UNITED STATES ARMY (1837–1840)
Regular Army Enlistment Register, R.G. 94, Military Service Records (NNCC), National Archives, Washington (GSA)

1843

5 May: letter from Johann Ernst Krieghoff of Mainberg to Wilhelm Sattler of Schweinfurt mentions that Cornelius Krieghoff owns an upholstery business in Rochester, New York

8–13 June: Krieghoff exhibition in Rochester, New York

1844

26 January–16 February: Krieghoff advertises as an artist in Toronto

9 October: in Paris, Krieghoff registers at the Louvre to make copies of paintings under the instruction of painter Michel-Martin Drölling (1786–1851)

29 November: Parliament opens in Montreal after moving from Kingston

1845

start of potato famine in Ireland, which led to massive immigration to North America

1846

10 February–24 November: Krieghoff advertises as an artist in Montreal

September: Lord Elgin is named Governor of the Province of Canada

1847

11 January to at least 11 February: Krieghoff exhibits 48 paintings with the Montreal Society of Artists

February (?): Krieghoff completes copy of portrait of Queen Victoria, after Hayter, for Legislative Assembly

April: three Krieghoff paintings at the Toronto Society of Arts Exhibition

September: Krieghoff paintings offered by Scobie & Balfour, Toronto

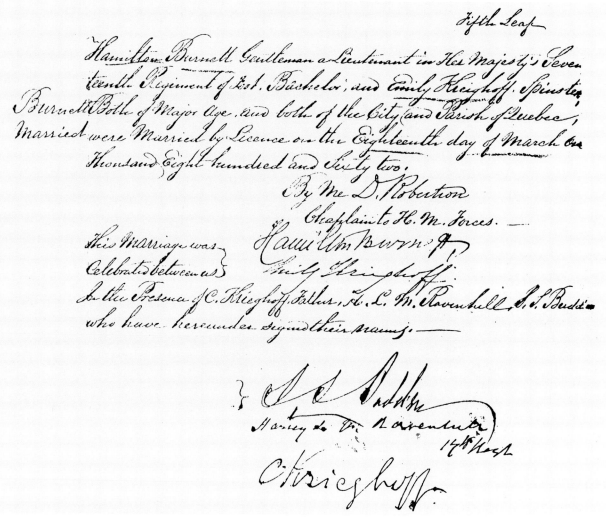

Figure 42 (top)
RECORD OF MARRIAGE OF EMILY KRIEGHOFF, DAUGHTER OF C. KRIEGHOFF, TO HAMILTON BURNETT, 18 MARCH 1862
Registre des archives judiciaires de Québec, Québec

Figure 43 (bottom)
The Daily Advertiser (Rochester), 30 May 1843

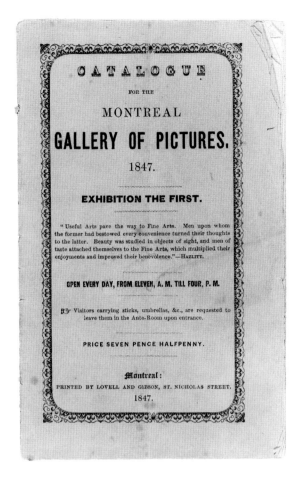

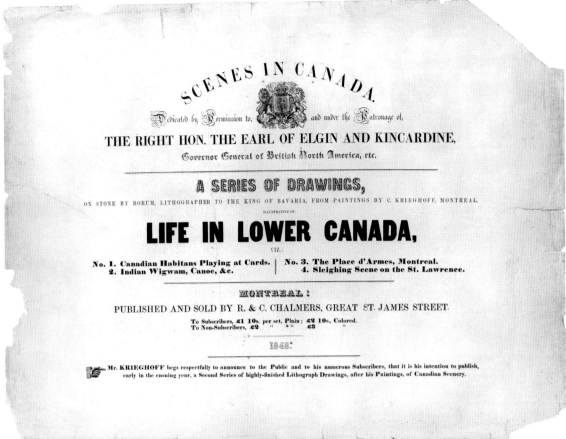

Figure 44 *(left)*
COVER OF CATALOGUE FOR THE
MONTREAL GALLERY OF PICTURES, 1847
Marion Wallace (née Sawyer), Kingston, Ontario

Figure 45 *(right)*
SCENES IN CANADA: A SERIES OF
DRAWINGS, ILLUSTRATIVE OF LIFE IN
LOWER CANADA, 1848
Collection of Peter Winkworth, London

1848

March: Baldwin–La Fontaine coalition government introduces practice of responsible government in Canada

25 February: sale at auction of two Krieghoff paintings by John Leeming

17 July–28 August: advertisement for sale of Krieghoff lithograph *Indians and Squaws of Lower Canada*

12 October–21 November: advertisements of forthcoming set of four Krieghoff lithographs in Scenes in Canada series

1849

Krieghoff resident on Current St-Mary, Montreal

25 April: introduction of the Rebellion Losses Bill leads to riots in Montreal, and the Parliament is burned

May: it is decided that Parliament should be moved from Montreal

October–December: one Krieghoff painting at the Western Art-Union Exhibition, Cincinnati

26 October: Krieghoff writes to the Honourable Hamnett Pinhey to obtain a commission to paint a portrait of the Queen

November: Government moves from Montreal to Toronto

16 November: sale at auction of approximately 12 Krieghoff paintings by John Leeming, Montreal

1850

Krieghoff resident on Belmont Street, Beaver Hall, Montreal

5 February: John Leeming exhibits 31 Krieghoff paintings at the Eighth Annual Festival, Mechanics' Institute, Montreal

22 February: sale at auction by John Leeming of 40 Krieghoff paintings

May: Krieghoff's parents move from Mainberg to Nürnberg

October: Krieghoff exhibits canvases at the Industrial Exhibition, Montreal, but wins first prize for a painting on a cast-iron table

1851

June: Krieghoff assists in repairs to Lewis's panorama of the Mississippi

July: announcement that Krieghoff and James Duncan plan to paint a panorama of Canada

10 September: sale at auction by Scott & Glassford, Montreal, of a number of Krieghoff paintings

October: Government moves from Toronto to Quebec City

2 October: sale at auction by Fisher & Armour, Montreal, of Krieghoff paintings not sold in September

1852

Krieghoff resident at Barclay Place, Montreal

April: Krieghoff's parents return to Schweinfurt following a lengthy visit to Montreal and New York

4 June: Krieghoff paintings included in sale at auction by Fisher & Armour

8 July: great fire of Montreal destroys 11,000 houses

1853

May–June: a Krieghoff resident on Aylmer Sreet, Montreal

12 May–17 August: advertisement for "Original Oil Painting ...Ice Cone at the Falls of Montmorency...at the Boston Piano Forte Store of Messrs. Owen...," Quebec

July: Grand Trunk Railway service begins between Montreal and Portland, Maine

September: Krieghoff exhibits at the Provincial Exhibition, Montreal, where he is awarded first prize for a painting in oil of a Canadian subject

1854

Krieghoff's studio at 25 St. John Sreet, without [the walls of the old city], residence on Cap Rouge Road, Quebec

6 June: reciprocity treaty is reached between the Province of Canada and the United States

14 September: Crimean War begins

September: Krieghoff exhibits at Provincial Exhibition, Quebec, where he wins first prize for a landscape in oil and a first prize for a study in oils

13 November: Lévis, opposite Quebec, is linked to Montreal by the Grand Trunk Railway

23 November: seigneurial system abolished in Canada East

1855

Krieghoff resident at 153 St. John Street, business address at Mount Pleasant, Quebec

1 January: Bytown is officially incorporated as a city, adopting the name Ottawa

January (first week): raffle of Krieghoff paintings at Mr. Sinclair's, Quebec

October: Government moves from Quebec City to Toronto

12 December: advertisement that Krieghoff is preparing a panorama of Canada

1856

23 February: Krieghoff petitions for government support to complete his panorama and related projects

30 March: the Treaty of Paris is signed, ending the Crimean War

27 October: opening of Grand Trunk Railway service between Montreal and Toronto

Figure 46
CORNELIUS KRIEGHOFF AND FRIENDS
(Krieghoff is on far right), 1856
albumen print, 17.5 × 23.2 cm
Notman Photographic Archives, McCord Museum of Canadian History, Montreal, gift of Walter H. Klinkhoff, before 1973 (MP-0000.2044)

1857

Krieghoff resident at 153 St. John Street, business address at Mount Pleasant, Quebec

May: two Krieghoff paintings at the Pennsylvania Academy of the Fine Arts Exhibition, Philadelphia

1858

Krieghoff resident at 11 Grande-Allée, Quebec

May: six Krieghoff paintings at the Pennsylvania Academy of the Fine Arts Exhibition, Philadelphia

September–October: four Krieghoff paintings at an exhibition in support of a building fund for St. Paul's Church, Yorkville, at Romain's Buildings, Toronto

1859

6 March: Krieghoff writes a letter to Alexander Galt, the minister of finance, protesting the 15 per cent duty charged on all prints imported into Canada

May: government moves from Toronto to Quebec City

4 October: one Krieghoff painting at the Maine Mechanic Association Exhibition, Portland, Maine

29 October–10 December: advertisement for two Krieghoff chromolithographs, *"Pour l'amour du Bon Dieu?"* and *"Va au Diable!"*

1860

one Krieghoff painting at the Lyceum Gallery, 548 Broadway, New York

two Krieghoff lithographs published in James Hodges, *Construction of the Great Victoria Bridge in Canada* (London: John Weale, 1860)

23 April: founding of the Art Association of Montreal

May: two Krieghoff paintings at the Pennsylvania Academy of the Fine Arts Exhibition, Philadelphia

August–September: Krieghoff exhibits at the Provincial Exhibition, Montreal

25 August: Victoria Bridge in Montreal is officially inaugurated by the Prince of Wales

1861

May: one Krieghoff painting at the Pennsylvania Academy of the Fine Arts Exhibition, Philadelphia

7 August: sale at auction by A.J. Maxham & Co., Quebec, of Krieghoff's collection of engravings and chromolithographs

19 November: sale at auction by A.J. Maxham & Co. of what is likely a collection of paintings selected by Krieghoff in New York; sale continued on the 30th

from 24 December: one Krieghoff painting at the Young Men's Association Exhibition, Buffalo, New York

1862

1 March: Krieghoff leases a house at 44 Grand-Allée, Quebec

18 March: marriage of Emily Krieghoff, daughter of the artist, to Lt. Hamilton Burnett, 17th Regiment of Foot

9 April: sale by auction of approximately 100 Krieghoff paintings by A.J. Maxham & Co.

May: two Krieghoff paintings at the Pennsylvania Academy of the Fine Arts Exhibition, Philadelphia

23 December: sale by auction of 31 Krieghoff paintings by A.J. Maxham & Co.

Figure 47
Jules Isaï Benoît dit Livernois
CORNELIUS KRIEGHOFF PHOTOGRAPHED IN QUEBEC, WHEN HE WAS 43 YEARS OLD, c. 1858
photograph taken from the original owned by John T. Ross of Quebec City, by Marius Barbeau (1934)
Canadian Museum of Civilization, Hull (image #98–98)

Figure 48
VENTE IMPORTANTE DE PEINTURES À
L'HUILE...
Journal de Québec 13 December 1862, p. 3

1863

21 February: Hamilton Burnett leases a cottage at 115 Grande-Allée West for 1 May occupancy

29 April: sale by auction of Krieghoff paintings, library, personal collections and furniture by A.J. Maxham & Co.

2 May: Hamilton Burnett sublets the Grand-Allée cottage to a Mr. De Courtenay

21 August: Krieghoff signs over power of attorney to Andrew John Maxham

22 August: Hamilton Burnett sells his commission and leaves the army

28 August: Toronto newspaper announcement that Krieghoff has just left Quebec because of ill health to reside in Italy or France

probably December: one Krieghoff painting at the Buffalo Fine Arts Academy Exhibition, Buffalo

14–22 December: three Krieghoff paintings at the Ladies' Hospital Relief Association Exhibition, Rochester

1864

11 February: three Krieghoff paintings in Art Association of Montreal annual exhibition

28 April: Krieghoff registers with the government the copyright for 13 photographs of his works

1 September: Charlottetown conference on Confederation

10 October: Quebec conference on Confederation

1865

seven works by Krieghoff published in William Notman's *Photographic Selections*

27 February: one Krieghoff painting at the Art Association of Montreal Exhibition

22 March–1 April: four Krieghoff paintings at the Toronto Mechanics' Institute Exhibition

14 April: President Lincoln is assassinated

May: 29 tinted photographs of Krieghoff paintings included as part of the Canadian contribution to the Dublin Exhibition

24 May: four Krieghoff paintings at the Hamilton and Gore Mechanics Institute Exhibition, Hamilton

26 May: End of American Civil War

Figure 49
Jules Isaï Benoît dit Livernois
CORNELIUS KRIEGHOFF AT HIS EASEL,
c. 1870
photograph taken from the original owned by John T. Ross of Quebec City, by Marius Barbeau (1934)
Canadian Museum of Civilization, Hull
(image #98–97)

20 October: Government moves from Quebec City to Ottawa

probably December: five Krieghoff paintings at the Buffalo Fine Arts Academy Exhibition, Buffalo

1866

20 March–2 April: three Krieghoff paintings at the Toronto Mechanics' Institute Exhibition

10–11 May: 11 Krieghoff paintings included in sale at auction by Jacob Graff & Co., Cincinnati

1867

two Krieghoff paintings at the Utica Art Association Exhibition, New York

5 February: three Krieghoff paintings at the Art Association of Montreal exhibition

9 February: death of Isabella Ludovica Wouters, Krieghoff's mother, in Schweinfurt

May–December: grouping of Krieghoff paintings at the Exposition Universelle, Paris

1 July: the British North America act creates the Dominion of Canada; John A. Macdonald becomes the first prime minister of Canada; the Parliament of Canada is permanently established in Ottawa

probably December: one Krieghoff painting included in the Buffalo Fine Arts Academy Exhibition, Buffalo

1868

25 April: announcement of sale at auction by A.J. Maxham of Krieghoff paintings from Europe, via Portland, Maine; apparently never held

28 May: death of Johann Ernst Krieghoff, Cornelius's father, in Schweinfurt

probably December: one Krieghoff painting included in exhibition of the Buffalo Fine Arts Academy

1869

11 November: sale at auction of Krieghoff paintings and a selection of original works and copies of contemporary artists chosen by Krieghoff, ordered from Paris by A.J. Maxham & Co.

1870

19 July: start of Franco-Prussian War

5 August: a Quebec newspaper notes that Krieghoff and family are in town on a visit

30 August: Krieghoff leases the two upper floors and garret of a house on Richelieu Sreet

26 October: sale at auction by A.J. Maxham & Co. of Krieghoff paintings and contemporary European paintings chosen by him

1871

1 May: Krieghoff moves into the top floor of a house at 6 3/4 Prevost Sreet

from 12 September: Krieghoff exhibits two works at Provincial Exhibition, Quebec, where he wins a prize for best landscape in oil

8 October: the Great Fire in Chicago

24 October: sale at auction by A.J. Maxham & Co. of Krieghoff's library

11 November: last of British army withdraws from Canada

28 November: sale at auction by A.J. Maxham & Co. of Krieghoff's paintings, furniture and other personal effects at his home on Prevost Street

1872

4 March: death of Cornelius Krieghoff at 721 West Jackson Sreet, Chicago

1906

2 September: death of Émilie Gauthier, wife of Krieghoff, in Denver, Colorado

1929

29 December: death of Emily Burnett, daughter of Krieghoff, in Denver, Colorado

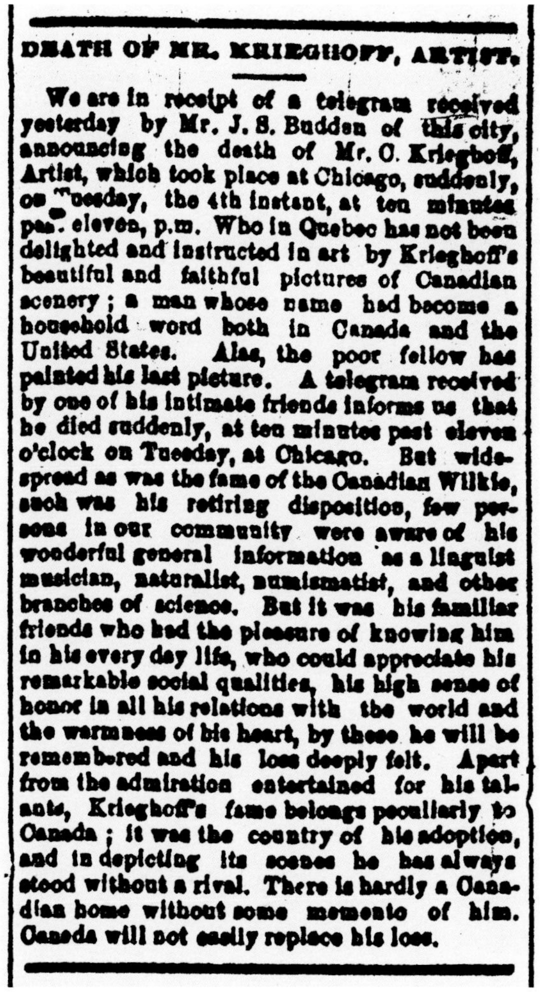

DEATH OF MR. KRIEGHOFF, ARTIST.

We are in receipt of a telegram received yesterday by Mr. J. S. Budden of this city, announcing the death of Mr. C. Krieghoff, Artist, which took place at Chicago, suddenly, on Tuesday, the 4th instant, at ten minutes past eleven, p.m. Who in Quebec has not been delighted and instructed in art by Krieghoff's beautiful and faithful pictures of Canadian scenery; a man whose name had become a household word both in Canada and the United States. Alas, the poor fellow has painted his last picture. A telegram received by one of his intimate friends informs us that he died suddenly, at ten minutes past eleven o'clock on Tuesday, at Chicago. But wide-spread as was the fame of the Canadian Wilkie, such was his retiring disposition, few persons in our community were aware of his wonderful general information as a linguist musician, naturalist, numismatist, and other branches of science. But it was his familiar friends who had the pleasure of knowing him in his every day life, who could appreciate his remarkable social qualities, his high sense of honor in all his relations with the world and the warmness of his heart, by these he will be remembered and his loss deeply felt. Apart from the admiration entertained for his talents, Krieghoff's fame belongs peculiarly to Canada; it was the country of his adoption, and in depicting its scenes he has always stood without a rival. There is hardly a Canadian home without some memento of him. Canada will not easily replace his loss.

Figure 50
"DEATH OF MR. KRIEGHOFF, ARTIST."
Morning Chronicle (Quebec), 7 March 1872

CATALOGUE

ARLENE GEHMACHER

Abbreviations

Exhibitions

ARTIST AND LAND 1973
Madison, Wisconsin, Elvehjem Art
Center, 11 April–23 May 1973; Hanover,
New Hampshire, Hopkins Center Art
Galleries, Dartmouth College, 22 June–1
August 1973; Austin, Texas, University Art
Museum, University of Texas, 26
August–7 October 1973, *The Artist and the
Land: Canadian Landscape Painting
1670–1930*.

ARTS IN FRENCH CANADA 1952
Quebec City, Musée de la Province de
Québec, 29 May–28 September 1952, *The
Arts in French Canada*.

ARTS IN FRENCH CANADA 1959
Vancouver, Vancouver Art Gallery, 12
July–23 August 1959, *The Arts in French
Canada*.

CANADIAN HERITAGE 1966
Vancouver, Vancouver Art Gallery, 3
September–30 October 1966, *Images for a
Canadian Heritage*.

CANADIAN PAINTING 1967
Ottawa, National Gallery of Canada (tour-
ing exhibition): Windsor, Art Gallery of
Windsor, 8 January–12 February 1967;
London, London Art Museum, 17
February–26 March 1967; Hamilton, Art
Gallery of Hamilton, 1 April–7 May 1967;
Kingston, Agnes Etherington Art Centre,
12 May–10 June 1967; Stratford,
Rothman's Art Gallery, 16 June–30 July
1967; Saskatoon, Mendel Art Gallery, 9
August–9 September 1967; Edmonton,
Edmonton Art Gallery, 15 September–10
October 1967; Victoria, Art Gallery of
Greater Victoria, 20 October–18
November 1967; Charlottetown,
Confederation Centre Art Gallery, 30
November–30 December 1967; Saint
John, N.B., New Brunswick Museum, 15
January–15 February 1968; Fredericton,
Beaverbrook Art Gallery, February–1968;

Quebec City, Musée du Québec, 15
March–15 April 1967, *Canadian Painting
1850–1950*.

CANADIANA 1942
New York, Grand Central Art Galleries,
6–18 April 1942, *Canadiana, An Exhibition
of Historical Prints, Water-Colour Drawings,
Oil Paintings and Maps*.

COLONIAL PAINTING 1964
Charlottetown, Fathers of Confederation
Building, June–October 1964, *A Century of
Colonial Painting: The Seven Years War to
Confederation*.

DEVELOPMENT OF PAINTING IN
CANADA 1945
Toronto, Art Gallery of Toronto, January
1945; Montreal, Art Association of
Montreal, February 1945; Ottawa,
National Gallery of Canada, March 1945;
Quebec City, Musée de la Province de
Québec, April 1945, *The Development of
Painting in Canada*.

DUPLESSIS 1991
Quebec City, Musée du Québec, 16–31
May 1991, *La collection Duplessis*.

EARLY CANADIAN PORTRAITS 1969
Ottawa, National Gallery of Canada (touring exhibition), 5 September 1969–31 May
1970, *Early Canadian Portraits*.

ELEVEN ARTISTS 1960
Montreal, Montreal Museum of Fine Arts,
8 September–2 October 1960, *Eleven Artists
in Montreal 1860–1960*.

EVERYMAN'S CANADA 1962
Ottawa, National Gallery of Canada,
May–September 1962; Quebec City,
Musée de la Province de Québec,
July–August 1963; Winnipeg, Winnipeg
Art Gallery, September 1963; Vancouver,
University of British Columbia,
October–November 1963; Victoria, Art
Gallery of Greater Victoria, November–
December 1963; Windsor, Willistead Art
Gallery, December 1963–January 1964;

Kingston, Agnes Etherington Art Centre, Queen's University, January–February 1964; Regina, Norman Mackenzie Art Gallery, February–March 1964, *Everyman's Canada, Paintings and Drawings from the McCord Museum of McGill University.*

EXPOSITION DE PEINTURES 1920
Quebec City, Académie commerciale, 25 October–1 November 1920, *Exposition de Peintures et Dessins.*

FRENCH IN AMERICA 1951
Detroit, Detroit Institute of Arts, 14 July–16 September 1951, *The French in America, 1520–1880.*

GERMAN IMMIGRANT PAINTERS 1975
Boston, Goethe Institute, July 1975–1976, *America through the Eyes of German Immigrant Painters.*

INAUGURAL EXHIBITION AGT 1926
Toronto, Art Gallery of Toronto, 29 January–28 February 1926, *Inaugural Exhibition.*

KRIEGHOFF AGT 1934
Toronto, Art Gallery of Toronto, 5–29 January 1934, *Paintings by Cornelius Krieghoff.*

KRIEGHOFF BAG 1961
Fredericton, Beaverbrook Art Gallery, September 1961, *Cornelius Krieghoff, ca. 1815–1872.*

KRIEGHOFF CNE 1955
Toronto, Canadian National Exhibition, 26 August–10 September 1955, *Exhibition of Paintings and Sculpture.*

KRIEGHOFF GLENHYRST 1968
Brantford, Ontario, Glenhyrst, the Art Gallery of Brantford, 5–29 October 1968, *The World of Cornelius Krieghoff.*

KRIEGHOFF MM 1972
Montreal, McCord Museum, 30 November 1972–23 April 1973; Toronto, Royal Ontario Museum, 10 May–15 August

1973; Paris, Canadian Cultural Centre, 1973; Brussels, Canadian Embassy, 1974; London, Canada House, 6 March–1 May 1974; Ottawa, Public Archives of Canada, 12 June–2 September 1974, *Scenes in Canada: C. Krieghoff, Lithograph Drawings After His Paintings of Canadian Scenery 1848–1862.*

KRIEGHOFF MORGAN 1952
Montreal, Henry Morgan & Co. Ltd, Antique Salon, 16–23 January 1952, [*Cornelius Krieghoff*].

KRIEGHOFF MQ 1971
Quebec City, Musée du Québec, 29 September–31 October 1971, *Cornélius Krieghoff 1815–1872.*

KRIEGHOFF MQ 1985
Quebec City, Musée du Québec, 12 June–22 September 1985, *Cornélius Krieghoff et le XIXe siècle : la peinture au Québec (1830–1880).*

KRIEGHOFF NGC/AAM 1934
Ottawa, National Gallery of Canada, 15 February– March 1934; Montreal, Art Association of Montreal, 16 March–22 April 1934, *Exhibition of Paintings by Cornelius Krieghoff 1815–1872.*

KRIEGHOFF Place des Arts 1976
Montreal, Place des Arts, 2 November–5 December 1976, *Cornelius Krieghoff.*

KRIEGHOFF ROM 1951
Toronto, Royal Ontario Museum, 7 November 1951–21 May 1952, *Oil Paintings and Watercolours of Early Canada.*

KRIEGHOFF ROM 1958
Toronto, Royal Ontario Museum, 22 March–4 October 1958, *Krieghoff, Kane and Bartlett: Three Pioneer Painters of Canada.*

KRIEGHOFF ROM 1968
Toronto, Royal Ontario Museum, May–15 July 1968, *Cornelius Krieghoff.*

KRIEGHOFF ROM 1971
Toronto, Royal Ontario Museum, 16 December 1971–12 March 1972, *Krieghoff and His Contemporaries.*

KRIEGHOFF ROM 1975
Toronto, Royal Ontario Museum, 20 September–1 December 1975, *Cornelius Krieghoff (1815–1872): Genre Painter of Early Canada.*

KRIEGHOFF ROM 1979
Toronto, Royal Ontario Museum, 23 February–6 June 1979, *Life in Lower Canada–Cornelius Krieghoff and His Contemporaries.*

KRIEGHOFF ROM 1994
Toronto, Royal Ontario Museum, 10 September 1994–9 July 1995; Washington, D.C., The Art Gallery of the Canadian Embassy, 5 October 1995–6 January 1996, *Krieghoff's Canada: An Artist's View 1844–1872.*

KRIEGHOFF STEVENS 1943
Montreal, Stevens Art Gallery, 20 November–11 December 1943, *Exhibition of Canadiana by Cornelius Krieghoff.*

KRIEGHOFF WILLISTEAD 1963
Windsor, Willistead Art Gallery, 6–31 January 1963; London, London Art Museum, 7 February–11 March 1963; Hamilton, Art Gallery of Hamilton, 5–31 March 1963, *Cornelius Krieghoff ca. 1815–1872.*

KRIEGHOFF WIMODAUSIS 1957
Toronto, Wimodausis Club, Casa Loma, 4–7 November 1957, Antique and Treasure Mart [*Cornelius Krieghoff Paintings from the Boylen Collection*].

MACAMIC TO MONTREAL 1974
Montreal, Man and His World, 20 June–2 September 1974, *From Macamic to Montreal: People and Places in Quebec.*

MAÎTRES CANADIENS 1989
Quebec City, Musée du Séminaire de Québec, 15 September–5 November 1989, *Les Maîtres canadiens de la collection Power Corporation du Canada 1850–1950.*

MILESTONES 1961
London, London Art Museum, 19 January–25 February 1961, *The Face of Early Canada: Milestones of Canadian Painting.*

MQ CINQUANTE ANNÉES 1983
Quebec City, Musée du Québec, 2 November 1983–4 March 1984, *Le Musée du Québec, 1933–1983. Cinquante années d'acquisitions.*

MSA 1847
Montreal, Montreal Society of Artists, mid January–mid February 1847, *Montreal Gallery of Pictures.*

PAINTER AND THE NEW WORLD 1967
Montreal, Montreal Museum of Fine Arts, 9–30 July 1967, *The Painter and the New World.*

PAINTING IN QUEBEC 1991
Quebec City, Musée du Québec, 16 October 1991–5 January 1992; Ottawa, National Gallery of Canada, 31 January–29 March 1992; Vancouver, Vancouver Art Gallery, 29 April–23 June 1993; Halifax, Art Gallery of Nova Scotia, 1 August–27 September 1992; Montreal, Montreal Museum of Fine Arts, 29 October 1992–3 January 1993, *Painting in Quebec 1820–1850: New Views, New Perspectives.*

PEINTURE TRADITIONNELLE 1967
Quebec City, Musée du Québec, July–September 1967, *Sculpture, peinture, orfèvrerie traditionnelles du Québec.*

PEOPLE AND PLACES 1982
Toronto, Royal Ontario Museum, 25 November 1982–25 September 1983, *People and Places: Early Canadian Painters.*

QUÉBEC VUE 1994
Quebec City, Musée du Québec, 1 June–21 August 1994, *Québec, plein la vue.*

THREE HUNDRED YEARS 1967
Ottawa, National Gallery of Canada, 12 May–17 September 1967, *Three Hundred Years of Canadian Art.*

THROUGH CANADIAN EYES 1976
Calgary, Glenbow-Alberta Institute, 22 September–24 October 1976, *Through Canadian Eyes: Trends and Influences in Canadian Art, 1815–1965.*

TREASURES 1962
Toronto, Royal Ontario Museum, 25 September 1962–25 September 1963, *Treasures of Canadiana.*

WINTER KING 1988
Banff, Alberta, Whyte Museum of the Canadian Rockies, 26 January–6 March 1988; London, London Regional Art Gallery, 9 April–24 May 1988; Windsor, Windsor Art Gallery, 4 June–10 July 1988; Montreal, McCord Museum, 16 September–31 October 1988, *When Winter Was King: The Image of Winter in 19th Century Canada.*

Literature

AGO CAN COLL 1970
Art Gallery of Ontario, *The Canadian Collection.* Toronto: McGraw-Hill, 1970.

BARBEAU 1934
Barbeau, Marius. *Cornelius Krieghoff: Pioneer Painter of North America.* Toronto: The Macmillan Company of Canada, 1934.

BARBEAU 1936
Barbeau, Marius. "Merry-Making." In *Quebec: Where Ancient France Lingers.* Toronto: Macmillan Company of Canada, 1936.

BARBEAU 1948
Barbeau, Marius. *Cornelius Krieghoff.* The Canadian Art Series. Toronto: The Ryerson Press, 1948.

BARBEAU 1962
Barbeau, Marius. *Cornelius Krieghoff.* The Gallery of Canadian Art, no. 1 [Toronto]: McClelland and Stewart Limited, 1962.

BARBEAU CGJ 1934
Barbeau, Marius. "Krieghoff Discovers Canada." *Canadian Geographical Journal* 8, no. 3 (March 1934): 100–113.

BARBEAU NGC 1934
Barbeau, Marius. *Exhibition of Paintings by Cornelius Krieghoff* (ex. cat.) Ottawa: The National Gallery of Canada, 1934.

BARBEAU RSC 1934
Barbeau, Marius. "Krieghoff découvre le Canada." *Proceedings and Transactions of the Royal Society of Canada,* section 1, 3d series, vol. 28 (May 1934): 111–18.

BARBEAU STAR MONTREAL 1934
Barbeau, Marius. "Krieghoff's Early Canadian Scenes Varied, Resourceful, Embracing." *Star* (Montreal), 17 March 1934.

BÉLAND ET AL. 1992
Béland, Mario., ed. *Painting in Québec 1820–1850. New Views, New Perspectives* (ex. cat.). Québec: Musée du Québec, 1992.

CARTER 1967
Carter, David G. *The Painter and the New World* (ex. cat.). Montreal: Montreal Museum of Fine Arts, 1967.

CAVELL/REID 1988
Cavell, Edward, and Dennis Reid. *When Winter Was King: The Image of Winter in 19th Century Canada* (ex. cat.). Banff: The Whyte Museum of the Canada Rockies in association with Altitude Publications, 1988.

CHAUVIN 1934
Chauvin, Jean. "Cornelius Krieghoff, imagier populaire." *La Revue Populaire* (June 1934): 6–7.

COOKE 1961
Cooke, Edwy. *Cornelius Krieghoff, ca. 1815–1872* (ex. cat.). Fredericton: Beaverbrook Art Gallery, [1961].

CURATOR 1961
"Curator Explains Canvases." *Gleaner* (Fredericton), 2 September 1961.

FAIRCHILD 1908
Fairchild, G.M. *Gleanings from Quebec.* Quebec City: Frank Carrel, 1908.

GUTTENBERG 1954
Guttenberg, A. Ch. de. "Cornelius Krieghoff." *Revue de l'Université d'Ottawa* 24, no. 1 (1954): 90–108.

HARDING 1975
Harding, Anneliese. *America through the eyes of German Immigrant Painters* (ex. cat.) Boston: Goethe Institute, 1975.

HARPER 1962
Harper, J. Russell. *Everyman's Canada: Paintings and Drawings from the McCord Museum of McGill University* (ex. cat.). Ottawa: Roger Duhamel, Queen's Printer, 1962.

HARPER 1977
Harper, J. Russell. *Painting in Canada: A History.* 2d ed. Toronto: University of Toronto Press, 1977.

HARPER 1979
Harper, J. Russell. *Krieghoff.* Toronto: University of Toronto Press, 1979.

HARPER FARM 1977
Harper, J. Russell. *Cornelius Krieghoff: The Habitant Farm.* (Masterpieces in the National Gallery of Canada, no. 9). Ottawa: National Gallery of Canada, 1977.

HARPER PAINTING 1966
Harper, J. Russell. *Painting in Canada: A History.* Toronto: University of Toronto Press, 1966.

HARPER PEINTURE 1966
Harper, J. Russell. *La peinture au Canada des origines à nos jours.* Québec: Presses de l'Université Laval, 1966.

HARPER THREE CENTURIES 1962
Harper, J. Russell. "Three Centuries of Canadian Painting." *Canadian Art* 19, no. 6 (November/December 1962): 405–52.

HUBBARD 1963
Hubbard, R.H. *The Development of Canadian Art.* Ottawa: Queen's Printer ("Published for the Trustees of the National Gallery of Canada"), [1963].

HUBBARD/OSTIGUY 1967
Hubbard, R.H., and J.R Ostiguy. *Three Hundred Years of Canadian Art* (ex. cat.). Ottawa: The National Gallery of Canada, 1967.

JOUVANCOURT 1971
Jouvancourt, Hugues de. *Cornelius Krieghoff.* Translation and adaptation by Nancy Côté. Montréal: Éditions de la Frégate, 1971 (deluxe edition).

JOUVANCOURT 1973
Jouvancourt, Hugues de. *Cornelius Krieghoff.* Translation and adaptation by Nancy Côté. Toronto: Musson, 1973 (trade edition).

JOUVANCOURT 1979
Jouvancourt, Hugues de. *Cornelius Krieghoff.* Montréal: Stanké, 1979 (trade edition).

JUNEAU 1971
Juneau, André. *Cornélius Krieghoff 1815–1872* (ex.cat.). Québec: Musée du Québec, 1971.

KAREL 1991
Karel, David. *La collection Duplessis.* (ex. cat.) Québec: Musée du Québec, 1991.

KRIEGHOFF GAZETTE MONTREAL 1952
"Paintings by Krieghoff Showing at Morgan's." *Gazette* (Montreal), 17 January 1952, 17.

KRIEGHOFF STAR MONTREAL 1952
"Krieghoff." *Star* (Montreal), 26 January 1952.

LEEMING COURIER MONTREAL 1850
"By John Leeming. 40 Valuable Oil Paintings by 'Kreighoff' [sic]." (advertisement), *Morning Courier* (Montreal), 18 February 1850.

LIFE IN LOWER CANADA 1979
Life in Lower Canada Cornelius Krieghoff and his Contemporaries (ex. brochure). Toronto: Royal Ontario Museum, 1979.

MACLEAN'S 1955
"The Rebirth of a Fascinating Painter." *Maclean's*, 24 December 1955: 13–19, [46] (reprinted with additions in a portfolio format, 1955).

McINNIS 1941
McInnis, Graham. "Winter's Mantle." *New World* (February 1941).

MMFA CAT 1960
Montreal Museum of Fine Arts. *Catalogue of Paintings.* Montreal: Montreal Museum of Fine Arts, 1960.

NGC CAT 1960
National Gallery of Canada, *Catalogue of Paintings and Sculpture, Vol. 3, Canadian School.* Toronto: University of Toronto Press, 1960.

NGC CAT 1994
Catalogue of the National Gallery of Canada, Ottawa: Canadian Art, Vol. 2, G-K. Ottawa: The National Gallery of Canada, 1994.

NOTMAN 1865
Notman's Photographic Selections. Second series. Montreal: W. Notman, 1865.

PENCIER 1995
Pencier, Honor de. *Krieghoff's Canada: An Artist's View, 1844–1872* (ex. brochure). Washington, D.C.: The Art Gallery of the Canadian Embassy, 1995.

PORTER/PRIOUL 1994
Porter, John, and Didier Prioul. *Québec, plein la vue* (ex. cat.). Québec: Musée du Québec, 1994.

REID 1973
Reid, Dennis. *A Concise History of Canadian Painting.* Toronto: Oxford University Press, 1973.

REID 1988
Reid, Dennis. *A Concise History of Canadian Painting.* 2d ed. Toronto: Oxford University Press, 1988.

ROBSON 1937
Robson, Albert H. *Cornelius Krieghoff.* Toronto: The Ryerson Press, 1937.

ROMBOUT 1962
Rombout, Louis. "Cornelius Krieghoff." *Atlantic Advocate* 53, no. 4 (December 1962): 42–43, 45, 48.

SIG SAM COLL 1948
Catalogue of the Sigmund Samuel Collection, Canadiana and Americana. Compiled by Charles W. Jefferys. Toronto/Halifax/Vancouver: Ryerson Press, 1948.

SMALL 1866
Small, H. Beaufort, compiler. *The Canadian Handbook and Tourist's Guide....* Montreal: M. Longmoore, 1866.

SPENDLOVE 1958
Spendlove, F. St. George. *The Face of Early Canada: Pictures of Canada Which Have Helped to Make History.* Toronto: The Ryerson Press, 1958.

STEVENS GAZETTE MONTREAL 1943
"Stevens Gallery Canadiana Show Features the Art of Krieghoff." *Gazette* (Montreal), 20 November 1943, 10.

THIBAULT 1983
Thibault, Claude. *Musée du Québec: 500 Œuvres choisies* (ex. cat.). Québec: Musée du Québec, 1983.

TRUDEL 1967
Trudel, Jean. *Peinture traditionnelle du Québec* (ex. cat.). Québec: Musée du Québec/Ministère des Affaires Culturelles, 1967.

VÉZINA 1972
Vézina, Raymond. *Cornelius Krieghoff, Peintre de mœurs (1815–1872).* Ottawa: Éditions du Pélican, 1972.

VÉZINA 1974
Vézina, Raymond. "Attitude esthétique de Cornelius Krieghoff au sein de la tradition picturale canadienne-française." *RACAR* 1, no. 1 (1974): 47–59.

WILLIAMSON 1976
Williamson, Moncrieff. *Through Canadian Eyes: Trends and Influences in Canadian Art 1815–1965* (ex. cat.). Calgary: Glenbow-Alberta Institute, 1976.

WINKWORTH 1972
Winkworth, Peter. *Scenes in Canada: C. Krieghoff, Lithograph Drawings After His Paintings of Canadian Scenery 1848–1862* (ex. cat.). Montreal: McCord Museum, 1972.

Boucherville 1840–41

1

ÉTIENNE SÉVÈRE FILIATRAULT, 1840–41
watercolour on paper, 21.5 × 19.2 cm
LR: C. Krieghoff pinx
LC: E.S. Filiatrault

Musée du Québec, Québec, purchased 1997, in memory of Jacques Labrecque, folklorist (97.10)

Provenance
Étienne Sévère Filiatrault, Boucherville, Quebec, presumably commissioned from the artist, 1840–41; Marie Flore Malvina Filiatrault (daughter of E.S. Filiatrault), St. Benoît, Quebec, by succession 1843; Berthe Rhéaume (adopted daughter of M.F.M. [Filiatrault] Mignault), St. Eustache, Quebec, by succession 1915; M. Jacques Labrecque (son of B. Rhéaume), Les Éboulements, Quebec, by succession; Mrs. Michelle Duquette (wife of J. Labrecque), Les Éboulements, by succession 1995; MQ, purchase, 1997.

2

MADAME ÉTIENNE SÉVÈRE FILIATRAULT, NÉE MARTINE BRIEN DIT DESROCHERS, 1840–41
watercolour on paper, 22.0 × 19.0 cm
LR: C. Krieghoff
LC: M^{de} M. Filiatrault

Musée du Québec, Québec, purchased 1997, in memory of Jacques Labrecque, folklorist (97.11)

Provenance
Étienne Sévère Filiatrault, Boucherville, Quebec, presumably commissioned from the artist, 1840–41; Marie Flore Malvina Filiatrault (daughter of E.S. Filiatrault), St. Benoît, Quebec, by succession 1843; Berthe Rhéaume (adopted daughter of M.F.M. [Filiatrault] Mignault), St. Eustache, Quebec, by succession 1915; M. Jacques Labrecque (son of B. Rhéaume), Les Éboulements, Quebec, by succession;

Mrs. Michelle Duquette (wife of J. Labrecque), Les Éboulements, by succession 1995; MQ, purchase, 1997.

Toronto 1844

3

WILLIAM WILLIAMSON AND HIS SON ALEXANDER, 1844
oil on canvas, 102.0 × 87.4 cm

Royal Ontario Museum, Toronto, purchased 1978, Sigmund Samuel Trust (978.289.1)

Provenance
William Williamson, Toronto, commissioned from the artist; Jessie (Williamson) Hoskin (daughter of W. and M. Williamson), Toronto, by succession; Alfred E. Hoskin (husband of J. [Williamson] Hoskin), Winnipeg, by succession 1931; James A.E. Hoskin (son of A.E. Hoskin), Carman, Manitoba, by succession by May 1960; ROM, purchase, 1978.

Exhibitions
Toronto, Royal Ontario Museum, 7 April–10 September 1978, *Early Canadian Faces.*

Literature
BARBEAU 1934, 33, 130; J.A.E. Hoskin, "Portraits by Krieghoff" (letter to the editor), *Country Life* (London), 22 September 1960: 633, (repr.); JOUVANCOURT 1971 and JOUVANCOURT 1973, 35; Marilyn Lindon, "Face our past with ROM show of early portraits," *Sun* (Toronto), 13 April 1978, 74; HARPER 1979, 13; JOUVANCOURT 1979, 54.

4

MARGARET ERSKINE WILLIAMSON AND HER DAUGHTER JESSIE, 1844
oil on canvas, 102.0 × 87.4 cm
LR: C.Krieghoff 44

Royal Ontario Museum, Toronto, purchased 1978, Sigmund Samuel Trust (978.289.2)

Provenance
William Williamson, Toronto, commissioned from the artist; Jessie (Williamson) Hoskin (daughter of W. and M. Williamson), Toronto, by succession; Alfred E. Hoskin (husband of J. [Williamson] Hoskin), Winnipeg, by succession 1931; James A.E. Hoskin (son of A.E. Hoskin), Carman, Manitoba, by succession by May 1960; ROM, purchase, 1978.

Exhibitions
Toronto, Royal Ontario Museum, 7 April–10 September 1978, *Early Canadian Faces.*

Literature
BARBEAU 1934, 33, 130; J.A.E. Hoskin, "Portraits by Krieghoff" (letter to the editor), *Country Life* (London), 22 September 1960: 633, (repr.); JOUVANCOURT 1971 and JOUVANCOURT 1973, 35; Marilyn Lindon, "Face our past with ROM show of early portraits," *Sun* (Toronto), 13 April 1978, 74; HARPER 1979, 11 (repr.), 13; JOUVANCOURT 1979, 54.

Montreal 1846–53

MSA 1847

5

MARINE VIEW—MOONLIGHT (after Curt Grolig), c. 1845
oil on canvas, 60.5 × 91.0 cm
LR: C. Krieghoff

National Gallery of Canada, Ottawa, gift of Dr. Max Stern, Montreal, 1983 (28426)

Provenance
Max Stern, Montreal; NGC, gift, 1983.

Exhibitions
MSA 1847, no. 121, as "Marine View—Moonlight."

Literature
BARBEAU 1934, 27; "Principal Acquisitions of Canadian Museums and Galleries 1983," *RACAR* 9, nos.1–2 (1984): 188 (repr.).

6

THE ARTIST'S STUDIO, c. 1845
oil on canvas, 44.7 × 54.0 cm
LL: C. Krieghoff

National Gallery of Canada, Ottawa, purchased 1902 (128)

Provenance
Honourable J.C. Patterson, Ottawa; NGC, purchase, 1902.

Exhibitions
Probably MSA 1847, no. 54, as "The Artist's Studio"; KRIEGHOFF NGC/AAM 1934, no. 88; Hartford, Connecticut, Wadsworth Athenaeum, 9 November–31 December 1949, *Pictures within Pictures*, no. 25; KRIEGHOFF BAG 1961, no. 1; KRIEGHOFF WILLISTEAD 1963, no. 1; COLONIAL PAINTING 1964, no. 29; KRIEGHOFF MQ 1971, no. 11.

Literature
Probably H.N., "Montreal Gallery of Paintings" (letter to the editor), *Pilot and Journal of Commerce* (Montreal), 29 January 1847, 2; BARBEAU 1934, 49, 124; Charles C. Cunningham, "Painting paintings of paintings," *Art News* 48, no. 7, part 1 (November 1949): 35 (repr.); NGC CAT 1960, 161 (repr.); COOKE 1961, (repr. no. 1); BARBEAU 1962, (repr. plate 7); HUBBARD 1963, 59; JOUVANCOURT 1971 and JOUVANCOURT 1973, 12 (repr.); JUNEAU 1971, 14 (repr.); VÉZINA 1972, (repr. fig. 38); JOUVANCOURT 1979, 29 (repr.); NGC CAT 1994, 384 (repr.).

7

THE WINETASTERS (after Johann Hasenclever), c. 1846
oil on canvas, 35.3 × 50.3 cm
LR: C. Krieghoff/after/Hasenclever

The Thomson Collection (P-C-65)

Provenance
Leslie W. Lewis, purchased in London (at Colnaghi?) c. 1931; Mrs. George McLaughlin; Percy Smith; Allen E. Rosen, Toronto; Kenneth R. Thomson, Toronto, purchased c. February 1964.

Exhibitions
MSA 1847, no. 148, as "The Winetasters."

Literature
"'The Wine Tasters,'" *Gazette* (Montreal), 22 December 1847, 2; "The Fine Arts" (advertisement), *Gazette* (Montreal), 2 December 1847, 3; BARBEAU 1934, 31; HARPER 1979, 6 (repr.).

8

STILL LIFE WITH FLOWERS, FRUIT AND CORN, 1846
oil on canvas, 97.7 × 78.0 cm
LR: C. Krieghoff 1846

Montreal Museum of Fine Arts, purchased 1967, Horsley and Annie Townsend Bequest (1967.1549)

Provenance
Berry-Hill Galleries, New York, in or before February 1965; MMFA, purchase, 1967.

Exhibitions
Probably MSA 1847, no. 118, as "Flower and Fruit-piece"; PAINTER AND THE NEW WORLD 1967, no. 194; Montreal, Montreal Museum of Fine Arts, 4–25 January 1968, *Recent Acquisitions*; KRIEGHOFF MQ 1971, no. 20; PAINTING IN QUEBEC 1991, no. 148.

Literature
CARTER 1967, (repr. no. 194); VÉZINA 1972, (repr. fig. 81); JOUVANCOURT 1971 and JOUVANCOURT 1973, [61] (repr.); JUNEAU 1971, 20 (repr.); JOUVANCOURT 1979, 99 (repr.); BÉLAND ET AL. 1992, 342–43, (repr.); Hélène Lamarche, *Looking at the Collections of the Montreal Museum of Fine Arts* (Montreal: Montreal Museum of Fine Arts, 1992), 100, 101 (repr.).

9

THE PLAINS OF BABYLON (after Andrew Anthony Staunton), 1846
oil on canvas, 32.5 × 41.0 cm
LL: C.Krieghoff/after Stanton [sic]

The Collection of Power Corporation of Canada, Montreal

Provenance
Canada Steamship Lines, Montreal; PCC, purchase, 1981.

Exhibitions
MSA 1847, no. 42.

Literature
BARBEAU 1934, 28; BÉLAND ET AL. 1992, 340, 341 (repr., as "Landscape on the Nile").

10

AN OFFICER'S ROOM IN MONTREAL, 1846
oil on canvas, 44.5 × 63.5 cm
LL: C. Krieghoff./1846

Royal Ontario Museum, Toronto, gift of the Sigmund Samuel Endowment Fund, 1954 (954.188.2)

Provenance
Dr. A.A. Staunton, Montreal, possibly commissioned from the artist; Lt. John MacDonnell, Montreal, later London, England; Sir Reginald MacDonald, England; Lady MacDonald, Brighton, England, presumably by succession; Williams & Son, London, England, purchased at auction, Tansley's (Brighton), 24 January 1936, lot 68; Watson Art Galleries, Montreal, purchased 1 April 1936; Miss Helen Norton, Coaticook, Quebec, purchased (with two additional paintings) for $4,150 11 April 1936; ROM, gift, December 1954.

Exhibitions
MSA 1847, no. 103, as "An Officer's Room in Montreal"; KRIEGHOFF ROM 1958; CANADIAN HERITAGE 1966, no. 38; KRIEGHOFF GLENHYRST 1968, no. 19;

KRIEGHOFF ROM 1971; KRIEGHOFF ROM 1975; KRIEGHOFF ROM 1979, (repr.); PEOPLE AND PLACES 1982; PAINTING IN QUEBEC 1991, no. 147; KRIEGHOFF ROM 1994, no. 1.

Literature
"We have been much pleased ...," Gazette (Montreal), 15 January 1847, 2; SPENDLOVE 1958, 75; BARBEAU 1962, as "Lord Elgin's Montreal Office" (repr. plate 8); HARPER THREE CENTURIES 1962, 412 (repr.); Theodore Allen Heinrich, Art Treasures in the Royal Ontario Museum (Toronto: McClelland and Stewart, 1963), 190, 191 (repr.); "Canadian Painters: Cornelius Krieghoff 1815–72," The Auctioneer 8, no. 3 (April 1966): 7 (repr.); JOUVANCOURT 1971 and JOUVANCOURT 1973, facing 8 (repr.); VÉZINA 1972, (repr. fig. 39), 171; JOUVANCOURT 1979, 51 (repr.); HARPER 1979, 20–21, 22 (repr.), 44; LIFE IN LOWER CANADA 1979, (repr.); Mahonri Sharp Young, review of J.R. Harper, Krieghoff, Apollo 117, no. 225 (May 1983): 414; Valerie Grant, "Souvenir—Art or Artifact?," Rotunda 19, no. 1 (Summer 1986): 13 (repr.); Jean Trudel, "Le Musée des traces d'Irene F. Whittome: L'imaginaire comme objet de curiosité," Parachute, no. 57 (January, February, March 1990): 6–7, (repr.); Jean Trudel, "The Montreal Society of Artists, Une galerie d'art contemporain à Montréal en 1847," Journal of Canadian Art History 13, no. 1 (1990): 63 (repr.); BÉLAND ET AL. 1992, 339–41, (repr.); PENCIER 1995, (repr.).

11

BREAKING LENT (or A FRIDAY'S SURPRISE), 1847
oil on canvas, 36.3 × 54.3 cm
LR: C. Krieghoff. 1847

The Thomson Collection (P-C-672)

Provenance
Watson Art Galleries, Montreal; Ward C. Pitfield, Saraguay, Quebec, purchased for $2,500 23 December 1937; Grace Pitfield (wife of W.C. Pitfield), by succession; Kenneth R. Thomson, Toronto, pur-

chased from the estate of Grace Pitfield 9 February 1987.

Exhibitions
Possibly MSA 1847, no. 122, as "Canadian Interior; a Friday's Surprise"; KRIEGHOFF MORGAN 1952; KRIEGHOFF BAG 1961, no. 41.

Literature
"Breaking Lent," Gazette (Montreal), 5 March 1938, 20, (repr.); "Le Carême qu'on brise," La Presse (Montreal), 5 March 1938, 7 (Magazine illustré) (repr.); KRIEGHOFF STAR MONTREAL 1952; MACLEAN'S 1955, 15 (repr.), portfolio (repr. plate VI); JOUVANCOURT 1971 and JOUVANCOURT 1973, 29 (repr.); HARPER 1979, 29, 31 (repr.); JOUVANCOURT 1979, 51 (repr.).

Montreal 1846–53

Representations of Habitants

12

HABITANT SLEIGH, VIEW NEAR THE CANADA LINE, c. 1847
oil on canvas, 64.1 × 92.0 cm
LL: C(K superimposed)

The Thomson Collection (P-C-669)

Provenance
Roy Art Galleries, Toronto; Fred A. Gaby, Toronto, purchased before January 1934; F.M. Gaby (son of F.A. Gaby), presumably by succession; Fred R. Gaby (son of F.M. Gaby), Toronto, presumably by succession; Kenneth R. Thomson, Toronto, purchased 2 January 1987.

Exhibitions
KRIEGHOFF AGT 1934, no. 207, as "Habitant Sleigh"; KRIEGHOFF NGC/AAM 1934, no. 36; Toronto, Canadian National Exhibition, 24 August–8 September 1934, English Painting, Miniatures, and Sculpture; Canadian Painting and Sculpture ..., no. 262, as "View Near the Canada Line."

Literature
BARBEAU 1934, 104, as "Habitant Sleigh, 'View Near the Canada Line.'"

13

A GAME OF CARDS, 1848
oil on canvas, 26.3 × 32.6 cm
LL: C. Krieghoff/1848

National Archives of Canada, Ottawa, gift of the Estate of Charles Murphy, Ottawa, 1938 (C-011003)

Provenance
James Wilson & Co., art dealers, Ottawa; Honourable Charles Murphy, Ottawa, presumably purchased, 1922; NAC, gift, 1938.

Exhibitions
KRIEGHOFF AGT 1934, no. 270; KRIEGHOFF NGC/AAM 1934, no. 86; KRIEGHOFF MQ 1971, no. 9; Ottawa, Public Archives of Canada, 2 October–31 October 1984, The Painted Past, no. 22.

Literature
BARBEAU 1934, 125; HUBBARD 1963, 59; JOUVANCOURT 1971 and JOUVANCOURT 1973, 47 (repr.); JUNEAU 1971, 14 (repr.); VÉZINA 1972, (repr. fig. 62); HARPER 1979, 33 (repr.), 34; JOUVANCOURT 1979, 55 (repr.); Sylvia A. Antoniou et al., The Painted Past (ex. cat.) (Ottawa: Public Archives of Canada, 1984), 39, (repr. no. 22).

14

THE ICE BRIDGE AT LONGUE-POINTE, c. 1848
oil on canvas, 60.8 × 76.2 cm
LL: C. Krieghoff

National Gallery of Canada, Ottawa, gift of Geneva Jackson, Kitchener, Ontario, 1933 (4085)

Provenance
Henry Fletcher Joseph Jackson, Longueuil, Quebec, later Kitchener, Ontario, Montreal, and Brockville, Ontario, purchased from the artist; Mr. Jackson (brother of H.F.J. Jackson),

England, gift, for c. 20 years; Geneva Jackson, (daughter of H.F.J. Jackson), Kitchener, presumably by succession, before 1926; NGC, gift, 1933.

Exhibitions
INAUGURAL EXHIBITION AGT 1926, no. 193, as "Ice Bridge at Longueuil"; KRIEGHOFF AGT 1934, no. 275; KRIEGHOFF NGC/AAM 1934, no. 90; MILESTONES 1961; KRIEGHOFF BAG 1961, no. 3; CANADIAN PAINTING 1967, no. 1; KRIEGHOFF MQ 1971, no. 91.

Literature
BARBEAU CGJ 1934, 102, 104 (repr.); BARBEAU 1934, 104; A.Y. Jackson, A Painter's Country (Toronto: Clarke, Irwin & Co. Ltd., 1958), 1, 13–14; NGC CAT 1960, 163 (repr.); Clare Bice, Canadian Painting 1850–1950 (ex. cat.) (Ottawa: The National Gallery of Canada, 1967), 7 (repr.); JOUVANCOURT 1971 and JOUVANCOURT 1973, 16 (repr.); JUNEAU 1971, 53 (repr.); VÉZINA 1972, [50], [51] (repr.), (repr. fig. 57); REID 1973, 63, 64 (repr.); HARPER 1979, 35 (repr.), 36, 74; JOUVANCOURT 1979, 30 (repr.); REID 1988, 60, 61 (repr.); NGC CAT 1994, 384 (repr.).

15

CANADIAN INTERIOR, 1850
oil on canvas, 45.0 × 70.0 cm
LR: C. Krieghoff 1850.

Musée du Québec, Québec, gift of the Honourable Maurice Duplessis Estate, 1959 (59.629)

Provenance
Watson Art Galleries, Montreal; Honourable Maurice Duplessis, Trois-Rivières, purchased for $2,000 28 March 1947; Mrs. Jeanne-L. Balcer (sister of M. Duplessis), Trois-Rivières, by succession 1959; MQ, gift, 1959.

Exhibitions
PEINTURE TRADITIONNELLE 1967, no. 35, as "Intérieur canadien français"; KRIEGHOFF MQ 1971, no. 8; Montreal, Man and His World (Quebec Pavilion),

Summer 1974, Les Arts du Québec, no. 37; DUPLESSIS 1991.

Literature
Possibly LEEMING COURIER MONTREAL 1850, as "Interior, (Lower Canada), Candle Light"; Adam Shortt, Arthur G. Doughty, eds., Canada and Its Provinces, vol. 15, The Province of Quebec (Toronto: Glasgow, Brook & Co., 1914), 110 (repr., as "Interior of a French-Canadian Farmhouse"); William Bennett Munro, The Seigneurs of Old Canada, vol. 5 of Chronicles of Canada, ed. George M. Wrong and H.H. Langton (Toronto: Glasgow, Brook & Co., 1921), facing 106 (repr.); BARBEAU 1962, (repr. fig. 9), as "Interior at Old Pocane's"; TRUDEL 1967, 70, 71 (repr. detail); JUNEAU 1971, 14 (repr.); KAREL 1991, 53 (repr.).

16

HABITANT FAMILY WITH HORSE AND SLEIGH, 1850
oil on canvas, 46.0 × 67.5 cm
LR: C. Krieghoff./1850

The Thomson Collection (P-C-584)

Provenance
G. Blair Laing, Toronto; Randy Hoyt, purchased 31 May 1968; Dorothy R. Hoyt, Toronto, presumably by succession; Kenneth R. Thomson, Toronto, purchased 6 January 1982.

17

VILLAGE SCENE IN WINTER, 1850
oil on canvas, 66.5 × 92.7 cm
LR: C. Krieghoff 1850

The Thomson Collection (P-C-74)

Provenance
William M. Connor, Ottawa; G. Blair Laing ("Gilbert"), Toronto, purchased for £5,000 at auction, Sotheby's (London), Fine Eighteenth and Nineteenth Century Drawings and Paintings, 29 May 1963, lot 10

(repr.); Kenneth R. Thomson, Toronto, purchased 31 July 1963.

Literature
JOUVANCOURT 1971, facing 34 (repr.); JOUVANCOURT 1973, facing 15 (repr.); JOUVANCOURT 1979, 35 (repr.).

18

COTTAGE, ST. ANNE, c. 1850
oil on canvas, 46.0 × 67.0 cm
LR: C. Krieghoff

Musée du Québec, Québec, acquired before 1934 (34.257)

Provenance
Mrs. Richard Turner, Quebec City, before 1920; Scott & Son, Montreal, c. 1934; MQ, before 1934.

Exhibitions
EXPOSITIONS DE PEINTURES 1920, as "Old Farm House"; FRENCH IN AMERICA 1951, no. 91; Paris, Grands Magasins du Louvre, 17 January–22 February 1958, Exposition de la Province de Québec (Visages du Canada— Vallée du Saint Laurent); ARTS IN FRENCH CANADA 1959, no. 160; KRIEGHOFF MQ 1971, no. 6; KRIEGHOFF PLACE DES ARTS 1976; MQ CINQUANTE ANNÉES 1983, no. 79; KRIEGHOFF MQ 1985.

Literature
BARBEAU 1934, 103; Gérard Morisset, La peinture traditionnelle au Canada français (Ottawa: Le Cercle du Livre de France, 1960), facing 80 (repr.); JUNEAU 1971, 13 (repr.); THIBAULT 1983, 79, (repr.).

19

WHITE HORSE INN BY MOONLIGHT, 1851
oil on canvas, 101.1 × 124.7 cm
LR: C. Krieghoff/1851

National Gallery of Canada, Ottawa, gift of Gabrielle Coste, Marie Louise Savon, and Eugene Francis Coste, 1971, grandchildren of Thomas Dillon Tims, to whom this painting was given by the artist (16702)

Provenance
Thomas Dillon Tims, Quebec City, gift from the artist before 1855; Eugene Coste, Toronto, by succession before 26 November 1937; NGC, gift, 1971.

Exhibitions
GERMAN IMMIGRANT PAINTERS 1975.

Literature
ROBSON 1937, 12, [13] (repr.); McINNIS 1941, (repr.); GUTTENBERG 1954, 103–104; VÉZINA 1972, 69, 72, (repr. fig. 13–15), 111, 129; HARDING 1975, 36 (repr.); NGC CAT 1994, 385 (repr.).

20

FIDDLER AND BOY DOING JIG, 1852
oil on canvas, 38.2 × 32.4 cm
LR: C. Krieghoff/1852
verso, on canvas: Montreal 1852, von onkel Cornelius Krieghoff (now covered by lining)

The Thomson Collection (P-C-777)

Provenance
Unidentified owner, West Germany; Gerald Pencer, Toronto, purchased for $230,000 at auction, Sotheby's (Toronto), Important Canadian Art, 12–13 May 1987, lot 193, as "Canadian Interior" (repr.); Kenneth R. Thomson, Toronto, purchased for $175,000 at auction, Joyner's (Toronto), Important Canadian Art, 20–21 November 1990, lot 100 (repr.).

Literature
Daniel Francis, "How our schools taught us to look down on Quebeckers," Globe and Mail (Toronto), 13 September 1997, 3 (D) (repr.).

21

SLEIGH RACE ON THE ST. LAWRENCE AT QUEBEC, 1852
oil on canvas, 45.0 × 62.9 cm
LL: C Krieghoff.1852

The Thomson Collection (P-C-78)

Provenance
W. Scott and Sons, Montreal, c. 1934; Edward F. Sise, Montreal; Adèle Sise (sister of E.F. Sise), Montreal, by succession 1943; Hazen Sise (nephew of A. Sise), Montreal, purchased from the estate of Adèle Sise, c. 1960; Walter Klinkhoff Gallery, Montreal; Leslie W. Lewis, Toronto, purchased 29 April 1969; Kenneth R. Thomson, Toronto, purchased 1 May 1969.

Exhibitions
ELEVEN ARTISTS 1960, no. 7.

Literature
HARPER 1979, 60, 62 (repr.).

Montreal 1846–53

Representations of Natives

22

CAUGHNAWAGA INDIAN ENCAMPMENT AT A PORTAGE, 1844?
oil on canvas, 35.5 × 54.0 cm
LL: C. Krieghoff.1844

Royal Ontario Museum, Toronto, gift of Dr. Sigmund Samuel, 1949 (949.39.20)

Provenance
Unidentified owner, Ireland; Harry Wallace, purchase; Watson Art Galleries, Montreal; either I.W.C. Solloway, Montreal, purchased for $1,000 27 July 1934, or Lucien Beaugrand, Montreal, purchased for $550 2 January 1935; Sigmund Samuel, Toronto; ROM, gift, March 1949.

Exhibitions
Probably KRIEGHOFF ROM 1951; probably KRIEGHOFF ROM 1958; TREASURES 1962; probably KRIEGHOFF ROM 1968; KRIEGHOFF GLENHYRST 1968, no. 7; KRIEGHOFF MM 1972; KRIEGHOFF ROM 1975; KRIEGHOFF ROM 1979; KRIEGHOFF ROM 1994, no. 8.

Literature
BARBEAU 1934, 133, as "Indian Camp"; BARBEAU 1948, 7 (repr.); SIG SAM COLL 1948, 141 (repr., titled incorrectly "Indians and Squaws, Lower Canada"), 143, (titled incorrectly "Indian Wigwam in Lower Canada"; identified incorrectly as a lithograph); VÉZINA 1972, (repr. fig. 19); HARPER 1979, 46, (repr.), 48 (repr. detail).

23

A CAUGHNAWAGA INDIAN ENCAMPMENT, c. 1848
oil on canvas, 34.0 × 50.5 cm
LR: C.Krieghoff

Royal Ontario Museum, Toronto, gift of Dr. Sigmund Samuel, 1949 (949.39.17)

Provenance
W.W.C. Wilson, Montreal; Mrs. W.W.C. Wilson, Montreal, by succession before 1934; Blair Laing, Toronto, before January 1946; Leslie W. Lewis, Haynes Art Gallery, Toronto, probably purchased at auction, Walter M. Kearns and Son (Montreal), 19 April 1947; Sigmund Samuel, Toronto; ROM, gift, March 1949.

Exhibitions
Probably KRIEGHOFF ROM 1951; probably KRIEGHOFF ROM 1958; probably KRIEGHOFF ROM 1968; KRIEGHOFF GLENHYRST 1968, no. 11; KRIEGHOFF ROM 1975; KRIEGHOFF ROM 1979; PEOPLE AND PLACES 1982; PAINTING IN QUEBEC 1991, no. 150; KRIEGHOFF ROM 1994, no. 7.

Literature
BARBEAU 1934, 132, as "Indian Camp"; "A Caughnawaga Indian Encampment Near Montreal, ...," Gazette (Montreal), 12 April 1947, 14 (repr.); BARBEAU 1948, 5 (repr.); SIG SAM COLL. 1948, 142 (repr.), 143 (identified incorrectly as a lithograph); HARPER 1979, 45 (repr.); LIFE IN LOWER CANADA 1979, (repr.); BÉLAND ET AL. 1992, 345, (repr.).

24

INDIAN TRAPPER ON SNOWSHOES, c. 1849
oil on canvas, 38.7 × 30.5 cm
LL: C Krieghoff.

The Thomson Collection (P-C-81)

Provenance
Mr. Goodwin, Montreal area, purchased for $500 c. 1890; Mr. Goodwin Jr. (son of Mr. Goodwin), probably Montreal, wedding gift 1905; Mrs. Elvie B. Goodwin (wife of Mr. Goodwin Jr.), Wolfboro, New Hampshire, by succession; Leslie W. Lewis, Hayne's Art Gallery, Toronto, purchased 3 September 1949; Roy Thomson, Toronto, purchased before 16 April 1951; Kenneth R. Thomson, gift January 1960.

25

CAUGHNAWAGA WOMAN AND BABY, c. 1849
oil on canvas, 38.8 × 30.5 cm
LR: C Krieghoff

The Thomson Collection (P-C-80)

Provenance
Mr. Goodwin, Montreal area, purchased for $500 c. 1890; Mr. Goodwin Jr. (son of Mr. Goodwin), probably Montreal, wedding gift 1905; Mrs. Elvie B. Goodwin (wife of Mr. Goodwin Jr.), Wolfboro, New Hampshire, by succession; Leslie W. Lewis, Hayne's Art Gallery, Toronto, purchased 3 September 1949; Roy Thomson, Toronto, purchased before 16 April 1951; Kenneth R. Thomson, gift January 1960.

26

CHIEF TANAGHTE, DELEGATE TO LORD ELGIN AT MONTREAL, c. 1849
oil on canvas, 33.9 × 25.5 cm
LL: C. Krieghoff
verso, on upper stretcher: Tanaghte/Young Chief from Lake Superior/Copper Mines

The Thomson Collection (P-C-72)

Provenance
Mrs. Helen Pearson; Sidney Cooling, London, purchased for £700 at auction, Sotheby's (London), Eighteenth and Nineteenth Century Drawings, Paintings and Sculpture, 20 December 1961, lot 114, as "Tanaghte, Indian chief from Lake Superior copper mines, in ceremonial dress and wearing a Peace Medal, seen standing in a forest clearing"; Leslie W. Lewis, Toronto, purchased from Cooling Galleries, Toronto, 3 August 1962; Kenneth R. Thomson, Toronto, purchased 5 August 1962.

Literature
JOUVANCOURT 1971 and JOUVANCOURT 1973, 55 (repr.); HARPER 1979, 53, 54 (repr.); JOUVANCOURT 1979, 117 (repr.).

27

CAUGHNAWAGA INDIAN, c. 1850
oil on board, 31.4 × 24.6 cm
LL: C. Krieghoff

National Archives of Canada, Ottawa, acquired 1937 (C-003139)

Provenance
NAC, 15 February 1937.

Exhibitions
KRIEGHOFF MQ 1971, no. 34.

Literature
JOUVANCOURT 1971 and JOUVANCOURT 1973, 15 (repr.); JUNEAU 1971, 26 (repr.); JOUVANCOURT 1979, 5 (repr.).

28

INDIAN ENCAMPMENT BY A RIVER, c. 1850
oil on canvas, 57.5 × 70.0 cm
LR: C. Krieghoff

Kastel Gallery, Montreal

Provenance
Unidentified owner, United States, before November 1986; Kastel Gallery, Montreal, purchased for $160,000 at auction,

Sotheby's (Toronto), *Important Canadian Art and Jewellery*, 17–18 November 1986, lot 489 (repr.).

29

THE TRADER, 1850
oil on canvas, 45.5 × 60.6 cm
LR: C. Krieghoff. 1850

Art Gallery of Hamilton, gift of Mrs. C.H. Stearn, 1957 (1966.75.0)

Provenance
Richard Fuller, purchased c. 1884; Mary E. Fuller (daughter of R. Fuller), Hamilton, presumably by succession, by July 1906; Rosalynde F. Osborne (niece of M.E. Fuller; granddaughter of R. Fuller) (later Mrs. Clement H. Stearn), Hamilton, by succession by March 1927; AGH, gift, 1957.

Exhibitions
Hamilton, Dundurn Castle, 1 July–30 September 1906, *Art Loan Gallery of Hamilton*, no. 7, as "The Trader"; KRIEGHOFF AGT 1934, no. 259, as "The Fur Trader"; KRIEGHOFF NGC/AAM 1934, no. 100; KRIEGHOFF GLENHYRST 1968, no. 27; Hamilton, McMaster University Art Gallery, 5–7 March 1971, *Canadian Art*; Oshawa, Robert McLaughlin Gallery, 5–30 September 1973, *19th and 20th Century Painting and Sculpture from the Art Gallery of Hamilton*; Toronto, Zacks Gallery, York University, October 1975, *100 Years of Canadiana*.

Literature
Possibly LEEMING COURIER MONTREAL 1850, as "Indians Trading"; BARBEAU 1934, 144; BARBEAU 1962, (repr. fig. 13, as "The Fur Trader [Caughnawaga Indians]").

30

HURON INDIANS AT PORTAGE, 1850
oil on canvas, 71.1 × 84.0 cm
LL: C.Krieghoff.1850

Royal Ontario Museum, Toronto, gift of the Sigmund Samuel Endowment Fund, 1954 (954.188.3)

Provenance
Watson Art Galleries, Montreal; R.O. Sweezey, Montreal, purchased for $750 2 June 1924; Watson Art Galleries, Montreal, after January 1934; Harry Norton, Ayer's Cliff, Quebec, purchased for $2,200 17 November 1934; Miss Helen Norton, Coaticook, Quebec, later Boston, presumably by succession; ROM, purchase, December 1954.

Exhibitions
KRIEGHOFF NGC/AAM 1934, no. 149, as "Indian at a Portage"; possibly KRIEGHOFF ROM 1951; probably KRIEGHOFF ROM 1958; probably KRIEGHOFF ROM 1968; KRIEGHOFF GLENHYRST 1968, no. 1; KRIEGHOFF ROM 1975; Toronto, Art Gallery of Ontario, 12 December 1975–1 February 1976, *The Ontario Community Collects: A survey of Canadian painting from 1766 to the present*, no. 50 (repr.); KRIEGHOFF ROM 1979; PEOPLE AND PLACES 1982; KRIEGHOFF ROM 1994, no. 10.

Literature
BARBEAU STAR MONTREAL 1934, (repr.); BARBEAU CGJ 1934, 103 (repr.); BARBEAU 1934, facing 3 (repr.), 133, as "Indians at a Portage"; SPENDLOVE 1958, 75; JOUVANCOURT 1971 and JOUVANCOURT 1973, 34 (repr.), 70; William Forsey, *The Ontario Community Collects: A survey of Canadian painting from 1766 to the present* (ex. cat.) (Toronto: Art Gallery of Ontario, 1975), 108, [109] (repr.); HARPER PEINTURE 1966, 121 (repr.); HARPER 1977, 164 (repr.); HARPER 1979, 47 (repr.); JOUVANCOURT 1979, 61 (repr., incorrectly cited as "private collection"), 109; PENCIER 1995, (repr.).

Montreal 1846–53

Prints

31

INDIANS AND SQUAWS OF LOWER CANADA, 1848

Toronto and Quebec
lithograph with watercolour on paper (Crehen), 34.5 × 47.5 cm (image)

Royal Ontario Museum, Toronto, gift of Dr. Sigmund Samuel, 1947 (947.131.1)

Ottawa, Vancouver, and Montreal
lithograph with watercolour on paper (Crehen), 34.4 × 47.4 cm (image)

Collection of Peter Winkworth, London (ZAPTW 164)

32

FRENCH CANADIAN HABITANS PLAYING AT CARDS, 1848

Toronto and Quebec
lithograph with watercolour and gouache on paper (Borum), 34.1 × 49.1 cm (image)

Collection of Peter Winkworth, London (ZAPTW 240)

Ottawa, Vancouver, and Montreal
lithograph with watercolour on paper (Borum), 34.2 × 48.8 cm (image)

National Gallery of Canada, Ottawa, gift of Donald Maclaren, Ottawa, 1990 (30821)

33

INDIAN WIGWAM IN LOWER CANADA, 1848

Toronto and Quebec
lithograph with watercolour and gouache on paper (Borum), 34.4 × 48.8 cm (image)

Collection of Peter Winkworth, London (ZAPTW 241)

Ottawa, Vancouver, and Montreal
lithograph with watercolour on paper (Borum), 34.4 × 48.5 cm (image)

National Gallery of Canada, Ottawa, gift of Donald Maclaren, Ottawa, 1990 (30820)

34

PLACE D'ARMES À MONTRÉAL, 1848

Toronto and Quebec
lithograph on paper (Borum), 34.5 × 48.6 cm (image)

McCord Museum of Canadian History, Montreal, gift of Sir Frederick Williams-Taylor, accessioned after November 1950 (M19840)

Ottawa, Vancouver, and Montreal
lithograph on paper (Borum), 34.7 × 48.7 cm (image)

Collection of Peter Winkworth, London (ZAPTW 260)

35

SLEDGE RACE NEAR MONTREAL, 1848

Toronto and Quebec
lithograph with beige tint stone, on paper (Borum), 33.7 × 48.5 cm (image)

Royal Ontario Museum, Toronto, acquired 1960 (960.66.4)

Ottawa, Vancouver, and Montreal
lithograph with beige tint stone, on paper (Borum), 34.6 × 49.6 cm (image)

National Archives of Canada, Ottawa, purchased 1931 (C-013466)

36

ICE CUTTING, c. 1849

Toronto and Quebec
lithograph with watercolour on paper (Sarony & Major), 17.1 × 24.9 cm (image)

Collection of Peter Winkworth, London (ZAPTW 206)

Ottawa, Vancouver, and Montreal
lithograph with watercolour on paper (Sarony & Major), 17.1 × 24.4 cm (image)

National Archives of Canada, Ottawa, acquired from the W.H. Coverdale Collection of Canadiana, 1970 (C-040776)

37

SUGAR MAKING IN CANADA, c. 1849

Toronto and Quebec
lithograph with watercolour on paper
(Sarony & Major), 17.1 × 24.8 cm (image)

Collection of Peter Winkworth, London
(ZAPTW 208)

Ottawa, Vancouver, and Montreal
lithograph with watercolour on paper
(Sarony & Major), 17.0 × 24.7 cm (image)

Royal Ontario Museum, Toronto, purchased 1991, Sigmund Samuel Trust
(991.175.1)

38

UNTITLED (HUNTER AND TWO WOMEN), c. 1849

Toronto and Quebec
lithograph with watercolour on paper
(Sarony & Major), 17.1 × 24.4 cm (image)

Collection of Peter Winkworth, London
(ZAPTW 209)

Ottawa, Vancouver, and Montreal
lithograph with watercolour on paper
(Sarony & Major), 17.0 × 24.5 cm (image)

Royal Ontario Museum, Toronto, gift of the Sigmund Samuel Endowment Fund, 1957 (957.62.2)

39

UNTITLED (INDIAN PORTAGING A CANOE), c. 1849

Toronto and Quebec
lithograph with watercolour on paper
(Sarony & Major), 17.1 × 24.6 cm (image)

Collection of Peter Winkworth, London
(ZAPTW 207)

Ottawa, Vancouver, and Montreal
lithograph with watercolour on paper
(Sarony & Major), 17.0 × 24.4 cm (image)

Royal Ontario Museum, Toronto, gift of the Sigmund Samuel Endowment Fund, 1957 (957.62.1)

40

FRENCH CHURCH, PLACE D'ARMES, MONTREAL, c. 1850

Toronto and Quebec
lithograph with watercolour on paper
(Sarony & Major), 42.5 × 32.0 cm (image)

Royal Ontario Museum, Toronto, purchased 1981, Sigmund Samuel Trust
(981.61)

Ottawa, Vancouver, and Montreal
lithograph with watercolour on paper
(Sarony & Major), 44.2 × 33.4 cm (image)

National Archives of Canada, Ottawa, acquired from the W.H. Coverdale Collection of Canadiana, 1970 (C-040912)

Montreal 1846–53

Krieghoff's Circle

41

SEIGNEURY AT SAINTE-ANNE-DE-LA-PÉRADE, 1846
oil on canvas, 29.9 × 40.5 cm
LR: C. Krieghoff. 1846.

McCord Museum of Canadian History, Montreal, gift of David Campbell, 1992 (990.758.1.3)

Provenance
Honourable Edward Hale, Sherbrooke, Quebec, commissioned from the artist; William Amherst Hale (son of E. Hale), Sherbrooke, by succession; Gladys Hale (daughter of W.A. Hale), Sherbrooke, by succession; Miss Vera McCrae (niece of G. Hale; daughter of Alicia [Hale] McCrae), Sherbrooke, by succession; David Campbell, Toronto, purchased through Walter Klinkhoff Gallery,

Montreal, 1990; MMCH, gift, 1992.

Exhibitions
Montreal, McCord Museum of Canadian History, 19 June–15 November 1993, *New Acquisitions Part I*.

Literature
HARPER 1979, 18, (repr.).

42

KING'S WALDEN, HERTFORDSHIRE, 1846
oil on canvas, 31.0 × 41.2 cm

McCord Museum of Canadian History, Montreal, gift of David Campbell, 1992 (990.758.1.1)

Provenance
Honourable Edward Hale, Sherbrooke, Quebec, commissioned from the artist; William Amherst Hale (son of E. Hale), Sherbrooke, by succession; Gladys Hale (daughter of W.A. Hale), Sherbrooke, by succession; Miss Vera McCrae (niece of G. Hale; daughter of Alicia [Hale] McCrae), Sherbrooke, by succession; David Campbell, Toronto, purchased through Walter Klinkhoff Gallery, Montreal, 1990; MMCH, gift, 1992.

Exhibitions
Montreal, McCord Museum of Canadian History, 19 June–15 November 1993, *New Acquisitions Part I*.

43

LT. ROBERT MCCLURE, 1847
oil on canvas, 60.6 × 46.0 cm
LR: C. Krieghoff 1847

The Thomson Collection (P-C-665)

Provenance
Williams & Son, London, England, purchased for £115 at auction, Christie's (London), *Important Ancient and Modern

Pictures and Drawings*, 25 February 1938, lot 146, as "Sir Robert Le Mesurier McClure in Winter Costume holding a pipe"; Cooling Gallery, Toronto, purchased for £160 30 June 1939; Mr. and Mrs. F.R. Niblett, Toronto, purchased c. 1939; George S. (son of F.R. Niblett) and Vera Niblett, Toronto, presumably by succession; Kenneth R. Thomson, Toronto, purchased 3 December 1986.

44

CHARLES THEOPHILUS METCALFE, BARON METCALFE (AFTER ALVAH BRADISH), 1847
oil on canvas, 117.6 × 92.1 cm
LR: C. Krieghoff 1847

Musée du Château Ramezay, Montreal, gift of W.B. Mathewson, 1899 (1998.1865)

Provenance
W.B. Mathewson, Montreal; CR, gift, 1899

Exhibitions
Possibly Montreal, Numismatic and Antiquarian Society of Montreal, 15 December 1887, *Loan Exhibition of Canadian Historical Portraits and Other Objects Relating to Canadian Archaeology*, no. 89–263–664; Ottawa, National Gallery of Canada, 27 October–7 January 1967, *A Pageant of Canada*, no. 261; Kingston, Agnes Etherington Art Centre, Queen's University, 3 June–28 October 1973, *Heritage Kingston*, no. 176.

Literature
Possibly Numismatic and Antiquarian Society of Montreal, *Descriptive Catalogue of a Loan Exhibition of Canadian Historical Portraits and Other Objects Relating to Canadian Archaeology* (Montreal: Gazette Printing Co, 1887), 32; Thomas O'Leary, *Catalogue of the Château Ramezay Museum and Portrait Gallery* (Montreal: C.A. Marchand, 1901), 18; Roy Strong, *A Pageant of Canada* (ex. cat.) (Ottawa:

National Gallery of Canada, 1967), 293 (repr.); Douglas Stewart and Ian E. Wilson, *Heritage Kingston* (ex. cat.) (Kingston: Agnes Etherington Art Centre, 1973), 145 (repr.); HARPER 1979, 23.

Quebec 1853–63

Landscape

45

MONTMORENCY FALLS, 1853
oil on canvas, 91.4 × 121.9 cm
LL: C Krieghoff./Quebec. 1853

The Thomson Collection (P-C-116)

Provenance
W. Darling Campbell, Quebec City, probably from the artist; George S. Cantlie (son-in-law of W.D. Campbell), Montreal, presumably by succession, c. 1924; Mrs. H.G. Lafleur, Montreal, before September 1966; Walter Klinkhoff Gallery, Montreal, after 1967; Kenneth R. Thomson, Toronto, purchased through Leslie W. Lewis, Toronto, 22 July 1970.

Exhibitions
KRIEGHOFF AGT 1934, no. 223; KRIEGHOFF NGC/AAM 1934, no. 19; London, Tate Gallery, 15 October–15 December 1938, *A Century of Canadian Art*, no. 128; Montreal, Montreal Museum of Fine Arts, Junior Associates (Jamm), 15 April–7 May 1959, *History of Montreal, Painting*; CANADIAN HERITAGE 1966, no. 39; PAINTER AND THE NEW WORLD 1967, no. 267; KRIEGHOFF MM 1972, no. [12].

Literature
BARBEAU NGC 1934, facing 10 (repr.); R.B.F., "Krieghoff Exhibition Is Beautiful Record of Early Days in Canada," *Journal* (Ottawa), 16 February 1934, 16; CHAUVIN 1934, 7 (repr.); BARBEAU 1934, 117, as "Montmorency Falls"; Donald W. Buchanan, ed., *Canadian Painters* (Oxford & London: Phaidon Press, 1945), 23, (repr. plate 3); MACLEAN'S 1955, 18–19

(repr. cropped), portfolio (repr. cropped plate X); BARBEAU 1962, (repr. plate 18); Doris Shadbolt, *Images for a Canadian Heritage* (ex. cat.) (Vancouver: Vancouver Art Gallery, 1966), (repr.); CARTER 1967, (repr. no. 267); WINKWORTH 1972, (repr. no. [12]).

46

QUEBEC VIEWED FROM POINTE-LÉVIS, 1853
oil on canvas, 36.6 × 53.9 cm
LR: C Krieghoff 1853

Musée du Québec, Québec, purchased 1984, with the assistance of the government of Canada through the Cultural Property Export and Import Act (84.18)

Provenance
Lt. Alfred Torrens, Quebec City, later England, from the artist; Charles Walter Torrens (son of Lt. A. Torrens), England, later Quebec City (by 1916); Bertha (Blair) Torrens (wife of W.C. Torrens), Quebec City, presumably by succession, by May 1945; Norman Fairlie Blair (brother of B. [Blair] Torrens), by succession after 1 April 1968; Ronald E. Blair (son of N.F. Blair), London, England, by succession early 1969; MQ, purchase, 1984.

Exhibitions
KRIEGHOFF MQ 1985; PAINTING IN QUEBEC 1991, no. 256; QUÉBEC VUE 1994, no. 106.

Literature
BÉLAND ET AL. 1992, 556–58, (repr.); PORTER/PRIOUL 1994, 139 (repr.).

47

QUEBEC FROM POINTE-LÉVIS, 1853
oil on canvas, 36.0 × 53.5 cm
LL: C Krieghoff/1853

Royal Ontario Museum, Toronto, gift of Raymond A. Willis, Esq., 1955 (955.84)

Provenance
Raymond A. Willis, Toronto, by succession before 1948; ROM, gift, 11 June 1955.

Exhibitions
TREASURES 1962; KRIEGHOFF GLENHYRST 1968, no. 17; KRIEGHOFF MQ 1971, no. 23; KRIEGHOFF ROM 1975; KRIEGHOFF ROM 1979; PEOPLE AND PLACES 1982; KRIEGHOFF ROM 1994, no. 11.

Literature
JOUVANCOURT 1971 and JOUVANCOURT 1973, 37 (repr.); JUNEAU 1971, 20 (repr.); VÉZINA 1972, 53 (repr.); JOUVANCOURT 1979, [66]–67 (repr.); BÉLAND ET AL. 1992, 556–58, (repr.).

48

FALLS OF LORETTE, NEAR QUEBEC, 1854
oil on canvas, 31.1 × 38.6 cm
LL: C. Krieghoff
verso, on canvas: Falls of Lorette/near Quebec/C. Krieghoff 1854

Musée du Québec, Québec, purchased 1949 (49.101)

Provenance
Mrs. Charles C. Wilson, Quebec City; Mrs. Alfred E. (Wilson) Beck (daughter of Mrs. C.C. Wilson), Toronto, by succession before January 1934; G. Blair Laing, Toronto, before 16 June 1945; Continental Galleries, Montreal; MQ, purchase, 1949.

Exhibitions
KRIEGHOFF AGT 1934, no. 205; ARTS IN FRENCH CANADA 1952, no. 66; ARTS IN FRENCH CANADA 1959, no. 161; KRIEGHOFF BAG 1961, no 9; PEINTURE TRADITIONNELLE 1967, no. 34; KRIEGHOFF MQ 1971, no. 55; KRIEGHOFF PLACE DES ARTS 1976; MQ CINQUANTE ANNÉES 1983, no. 83; KRIEGHOFF MQ 1985.

Literature
BARBEAU 1934, 118; "Pictures for Lasting Pleasure" (advertisement for Laing Galleries), *Saturday Night* 60, no. 41 (16 June 1945): 17 (repr.); COOKE 1961, (repr., no. 9); TRUDEL 1967, 68, 69 (repr.); JUNEAU 1971, 33 (repr.); HARPER 1979, 116 (repr.), 117; THIBAULT 1983, 82, (repr.); Marie Delagrave, "Krieghoff et son

temps," *Le Soleil* (Quebec City), 3 August 1985, 3 (E), (repr.).

49

THE PASSING STORM, ST. FÉRÉOL, 1854
oil on canvas, 39.0 × 50.2 cm
LC: C. Krieghoff/Quebec 1854

National Gallery of Canada, Ottawa, purchased 1963 (15190)

Provenance
W. O'Connor, Quebec City, from the artist; Heber Budden, Quebec City, gift from John S. Budden (brother of H. Budden) c. 1897; Watson Art Galleries, Montreal, by August 1949; William M. Connor, Ottawa, purchased for $1,050 5 August 1949; NGC, purchase, 1963.

Exhibitions
KRIEGHOFF MQ 1971, no. 80

Literature
JOUVANCOURT 1971 and JOUVANCOURT 1973, 45 (repr.); JUNEAU 1971, 48 (repr.); HARPER 1979, 120, 122 (repr.); JOUVANCOURT 1979, 79 (repr.); NGC CAT 1994, 386 (repr.).

50

THE ST. ANNE FALLS NEAR QUEBEC FROM ABOVE AND LOOKING UPWARD, 1854-5
oil on canvas, 31.0 × 46.5 cm
LL: C Krieghoff 1854
verso, on canvas: Falls St. Ann's near Quebec/from above & looking upward C. Krieghoff 1855

National Gallery of Canada, Ottawa, purchased 1995 (37781)

Provenance
Possibly David H. Geggie, Quebec City; John Young, Quebec City; James Young, (nephew of John Young), Montreal, presumably by succession, by 1934; Continental Galleries, Montreal, possibly purchased at auction, Ward-Price

(Toronto), 14 May 1946; Gérald Martineau, Sillery, Quebec; Blandine D. Martineau (wife of G. Martineau), Sillery, by succession 1968; NGC, purchase, 1995.

Literature
BARBEAU 1934, 119; "Falls of Ste. Anne, Near Quebec," (advertisement for Ward-Price auction), *Globe and Mail* (Toronto), 14 May 1946, 5 (repr.).

51

THE ST. ANNE FALLS, 1855
oil on canvas, 40.0 × 48.6 cm
LL: C. Krieghoff. 1855.

National Gallery of Canada, Ottawa, purchased 1995 (37780)

Provenance
W.W.C. Wilson, Montreal; Mrs. W.W.C. Wilson, Montreal, by succession by 1924; possibly Stevens Art Gallery, Montreal, 1943; Continental Galleries, Montreal, before 17 July 1954; Gérald Martineau, Sillery, Quebec; Blandine D. Martineau (wife of G. Martineau), Sillery, by succession 1968; NGC, purchase, 1995.

Exhibitions
Possibly KRIEGHOFF STEVENS 1943.

Literature
BARBEAU 1934, 119, as "Ste. Anne Falls"; possibly STEVENS GAZETTE MONTREAL 1943; "Falls of Ste. Anne …," *Gazette* (Montreal), 17 July 1954, 20 (repr.).

52

VIEW OF QUEBEC FROM THE GRAND TRUNK RAILWAY STATION AT POINTE-LÉVIS, 1856
oil on canvas, 41.2 × 61.4 cm
LL: C Krieghoff 1856

Private collection

Provenance
Scott & Sons, Montreal, c. 1934; unidentified owner, Montreal; private collection.

Exhibitions
KRIEGHOFF MM 1972, no. [19]; PAINTING IN QUEBEC 1991, no. 257.

Literature
WINKWORTH 1972, (repr. no. [19]); Peter Winkworth, "Cornelius Krieghoff: Scenes in Canada," *Connoisseur* 185, no. 745 (March 1974): 212 (repr.); HARPER 1979, 143 (repr.), 144; BÉLAND ET AL. 1992, 556–58, (repr.).

53

IN THE JARDIN DE CARIBOU, BELOW QUEBEC, 1856
oil on canvas, 39.5 × 39.4 cm
LL: C Krieghoff
LL spandrel: In the/Jardin de/Caribou below/Quebec
verso, on stretcher: Le Jardin des Caribous

McCord Museum of Canadian History, Montreal, bequest of Arnold Wainwright, Q.C., 1967 (M967.100.13)

Provenance
Dominion Gallery, Montreal, before 22 December 1953; Arnold Wainwright, Montreal, purchased before 1962; MMCH, bequest, 1967.

Exhibitions
EVERYMAN'S CANADA 1962, no. 31;

54

THE ARTIST AT NIAGARA, 1858
oil on canvas, 38.2 × 51.5 cm
LR: C.Krieghoff

Art Gallery of Ontario, Toronto, gift of Charles and Lois Thomson, Milton, Ontario, in memory of Mr. and Mrs. H. Dewar Thomson, 1998 (98/20)

Provenance
Charles Wilson, Westmount, Quebec, before 1928; Roberta (Wilson) Thomson (niece of C. Wilson), by succession; Charles (son of R. Thomson) and Lois Thomson, Milton, Ontario, by succession; AGO, gift, 1998.

55

THE CHAUDIÈRE, 1858
oil on canvas, mounted on plywood, 51.1 × 74.9 cm
LR: C Krieghoff/Quebec 58

National Gallery of Canada, Ottawa, gift of Edith Wilson, Ottawa, 1923, in memory of Senator and Mrs. W.C. Edwards (2037)

Provenance
Edith Wilson, Ottawa; NGC, gift, 1923.

Exhibitions
KRIEGHOFF AGT 1934, no. 273; KRIEGHOFF NGC/AAM 1934, no. 92; KRIEGHOFF BAG 1961, no. 24; COLONIAL PAINTING 1964, no. 28; KRIEGHOFF MQ 1971, no. 54; ARTIST AND LAND 1973, no. 18.

Literature
BARBEAU CGJ 1934, 108 (repr.); BARBEAU 1934, 76, 118; NGC CAT 1960, 162 (repr.); BARBEAU 1962, (repr. plate 25; JOUVANCOURT 1971 and JOUVANCOURT 1973, 120 (repr.); JUNEAU 1971, 32 (repr.); R.H. Hubbard, *The Artist and the Land: Canadian Landscape Painting 1670–1930* (ex. cat.) (Madison, Wis.: University of Wisconsin, Elvehjem Art Center, 1973), 72, 73 (repr.); JOUVANCOURT 1979, 189 (repr.); NGC CAT 1994, 388 (repr.).

56

THE TUBULAR BRIDGE AT ST. HENRY'S FALLS, 1858
oil on canvas, 36.4 × 54.0 cm
LR: C Krieghoff/Quebec 1858

McCord Museum of Canadian History, Montreal, bequest of Arnold Wainwright, Q.C., 1967 (M967.100.1)

Provenance
Watson Art Galleries, Montreal; William M. Connor, Ottawa, purchased for $650 6 June 1944; Dominion Gallery, Montreal; Arnold Wainwright, Montreal, purchased 19 July 1958; MMCH, bequest, 1967.

Exhibitions
EVERYMAN'S CANADA 1962, no. 92; THREE HUNDRED YEARS 1967, no. 116; KRIEGHOFF MQ 1971, no. 51.

Literature
HARPER 1962, 65 (repr.); HUBBARD/OSTIGUY 1967, 72, 73 (repr.); JUNEAU 1971, 51 (repr.); HARPER 1979, 142 (repr.).

57

PORTAGE AT GRAND'MÈRE FALLS, c. 1860
oil on panel set in top of table, 22.4 × 33.0 cm
LL: CKrieghoff

Private collection, Guelph, Ontario

Provenance
Mr. and Mrs. Jules Loeb, Toronto; private collection, Guelph, Ontario, purchased 1997.

Literature
HARPER 1979, 55, 56 (repr.)

58

IN THE JARDIN DE CARIBOU, 50 MILES BELOW QUEBEC, 1861
oil on canvas, 53.6 × 47.3 cm
LR: C Krieghoff/Quebec 1861
verso, on canvas: In the 'Jardin des Cariboux'/50 miles below Quebec/ C Krieghoff (now covered by lining)

The Thomson Collection (P-C-574)

Provenance
W.D. Green; G. Blair Laing, Toronto, purchased for £62,000 at auction, Sotheby's (London), *Topographical Paintings, Watercolours, Drawings and Prints*, 28 May 1981, lot 101 (repr.); Kenneth R. Thomson, Toronto, purchased July 1981.

Literature
G. Blair Laing, *Memoirs of an Art Dealer 2* (Toronto: McClelland and Stewart, 1982), [33] (repr.).

59

JAM OF SAWLOGS, SHAWINIGAN
FALLS, 1861
oil on canvas, 45.5 × 66.0 cm
LR: C. Krieghoff. 1861.
UL spandrel: Jam of Sawlog_____ [let-
ters missing]/upper most fall/in the little
Shavangagan R/near the Great falls/of
Shavanagan, St. Mauri[ce] R./25 miles
above/Three Rivers, Canada/1861

The Thomson Collection (P-C-224)

Provenance
Frank Stevens, Stevens Art Gallery,
Montreal, before November 1943;
William M. Connor, Ottawa, purchased
c. 1943; "Holstein," purchased ("in
house"?) for £1,600 at auction, Sotheby's
(London), *Fine Eighteenth and Nineteenth
Century Drawings and Paintings*, 29 May
1963, lot 22 (repr.); Kenneth R. Thomson,
Toronto, purchased from William M.
Connor, Manotick, Ontario, 14 March
1972.

Exhibitions
Probably KRIEGHOFF STEVENS 1943.

Literature
Probably STEVENS GAZETTE MONTREAL
1943.

60

LAC LAURENT: AUTUMN, 1862
oil on canvas, 33.8 × 50.0 cm
LL: C Krieghoff 1862
verso, on canvas: Lke Laurent/Quebec

The Thomson Collection (P-C-168)

Provenance
Col. Gordon Russell, Quebec City, later
England, probably purchased 23
December 1862; Col. James Russell (son
of Col. G. Russell) of Lennox Mansions,
Portsmouth, England, presumably by suc-
cession; Watson Art Galleries, Montreal,
by August 1939; Herbert S. Sharp,
Summerside, P.E.I., purchased for $1,000
10 August 1939; T.G. Torrance,
Richmond, Quebec, purchased for $1,000

through Watson Art Galleries 30
November 1939; Kenneth R. Thomson,
Toronto, purchased through Christie
Manson & Woods (Canada) Ltd. 30
December 1970.

Literature
FAIRCHILD 1908, 73, as "Lake Laurent—
Autumn."

61

LANDSCAPE WITH DEER AND DOE,
1862
oil on canvas, 52.7 × 92.3 cm
LR: C Krieghoff. 1862

The Thomson Collection (P-C-618)

Provenance
Thomas Fraser, Quebec City; Septimus
Fraser (son of T. Fraser), Montreal, pre-
sumably by succession; G. Blair Laing,
Toronto; Mr. Harold A. Kopas, Toronto,
purchased c. 1960; Donald B. Kopas (son
of H.A. Kopas) and Suzanne Kopas,
Toronto, by succession; Kenneth R.
Thomson, purchased 9 January 1984.

Literature
BARBEAU 1934, 143, as "Wild Deer in
Autumn Scenery."

62

EARLY WINTER ON THE ST. ANNE'S,
BELOW QUEBEC, 1863
oil on canvas, 51.2 × 51.8 cm
LR: C Krieghoff./Quebec 63.
LR spandrel: Early Winter/On the St
Ann's/below Quebec

The Thomson Collection (P-C-531)

Provenance
Watson Art Galleries, Montreal; Norman
MacFarlane, Montreal, purchased for
$400 21 September 1923; H. Thomas
MacFarlane (grandson of N. MacFarlane),
Montreal, presumably by succession;
Kenneth R. Thomson, Toronto, pur-
chased 19 December 1979.

63

DERY'S BRIDGE, SALMON LEAP,
JACQUES CARTIER RIVER, 1863
oil on canvas, 33.3 × 49.1 cm
LR: C Krieghoff/1863
LR spandrel: Dery's Bridge/Salmon Leap/
Jacque [sic] Cartier

McCord Museum of Canadian History,
Montreal, bequest of Arnold Wainwright,
Q.C., 1967 (M967.100.6)

Provenance
Probably Watson Art Galleries, Montreal;
probably Frances F. Gill, Ottawa, purchased for $550 5 April 1947; Dominion
Gallery, Montreal, before 15 July 1958;
Arnold Wainwright, Montreal, purchased
by 25 July 1958; MMCH, bequest, 1967.

Exhibitions
Buffalo, Buffalo Fine Arts Academy, probably December 1865, *Works of Art*, no. 104,
as "Devil's Bridge, Jaque Carten [sic], The
Salmon-leap on that River"; EVERYMAN'S
CANADA 1962, no. 94; KRIEGHOFF MQ 1971,
no. 77.

Literature
Dorothy Pfeiffer, "Cornelius Krieghoff,"
Gazette (Montreal), 12 July 1958, 22 (repr.);
JUNEAU 1971, 44 (repr.); VÉZINA 1972,
(repr. fig. 73); HARPER 1979, 113.

64

VIEW OF QUEBEC CITY FROM
POINTE-LÉVIS, 1863
oil on canvas, 34.9 × 59.0 cm
LL: C Krieghoff
verso, on stretcher: View of Quebec from
south shore 1863. J.T. Dawson

Montreal Museum of Fine Arts, Miss
Mary Fry Dawson Bequest, 1954
(1954.1103)

Provenance
J.T. Dawson, Quebec City; Miss Mary Fry
Dawson, presumably by succession;
MMFA, bequest, 1954.

Exhibitions
Quebec City, Provincial Exhibition, 12–15
September 1871, [Fine Arts Department];
KRIEGHOFF BAG 1961, no. 35; KRIEGHOFF
WILLISTEAD 1963, no. 45; PAINTER AND THE
NEW WORLD 1967, no. 304; KRIEGHOFF MQ
1971, no. 22; Montreal, Museum of Fine
Arts, 3 May–5 August 1984, *Quebec City As
Seen Through the Eyes of Légaré, Holloway,
Krieghoff, Sewell…*; QUÉBEC VUE 1994, no.
117.

Literature
MMFA CAT 1960, 24; CARTER 1967, (repr.
no. 304); JOUVANCOURT 1971 and
JOUVANCOURT 1973, 133 (repr.); VÉZINA
1972, [142] (repr.); JUNEAU 1971, 20
(repr.); JOUVANCOURT 1979, [206]–07;
BÉLAND ET AL. 1992, 556–58, (repr.);
PORTER/PRIOUL 1994, 151 (repr.).

Quebec 1853–63

Krieghoff's Circle

65

THE STEAMSHIP QUEBEC, 1853
oil on canvas, 67.7 × 93.4 cm
LR: CKrieghoff pinx/1853

The Thomson Collection (P-C-714)

Provenance
Capt. A.M. Raddall, Quebec City, presum-
ably commissioned from the artist; possi-
bly Miss Raddall (daughter of A.M.
Raddall); Dr. William Rounding Franks,
Toronto, before June 1953; Hugh R.
Franks (son of W.R. Franks), Toronto,
presumably by succession; Kenneth R.
Thomson, Toronto, purchased for
$270,000 at auction, Sotheby's (Toronto),
Important Canadian Art, 31 May–1 June
1988, lot 175 (repr.).

Exhibitions
Ottawa, National Gallery of Canada, 2
June–13 September 1953, *Exhibition of
Canadian Painting to Celebrate the Coronation
of Her Majesty Queen Elizabeth II*, no. 34;
London, Commonwealth Institute, 1965,

Treasures; THREE HUNDRED YEARS 1967, no. III, (repr); KRIEGHOFF ROM 1971; KRIEGHOFF ROM 1975; THROUGH CANADIAN EYES 1976, no. 14; Toronto, Royal Ontario Museum, 23 November 1979–6 April 1980, *Sailing Canadian Waters*, no. 35.

Literature

R.H. Hubbard, "Growth in Canadian Art," in *The Culture of Contemporary Canada*, ed. Julian Park (Ithaca: Cornell University Press, 1957), 120; R.H. Hubbard, "The Discovery of Early Canadian Painting," *Art in America* 47, no. 3 (1959): 43, (repr.); BARBEAU 1962, (repr. fig. 17); R.H. Hubbard, "Recent Discoveries in Early Canadian Art," *Journal of the Royal Society of Arts* (November 1962): 931, (repr.); HUBBARD 1963, 61 (repr.); HUBBARD/OSTIGUY 1967, 68, 69 (repr.); Paul Duval, *High Realism in Canada* (Toronto/Vancouver: Clarke, Irwin & Company Limited, 1974), 15 (repr.); Robert H. Hubbard, "Artists in Common: Canadian–American Contacts," *RACAR* 3, no. 2 (1976): 40 (repr.); WILLIAMSON 1976, (repr.); 1979: HARPER 1979, [vi] (repr.), 60.

66

LT. ALFRED TORRENS AND HIS WIFE IN FRONT OF THE CITADEL, c. 1854
oil on canvas, 29.3 × 46.3 cm
LR: C Krieghoff

The Thomson Collection (P-C-715)

Provenance

Lt. Alfred Torrens, Quebec City, later England (1855), presumably commissioned from the artist; Charles Walter Torrens (son of A. Torrens), England, later Quebec City (by 1916), presumably by succession; Bertha (Blair) Torrens (wife of C.W. Torrens), Quebec City, by succession by May 1945; Lady Betty Ann (Torrens) Baker Wilbraham (niece of C.W. Torrens), by succession; Letitia Ann (Baker Wilbraham) Kirkbride (daughter of B-A. Baker Wilbraham), Sandbach,

Cheshire, England, by succession 1976; Kenneth R. Thomson, purchased for £70,000 at auction, Christie's (South Kensington), *Topographical Pictures*, 9 June 1988, lot 99 (repr.).

67

FRASER, WITH MR. MILLER UP, 1854
oil on canvas, 63.7 × 79.7 cm
LR: C. Krieghoff pxt/Quebec 1854
verso, on canvas: Portrait of Fraser rode by Mr. Miller./painted by C.Krieghoff Quebec 1854 (now covered by lining)

National Gallery of Canada, Ottawa, purchased 1964 (14609)

Provenance

W. Kirwan, Quebec City, commissioned from the artist, 1854; Mr. Kirwan, by succession; Dominion Gallery, purchased before September 1961; NGC, purchase, 1964.

Exhibitions

KRIEGHOFF BAG 1961, no. 8; KRIEGHOFF WILLISTEAD 1963, no. 8; THREE HUNDRED YEARS 1967, no. 115; EARLY CANADIAN PORTRAITS 1969, no. 11; KRIEGHOFF MQ 1971, no. 4; THROUGH CANADIAN EYES 1976, no. 11; PAINTING IN QUEBEC 1991, no. 152.

Literature

CURATOR 1961; HUBBARD/OSTIGUY 1967, 72, 73 (repr.); JOUVANCOURT 1971, facing 98 (repr.); JUNEAU 1971, 10 (repr.); VÉZINA 1972, 103, (repr. fig. 45); JOUVANCOURT 1973, between 83 and 85 (no pagination) (repr.); WILLIAMSON 1976, (repr.); HARPER 1979, 96, 104 (repr.); JOUVANCOURT 1979, 195 (repr.); BÉLAND ET AL. 1992, 347, (repr.); NGC CAT 1994, 386 (repr.).

68

ELIZABETH BICKELL, c. 1854
oil on canvas, 59.6 × 49.7 cm

National Gallery of Canada, Ottawa, purchased 1953 (6107)

Provenance

Mrs. G. Doak (direct descendant of Bickell), Lennoxville, Quebec, presumably by succession, before 1952; R.A. Davies, Morgan & Co., (Antique Salon), Montreal, before 16 April 1952; NGC, purchase, 1953.

Exhibitions

Montreal, Morgan & Co., Antique Salon, c. 12 April 1952, [*Canadian and Continental Painters*]; KRIEGHOFF BAG 1961, no. 7.

Literature

"Mr. and Mrs. John Bicknell [sic] …," *Gazette* (Montreal), 12 April 1952, 16, (repr.); NGC CAT 1960, 164; ROMBOUT 1962, 47 (repr.); NGC CAT 1994, 385 (repr.).

69

JOHN PALMER BICKELL, 1854
oil on canvas, 61.2 × 51.1
LL: C Krieghoff 1854

National Gallery of Canada, Ottawa, purchased 1953 (6106)

Provenance

Mrs. G. Doak (direct descendant of Bickell), Lennoxville, Quebec, presumably by succession, before 1952; R.A. Davies, Morgan & Co., (Antique Salon), Montreal, before 16 April 1952; NGC, purchase, 1953.

Exhibitions

Montreal, Morgan & Co., Antique Salon, c. 12 April 1952, [*Canadian and Continental Painters*]; KRIEGHOFF BAG 1961, no. 6; EARLY CANADIAN PORTRAITS 1969, no. 12; KRIEGHOFF MQ 1971, no. 2.

Literature

"Mr. and Mrs. John Bicknell [sic] …," *Gazette* (Montreal), 12 April 1952, 16, (repr.); NGC CAT 1960, 164 (repr); ROMBOUT 1962, 47 (repr.); JOUVANCOURT 1971, verso III (repr.); JUNEAU 1971, 10 (repr.); VÉZINA 1972, (repr. fig. 40); JOUVANCOURT 1973, between 111 and 113 (no pagination) (repr.); JOUVANCOURT 1979, 179 (repr.); NGC CAT 1994, 385 (repr.).

70

SELF-PORTRAIT, 1855
oil on canvas, 28.8 × 24.8 cm
LL: C Krieghoff 1855
LR: C Krieghoff/1855

National Gallery of Canada, Ottawa, purchased 1920 (1657)

Provenance

John McDougall, Montreal, from the artist; Edgar Mill McDougall (son of J. McDougall), Montreal, presumably by succession; Miss Agnes K. McDougall (sister of E.M. McDougall), Montreal, presumably by succession; NGC, purchased through Scott & Sons, Montreal, consignors for the McDougall estate, 1920.

Exhibitions

INAUGURAL EXHIBITION AGT 1926, no. 190; KRIEGHOFF AGT 1934, no. 275A; KRIEGHOFF NGC/AAM 1934, no. 89; KRIEGHOFF WILLISTEAD 1963, no. 12; KRIEGHOFF MQ 1971, no. 1; GERMAN IMMIGRANT PAINTERS 1975.

Literature

BARBEAU NGC 1934, facing 5 (repr.); BARBEAU 1934, 131; BARBEAU 1948, 15 (repr); MACLEAN'S 1955, 13 (repr.), portfolio (repr. plate I); NGC CAT 1960, 161 (repr.); BARBEAU 1962, (repr. back cover); HARPER THREE CENTURIES 1962, 412 (repr.); ROMBOUT 1962, 48 (repr.); HARPER PAINTING 1966, 121 (repr.); JOUVANCOURT 1971 and JOUVANCOURT 1973, facing I (repr.), 102–103; JUNEAU 1971, 10 (repr.); VÉZINA 1972, (repr. fig. I); REID 1973, 65 (repr.), 66; HARDING 1975, 37 (repr.); HARPER 1979, xii (repr.); JOUVANCOURT 1979, facing I (repr.), 154; Dalhousie Art Gallery, *Selections from the Sobey Collections, Part I: Cornelius Krieghoff (1815–1872)* (ex. brochure) (Halifax: Dalhousie Art Gallery, Dalhousie University, 1983), (repr. fig. I); REID 1988, 63 (repr.); NGC CAT 1994, 386 (repr.).

71

ANDREW JOHN MAXHAM, 1856
oil on canvas, 35.8 × 29.0 cm
LR: C. Krieghoff 1856
verso, on canvas: A. J. MAXHAM
Esq/Quebec/Auctineer [sic]/By C. Kraigoff
[sic]

Musée du Québec, Québec, acquired
before 1934 (34.268)

Provenance
Andrew John Maxham, from the artist;
George Gale, Quebec City; MQ, before
1934.

Exhibitions
Quebec City, Musée de la Province de
Québec, 26 September–28 October 1948,
Québec il y a cent ans; ARTS IN FRENCH
CANADA 1952, no. 67, incorrectly titled
"Portrait de John Budden"; MQ
CINQUANTE ANNÉES 1983, no. 95;
KRIEGHOFF MQ 1985.

Literature
BARBEAU 1934, 32; FAIRCHILD 1908, 70;
THIBAULT 1983, 92 (repr.).

72

THE COUNTRY HOUSE OF CAPT.
JOHN WALKER, NEAR QUEBEC, 1857
oil on canvas, 45.7 × 68.9 cm
LL: C. Krieghoff Quebec 57

Musée du Québec, Québec, gift of the
Honourable Maurice Duplessis Estate,
1959 (59.584)

Provenance
Capt. John Walker, commissioned from
the artist, 1857; Mrs. M. Harvey-Cant
(granddaughter of Capt. J. Walker),
England, presumably by succession,
before 1954; Dominion Gallery, Montreal,
(probably "Rozendaal," purchased for
£600 at auction, Sotheby's [London],
*Modern and Eighteenth Century Paintings and
Drawings*, 17 March 1954, lot 162);
Honourable Maurice Duplessis, Trois-
Rivières, 1954; Mrs. Jeanne-L. Balcer

(sister of M. Duplessis), Trois-Rivières,
by succession 1959; MQ, gift, 1959.

Exhibitions
KRIEGHOFF MQ 1971, no. 21; MQ
CINQUANTE ANNÉES 1983, no. 85;
KRIEGHOFF MQ 1985; DUPLESSIS 1991.

Literature
JOUVANCOURT 1971 and JOUVANCOURT 1973,
122 (repr.); JUNEAU 1971, 20 (repr.);
HARPER 1979, 18 (repr.); JOUVANCOURT
1979, 57 (repr.); THIBAULT 1983, 84;
KAREL 1991, 54 (repr.).

73

THE NARROWS ON LAKE ST.
CHARLES, 1859
oil on canvas, 36.0 × 53.0 cm
LR: C.Krieghoff. Quebec 59
verso, on upper frame: Old Gabriel of
lake St. Charles/+ Mofin[?] Gibb,
Buddin[sic]/CKrieghoff pinxt[?]

The Thomson Collection (P-C-703)

Provenance
Presumably James Gibb, Quebec City,
presumably from the artist; Mrs. David A.
Ross (widow of J. Gibb), presumably by
succession; Frank W. Ross (no relation)
Quebec City, gift in lieu of payment
before May 1923; F. Donald Ross (son of
F.W. Ross), Quebec City, by succession
1966; Kenneth R. Thomson, Toronto,
purchased 22 March 1988.

Exhibitions
KRIEGHOFF NGC/AAM 1934, no. 133, as
"Lake St. Charles."

Literature
SMALL 1866, facing 46 (repr.); BARBEAU
1934, 120; HARPER 1979, 145, 149 (repr.).

74

DEATH OF THE MOOSE AT SUNSET.
LAKE FAMINE SOUTH OF QUEBEC,
1859
oil on canvas, 36.0 × 53.0 cm

LR: C Krieghoff/Quebec 1859
verso, LR on stretcher: Ayos [unclear]
Gibb Krieghoff J Budden

Glenbow Collection, Calgary, Alberta,
anonymous donation, 1981 (81.7.1)

Provenance
John S. Budden, Quebec City; James
Gibb, Quebec City; Mrs. David A. Ross
(widow of J. Gibb), presumably by succession; Frank W. Ross (no relation),
Quebec City, gift in lieu of payment
before May 1923, until at least 6 November
1952; undisclosed owner; GC, gift, 1981.

Exhibitions
KRIEGHOFF NGC/AAM 1934, no. 132.

Literature
NOTMAN 1865, plate 31, as "Death of the
Moose at sunset. Lake Famine South of
Quebec"; BARBEAU STAR MONTREAL 1934,
(repr.); BARBEAU RSC 1934, [120] (repr.);
BARBEAU 1934, 129; BARBEAU 1936, 124
(repr.); BARBEAU 1948, 19 (repr. as
"Hunting the Moose in the Laurentians");
HARPER 1979, 102 (repr.), 108, 145, 147
(repr. detail); John Porter, "The Market
for Paintings: Basic Needs versus Artistic
Taste," BÉLAND ET AL. 1992, 30 (repr.);
Joan M. Schwartz, "William Notman's
hunting photographs, 1866," *The Archivist*,
no. 117 (1998): 26, 28.

75

THE ARTIST PAINTING, c. 1860
oil on canvas, 23.0 × 33.0 cm
LL: C Krieghoff/Krieg

The Thomson Collection (P-C-279)

Provenance
Unidentified owner, Strasbourg, France;
unidentified owner, near Nîmes, France;
Jon Nicholas Streep, New York, purchased
October 1972; Kenneth R. Thomson,
purchased 22 May 1974.

Literature
HARPER 1979, 145, 148 (repr.).

76

THE PETS AND THE MATERIALS,
1860
oil on canvas, 26.8 × 31.8 cm
LR: C Krieghoff./1860.
verso, on canvas: "The pets & the materials"/Presented/To his Friends/Anny,
Christ f & Robt/O'Connor/in token of
regard & friendship/by their/sincere well-
wisher/C. Krieghoff. Quebec / Dec. 1860

National Gallery of Canada, Ottawa, gift
of Leonora D. McCarney, Ottawa, 1987, in
memory of her parents, Ethel and Frank
De Rice (29,785)

Provenance
Anny and Christopher O'Connor, Quebec
City, gift from the artist; John Breakey,
Breakeyville, Quebec; Ian Breakey (son of
J. Breakey), Breakeyville, presumably by
succession; Walter Klinkhoff Gallery,
Montreal, purchased for $12,000 at auc-
tion, Fraser Bros. (Montreal), 24
September 1975, lot 278 (repr.); Leonora
D. McCarney, Ottawa, purchase; NGC,
gift, 1987.

Literature
BARBEAU 1934, 149, as "Dining Table with
Two Prince Charles Spaniels"; HARPER
1979, 60, 63 (repr.), 64; J. Russell Harper,
"Krieghoff and Collectors," *Canadian
Antiques and Art Review* 1, no. 4 (December
1979/January 1980); 14–18, (repr.).

77

SPORTSMEN AT JACQUES CARTIER
FALLS, 1861
oil on canvas, 51.0 × 64.2 cm
LL: C. Krieghoff.. Quebec 1861

The Thomson Collection (P-C-575)

Provenance
James Gibb, Quebec City, presumably
from the artist; Mrs. David A. Ross (widow
of J. Gibb), Quebec City, presumably by
succession; Frank W. Ross (no relation),
Quebec City, gift in lieu of payment

before May 1923; Harold T. Ross (son of F.W. Ross), Sillery, Quebec, presumably by succession; Walter Klinkhoff Gallery, Montreal, purchased April 1967; Mrs. Harry A. (Suzanne) Willsie (later S. Brilliant-Fluehler), Montreal, purchased before June 1967; Kenneth R. Thomson, Toronto, purchased 27 July 1981.

Exhibitions
PAINTER AND THE NEW WORLD 1967, no. 268;

Literature
BARBEAU 1934, 144, as "Scene on the Jacques-Cartier by Moonlight"; CARTER 1967, (repr. no. 268).

Quebec 1853–63

Prints

78

THE ICE CONE AT THE FALLS OF MONTMORENCY NEAR QUEBEC, LOWER CANADA, IN 1853, 1853

Toronto and Quebec
colour lithograph on paper (Simpson), 40.0 × 58.6 cm (image)

Collection of Peter Winkworth, London (ZAPTW 170)

Ottawa, Vancouver, and Montreal
colour lithograph on paper (Simpson), 40.0 × 58.8 cm (image)

National Archives of Canada, Ottawa, acquired from the W.H. Coverdale Collection of Canadiana, 1970 (C-041048)

79

"POUR L'AMOUR DU BON DIEU?", 1858

Toronto and Quebec
chromolithograph on paper, 27.0 × 22.9 cm (image)

The Tennison family and Maydwell Manufacturing Company, Toronto

Ottawa, Vancouver, and Montreal
chromolithograph on paper, 26.8 × 27.0 cm (image)

Collection of Peter Winkworth, London (ZAPTW 178)

80

"VA AU DIABLE!", 1858

Toronto and Quebec
chromolithograph on paper, 27.0 × 22.9 cm (image)

The Tennison family and Maydwell Manufacturing Company, Toronto

Ottawa, Vancouver, and Montreal
chromolithograph on paper, 26.8 × 22.8 cm (image)

Collection of Peter Winkworth, London (ZAPTW 175)

81

INDIAN CHIEFS, 1860

Toronto and Quebec
Opposite page 9 in Construction of the Great Victoria Bridge in Canada (London: J. Weale, 1860).
colour lithograph (Kell Brothers), 20.2 × 28.9 cm (image)

Edward P. Taylor Research Library & Archives, Art Gallery of Ontario, Toronto, purchased with the assistance of the Walter and Duncan Gordon Charitable Foundation, 1997

Ottawa, Vancouver, and Montreal
From Construction of the Great Victoria Bridge in Canada (London: J. Weale, 1860).
colour lithograph (Kell Brothers), 22.2 × 29.0 cm (image)

National Archives of Canada, Ottawa, purchased 1921 (C-013467)

82

PASSENGERS AND MAIL, CROSSING THE RIVER, 1860

Toronto and Quebec
colour lithograph (Kell Brothers), 19.5 × 28.0 cm (image)

Royal Ontario Museum, Toronto, gift of Miss Mary B. Dickenson, 1962 (962.156.1)

Ottawa, Vancouver, and Montreal
Opposite page 78 in Construction of the Great Victoria Bridge in Canada (London: J. Weale, 1860).
colour lithograph (Kell Brothers), 19.5 × 28.1 cm (image)

Edward P. Taylor Research Library & Archives, Art Gallery of Ontario, Toronto, purchased with the assistance of the Walter and Duncan Gordon Charitable Foundation, 1997

83

VIEW OF QUEBEC, CANADA: FROM THE RAILWAY STATION OPPOSITE QUEBEC, THE CITY, 1862

Toronto, Quebec, Ottawa, Vancouver, and Montreal
lithograph with watercolour on paper, 41.2 × 60.3 cm (image)

Collection of Peter Winkworth, London (ZAPTW 153)

Quebec 1853–63

Single Figures

84

A LORETTE INDIAN, c. 1855
oil on canvas, 28.3 × 23.2 cm
LL: CKrieghoff

McCord Museum of Canadian History, Montreal, bequest of Arnold Wainwright, Q.C., 1967 (M967.100.9)

Provenance
Unidentified owner, Belfast; Dominion Gallery, Montreal (probably "Rozendaal," purchased as one of a pair for £504 at auction, Christie's [London], Modern Pictures, 12 June 1953, lot 111, as "A Lovetti [sic] Indian"); Arnold Wainwright, Montreal, purchase; MMCH, bequest, 1967.

Exhibitions
EVERYMAN'S CANADA 1962, no. 7; KRIEGHOFF MQ 1971, no. 19.

Literature
HARPER 1962, 19; JUNEAU 1971, 17 (repr.); VÉZINA 1972, (repr. cropped fig. 26).

85

A CAUGHNAWAGA WOMAN, c. 1855
oil on canvas, 28.0 × 23.1
LR: C Krieghoff

McCord Museum of Canadian History, Montreal, bequest of Arnold Wainwright, Q.C., 1967 (M967.100.10)

Provenance
Unidentified owner, Belfast; Dominion Gallery, Montreal, (probably "Rozendaal," purchased as one of a pair for £504 at auction, Christie's [London], Modern Pictures, 12 June 1953, lot 111, as "A Caughnawaja [sic] Squaw"); Arnold Wainwright, Montreal, purchase; MMCH, bequest, 1967.

Exhibitions
KRIEGHOFF MQ 1971, no. 36.

Literature
JUNEAU 1971, 26 (repr.); VÉZINA 1972, (repr. fig. 33).

86

INDIAN WOMAN, MOCCASIN SELLER, c. 1855
oil on canvas, 28.4 × 23.4 cm
LL: C Krieghoff

The Thomson Collection (P-C-678)

Provenance
John H. Price, Montreal; Kenneth R. Thomson, Toronto, purchased 25 March 1987.

Literature
Possibly BARBEAU 1934, 147.

87

THE TRAPPER, c. 1855
oil on canvas, 28.5 × 23.5 cm
LL: C Krieghoff.

The Thomson Collection (P-C-499a)

Provenance
William Hedley Anderson, Quebec City; Mathew Wheatley Anderson (son of W.H. Anderson), England, presumably by succession; Percival Hedley Anderson (son of M.W. Anderson), England, and his two sisters, South Wales, presumably by succession; Mrs. E.H. (Anderson) Williams (daughter of P.H. Anderson), United Kingdom, presumably by succession; Kenneth R. Thomson, Toronto, purchased through Doug Armour of Brawley Cathers Limited, 27 April 1979.

88

HEAD OF A HABITANT, c. 1855
oil on canvas, 33.5 × 25.6 cm
LR: C Krieghoff

Montreal Museum of Fine Arts, Mrs. J.H.R. Molson Bequest, 1910 (1910.307)

Provenance
Mrs. John H.R. Molson, Montreal; MMFA, bequest, 1910.

Exhibitions
KRIEGHOFF MORGAN 1952; KRIEGHOFF BAG 1961, no. 66; KRIEGHOFF WILLISTEAD 1963, no. 44; PAINTER AND THE NEW WORLD 1967, no. 263; KRIEGHOFF MQ 1971, no. 48; MACAMIC TO MONTREAL 1974.

Literature
BARBEAU 1934, 122; MMFA CAT 1960, 23; CARTER 1967, (repr., no. 263); JUNEAU

1971, 30 (repr.); JOUVANCOURT 1971 and JOUVANCOURT 1973, 46 (repr.); JOUVANCOURT 1979, 80 (repr.).

89

HEAD OF A HABITANT, c. 1855
oil on canvas, 30.5 × 25.4 cm

Montreal Museum of Fine Arts, Mrs. J.H.R. Molson Bequest (1910.308)

Provenance
Mrs. John H.R. Molson, Montreal; MMFA, bequest, 1910.

Exhibitions
KRIEGHOFF MORGAN 1952; KRIEGHOFF WILLISTEAD 1963, no. 43; PAINTER AND THE NEW WORLD 1967, no. 264; KRIEGHOFF MQ 1971, no. 47; MACAMIC TO MONTREAL 1974.

Literature
BARBEAU 1934, 122; MMFA CAT 1960, 24; CARTER 1967, (repr. no. 264); JUNEAU 1971, 30 (repr.); VÉZINA 1972, (repr. fig. 95).

90

THE INDIAN MOCCASIN SELLER, c. 1855
oil on canvas, 28.5 × 23.5 cm
LL: CKrieghoff

The Thomson Collection (P-C-499b)

Provenance
William Hedley Anderson, Quebec City; Mathew Wheatley Anderson (son of W.H. Anderson), England, presumably by succession; Percival Hedley Anderson (son of M.W. Anderson), England, and his two sisters, South Wales, presumably by succession; Mrs. E.H. (Anderson) Williams (daughter of P.H. Anderson), United Kingdom, presumably by succession; Kenneth R. Thomson, Toronto, purchased through Doug Armour of Brawley Cathers Limited 27 April 1979.

91

THE WOODCUTTER, 1857
oil on canvas, 28.2 × 23.3 cm
LL: C Krieghoff
verso, on canvas: Presented/to/Eveline A. Dudley/by "HARRY"/Augt 3D, 1858 (now covered by lining)

The Thomson Collection (P-C-727)

Provenance
Eveline A. Dudley, gift from "Harry," 1858; Salander-O'Reilly Galleries, New York, purchased at auction, William Doyle Galleries (New York), *American Paintings and Sculpture*, 5 April 1989, lot 47 (repr.); Kenneth R. Thomson, Toronto, purchased 12 April 1989.

92

HUNTER IN A BLIZZARD, c. 1858
oil on canvas, 28.5 × 23.5 cm
LL: CKrieghoff.

The Thomson Collection (P-C-717)

Provenance
Henry F. Hall, believed by succession; John W.F. Hall (son of H.F. Hall), Ottawa, by succession before 23 February 1956; Kenneth R. Thomson, purchased for $38,000 at auction, Empire Industries Inc. (Montreal), *Art, Antiques and Collectibles*, 27–29 June 1988, lot 283.

93

INDIAN TRAPPER ON SNOWSHOES, 1858
oil on canvas, 28.2 × 23.0 cm
LL: C Krieghoff/Quebec 58

The Thomson Collection (P-C-231)

Provenance
Unidentified owner, England; G. Blair Laing, Toronto, purchased for $9,000 at auction, Christie's (Montreal), "Important Paintings, Drawings, Watercolours ...," 27 April 1972, lot 80, as "Indian Hunter with Gun"

(repr.); Kenneth R. Thomson, Toronto, purchased 18 May 1972.

94

"POUR LE BON DIEU?", 1859
oil on canvas, 26.7 × 21.6 cm
LR: C. Krieghoff 1859

Kastel Gallery, Montreal

Provenance
Kaspar Gallery, Toronto; Kastel Gallery, Montreal, purchased c. 1981.

95

"VA AU DIABLE!", 1859
oil on canvas, 26.7 × 21.6 cm
LL: C Krieghoff/Quebec

Kastel Gallery, Montreal

Provenance
Kaspar Gallery, Toronto; Kastel Gallery, Montreal, purchased c. 1981.

96

CALLING THE MOOSE, c. 1860
oil on canvas, 27.0 × 21.5 cm
LR: CKrieghoff.

The Thomson Collection (P-C-66)

Provenance
Dr. Reginald Hearn, London; Sidney Cooling (brother-in-law of R. Hearn), London; Mrs. B.A. Dunlap, Toronto, purchase; Dr. Fred Stone, Buffalo, purchased from the estate of B.A. Dunlap; Leslie W. Lewis, Toronto, purchase; Kenneth R. Thomson, Toronto, purchased 1 October 1961.

97

HUNTER RESTING GUN ON A SNOWSHOE, c. 1860
oil on canvas, 28.5 × 23.0 cm
LR: CKrieghoff.

The Thomson Collection (P-C-452)

Provenance
Unidentified owner, England; G. Blair Laing, Toronto; Kenneth R. Thomson, Toronto, purchased 3 January 1978.

98

GOING TO MARKET, c. 1860
oil on canvas, 28.2 × 23.0 cm
LL: C Krieghoff

The Thomson Collection (P-C-675)

Provenance
Ward C. Pitfield, Cartierville, Quebec, probably by November 1934; Grace Pitfield (wife of W.C. Pitfield), by succession; Kenneth R. Thomson, Toronto, purchased from the estate of Grace Pitfield 9 February 1987.

Exhibitions
KRIEGHOFF BAG 1961, no. 102.

Literature
Probably BARBEAU 1934, 124.

99

THE OLD POACHER, c. 1860
oil on canvas, 28.3 × 23.1 cm
LL: C.Krieghoff

The Thomson Collection (P-C-291)

Provenance
Watson Art Galleries, Montreal; William M. Connor, Ottawa, purchased for $350 21 July 1937; Kenneth R. Thomson, purchased 19 December 1974.

100

THE BERRY SELLER, 1860
oil on canvas, 28.8 × 23.6 cm
LL: C Krieghoff
verso, on lower stretcher: Fr. Canad[n] Berries seller/returning home Quebec 1860

National Archives of Canada, Ottawa, acquired before 1922 (C-010698)

Provenance
NAC, before 1922.

101

LORETTE CARIBOU HUNTER, 1862
oil on canvas, 28.4 × 23.2 cm
LR: C Krieghoff./Quebec 1862

The Thomson Collection (P-C-677)

Provenance
John H. Price, Montreal; Kenneth R. Thomson, Toronto, purchased 25 March 1987.

102

THE INDIAN HUNTER, 1866
oil on canvas, 28.3 × 23.5 cm
LL: C Krieghoff. 1866

The Thomson Collection (P-C-175a)

Provenance
R. Harcourt Smith, Quebec City; A.H.C. Smith (grandson of R.H. Smith), Quebec City, presumably by succession; Mrs. A.H.C. Smith, Quebec City, presumably by succession; Kenneth R. Thomson, purchased through Leslie W. Lewis for $10,500 at auction, Christie's (Montreal), *Fine Canadian Paintings …*, 21–22 April 1971, lot 25 (repr.).

Literature
BARBEAU 1934, 146.

Quebec 1853–63

Representations of Natives

103

INDIAN ENCAMPMENT AT BIG ROCK, c. 1853
oil on canvas, 32.4 × 55.5 cm
CR: C Krieghoff

The Thomson Collection (KRT-C-5)

Provenance
N.R. Coysh; G. Blair Laing, Toronto, purchased through Williams & Son, London, for £6,000 at auction, Sotheby's

(London), *Fine Nineteenth and Twentieth Century British and Continental Paintings*, 12 February 1969, lot 146, as "Indian Encampment Above a River" (repr.); R.B. Love, Calgary, purchase; Kenneth R. Thomson, Toronto, purchased 13 March 1975.

104

THE HUNTERS, 1854
oil on canvas, 38.4 × 50.2 cm
LL: C Krieghoff/1854

McCord Museum of Canadian History, Montreal, bequest of Arnold Wainwright, Q.C., 1967 (M967.100.3)

Provenance
Miss Agnes Wainwright, Montreal; Arnold Wainwright (nephew of A. Wainwright), Montreal, presumably by succession; MMCH, bequest, 1967

Exhibitions
KRIEGHOFF MQ 1971, no. 56.

Literature
JUNEAU 1971, 36 (repr.).

105

PORTAGE NEAR FALLS OF GRAND'MÈRE, ST. MAURICE RIVER, 1855
oil on canvas, 53.2 × 61.1 cm
LL: C. Krieghoff
verso, on canvas: Portage near/Falls of Grande Mere/St Maurice River Ca/C. Krieghoff–1855 (now covered by lining)

The Collection of Power Corporation of Canada, Montreal

Provenance
Possibly Watson Art Galleries, Montreal; possibly Harry Snyder, Montreal, purchased for $600 10 October 1934; J.A. Dakin, Dorval; Walter Klinkhoff Gallery, Montreal, purchased January 1969; PCC, purchase, 1969.

Literature
JOUVANCOURT 1971 and JOUVANCOURT 1973, 88 (repr.); JOUVANCOURT 1979, 157 (repr.).

106

INDIANS DANCING, 1855
oil on academy board, 18.9 × 30.3 cm
LL: C. Krieghoff 1855

National Archives of Canada, Ottawa, acquired before 1934 (C-146150)

Provenance
NAC, before 1934.

Exhibitions
KRIEGHOFF AGT 1934, no. 266; KRIEGHOFF NGC/AAM 1934, no. 107.

Literature
BARBEAU 1934, 134; JOUVANCOURT 1971 and JOUVANCOURT 1973, 53 (repr.); JOUVANCOURT 1979, 87 (repr.).

107

THE INDIAN CAMPSITE, 1857
oil on canvas, 38.5 × 51.2 cm
LR: C Krieghoff/Quebec 57

The Thomson Collection (P-C-333)

Provenance
M.J. Boylen, Toronto; Murphy Corporation Limited, Nassau, Bahamas; Kenneth R. Thomson, Toronto, purchased 4 September 1975.

Exhibitions
KRIEGHOFF CNE 1955, no. 16, as "Indian Camp Site"; KRIEGHOFF WIMODAUSIS 1957; KRIEGHOFF BAG 1961, no. 88.

108

TAKING SHELTER FROM THE STORM, 1857
oil on canvas, 33.3 × 46.0 cm
LL: CKrieghoff/Quebec 57

The Thomson Collection (P-C-616)

Provenance
Blair Laing, Toronto, purchased at auction, Barridoff Galleries, Portland, Maine, November 1983, lot 78; Kenneth R. Thomson, Toronto, purchased 5 January 1984.

109

IN THE THOUSAND ISLANDS, c. 1858
oil on canvas, 34.0 × 50.8 cm
LC: C. Krieghoff

Art Gallery of Ontario, Toronto, bequest of Mrs. H.M. Mowat, Toronto, 1939 (2533)

Provenance
Mr. Howard, Quebec City, c. 1858; Mr. Herbert M. Mowat, Toronto, purchased 1877; Mrs. Mary (Skeaff) Mowat (wife of H.M. Mowat), Toronto, presumably by succession; AGO, bequest, 1939.

Exhibitions
Toronto, Art Museum of Toronto, 24 January–22 February 1911, *Loan Collection of Paintings by Deceased Canadian Artists*, no. 142, as "Scene in the Thousand Islands"; FRENCH IN AMERICA 1951, no. 89; KRIEGHOFF BAG 1961, no. 76; KRIEGHOFF WILLISTEAD 1963, no. 5.

Literature
BARBEAU 1934, 138; AGO CAN COLL 1970, 235; JOUVANCOURT 1971 and JOUVANCOURT 1973, 76 (repr.); JOUVANCOURT 1979, 124 (repr.).

110

INDIANS IN THE EMPLOY OF THE HUDSON'S BAY COMPANY AT A PORTAGE, 1858
oil on canvas, 40.6 × 50.8 cm
LL: C Krieghoff/Quebec 58
verso, on upper stretcher: Indians Employ of the/Hudson Bay Co at the/Portage

The Thomson Collection (P-C-656)

Provenance
Mr. Mitchell, purchased for £78 at auction, Dowell's (Edinburgh), 18 February 1933, as "Indians in the Employ of the Hudson Bay Company at a Portage"; Watson Art Galleries, Montreal, by 1934; Miss Helen Norton, Ayers Cliff, Quebec; Walter Klinkhoff Gallery, Montreal, purchase; Mr. and Mrs. Mel Dobrin, Montreal, purchased by 1971; Kenneth R. Thomson, Toronto, purchased for $130,000 at auction, Fraser Bros. (Montreal), *Canadian Art*, 23 October 1986, lot 83 (repr.).

Literature
BARBEAU 1934, 138, as "Portage," 1855; JOUVANCOURT 1971 and JOUVANCOURT 1973, 78 (repr.); JOUVANCOURT 1979, 155 (repr.).

111

INDIANS HUNTING A CARIBOU, c. 1860
oil on canvas, 45.7 × 38.0 cm
LL: CKrieghoff.

The Thomson Collection (P-C-244)

Provenance
Probably William Hedley Anderson, Quebec City; Mathew Wheatley Anderson (son of W.H. Anderson), England, probably by succession; Mrs. E.H. Williams (granddaughter of M.W. Anderson), United Kingdom, by succession; G. Blair Laing, Toronto, purchased through Williams & Son, London, for £3,780 at auction, Christie's (London), *Important English Pictures*, 18 November 1966, lot 52, as "A Wooded Winter Landscape" (repr.); Kenneth R. Thomson, Toronto, purchased 10 January 1973.

112

LAKE MEMPHREMAGOG, c. 1860
oil on canvas, 23.0 × 28.1 cm
LR: C Krieghoff
verso, on canvas: L. Memphremagog; verso, on stretcher: Unt by H.J. Scott [?]

The Thomson Collection (P-C-874)

Provenance
Henry Stewart Scott, Quebec City; Erskine Guthrie Scott, Quebec City, by succession 1883; Herbert Erskine Scott, Quebec City, by succession c. 1915; Marjorie (Swift) Scott (niece of H.E. Scott), by succession 1949; Michael B. Scott (son of M. Scott), St. Lambert, Quebec; Kenneth R. Thomson, Toronto, purchased 4 December 1992.

113

INDIAN HUNTERS ON THE ST. MAURICE RIVER, 1860
oil on canvas, 46.7 × 43.1 cm
LR: C.Krieghoff 60
verso, on canvas: On the ST Maurice Rr/Canada

The Collection of Power Corporation of Canada, Montreal

Provenance
Possibly Mr. Wood; Quebec City; possibly Col. William Wood (son of Mr. Wood), Quebec City, presumably by succession; Canada Steamship Lines, Montreal, between 1939 and 1942; PCC, purchase 1981.

Exhibitions
CANADIANA 1942, no. 81, as "Hunting Scene on the St. Maurice"; MAÎTRES CANADIENS 1989, no. 36.

Literature
JOUVANCOURT 1971 and JOUVANCOURT 1973, 136 (repr.); HARPER 1979, 135 (repr.); JOUVANCOURT 1979, 210 (repr.).

114

CHIPPEWAS ON LAKE SUPERIOR, 1860
oil on canvas, 40.6 × 61.3 cm
LL: C. Krieghoff/1860
verso, on canvas: Chippawa [sic] on Lake Superior (now covered by lining)

The Thomson Collection (P-C-314)

Provenance
John Hamilton, Quebec City, presumably purchased from John Budden; John Hamilton (son of J. Hamilton), Quebec City, presumably by succession, before 1934; Harold Pfeiffer, Quebec City; Watson Art Galleries, Montreal, purchased for $2,200 10 March 1955; Dr. and Mrs. M.J. Boylen, Toronto, purchased for $3,500 17 May 1955; Murphy Corporation Limited, Nassau, Bahamas; Kenneth R. Thomson, Toronto, purchased 4 September 1975.

Exhibitions
EXPOSITION DE PEINTURES 1920, as "Camp Indien"; KRIEGHOFF NGC/AAM 1934, no. 42, as "Chippawa Indians, Lake Superior"; KRIEGHOFF CNE 1955, no. 38, as "Chippawa Indians at Council Rock"; KRIEGHOFF WIMODAUSIS 1957; KRIEGHOFF BAG 1961, no. 80.

Literature
BARBEAU 1934, 137; COOKE 1961, (repr. no. 80); JOUVANCOURT 1971 and JOUVANCOURT 1973, 135, 138 (repr.); JOUVANCOURT 1979, 212, (repr.).

115

INDIAN HUNTERS, 1861
oil on canvas, 23.2 × 28.3 cm
LL: C Krieghoff/Quebec 1861

The Thomson Collection (P-C-331)

Provenance
Possibly unidentified Lady owner, England; Cooling Galleries, London, purchased for £280 at auction, Sotheby's (London), *Modern Drawings and Paintings*, 15 October 1952, lot 55, as "Autumn Landscape"; Dr. and Mrs. M.J. Boylen, Toronto, purchased before August 1955; Murphy Corporation Limited, Nassau, Bahamas; Kenneth R. Thomson, Toronto, purchased, 1975.

Exhibitions
KRIEGHOFF CNE 1955, no. 17, as "Indians Preparing Meal"; KRIEGHOFF WIMODAUSIS 1957; KRIEGHOFF BAG 1961, no. 84, as "Indian Hunters."

116

AFTER THE KILL, 1861
oil on canvas, 20.5 × 34.5 cm
LR: C Krieghoff/1861

The Thomson Collection (P-C-69)

Provenance
J.R. Wood, Surrey, England, before 1951;
Allen E. Rosen, Toronto; Kenneth R.
Thomson, Toronto, purchased 14
December 1960.

117

SHOOTING THE RAPIDS, 1861
oil on canvas, 23.2 × 28.3 cm
LR: C. Krieghoff 1861
verso, on stretcher: C M Strather [crossed
out] For Edith Strather Smith

National Archives of Canada, Ottawa,
acquired before 1934 (C-146152)

Provenance
NAC, before 1934.

Literature
BARBEAU 1934, 140; JOUVANCOURT 1971,
144 (repr.); VÉZINA 1972, (repr. fig. 51);
JOUVANCOURT 1973, facing 113 (repr.);
JOUVANCOURT 1979, 97 (repr.).

118

CANADIAN AUTUMN, VIEW ON THE
ROAD TO LAKE ST. JOHN, 1862
oil on canvas, 56.8 × 88.4 cm
LL: C. Krieghoff/Quebec 1862

Private collection

Provenance
John S. Budden, Quebec City; James
Gibb, Quebec City; Mrs. David A. Ross
(widow of J. Gibb), Quebec City, presumably by succession; Frank W. Ross (no
relation), Quebec City, gift in lieu of payment before May 1923; F. Donald Ross
(son of F.W. Ross), Quebec City, by succession; private collection.

Literature
NOTMAN 1865, plate 35, as "Canadian
Autumn, View on the Road to Lake St.

John; SMALL 1866, facing 130, as "Indian
Camp on the Road to Lake St. John";
BARBEAU 1934, 137.

119

ON LAKE LAURENT, 1863
oil on canvas, 36.2 × 54.0 cm
LR: C Krieghoff/Quebec 1863
UR, under liner: On Lake Laurent

The Thomson Collection (P-C-746)

Provenance
Unidentified owner, Paris, France;
Kenneth R. Thomson, Toronto, purchased for $110,000 at auction, Sotheby's
(Toronto), Important Canadian Art, 7
November 1989, lot 80A (repr.).

Quebec 1853–63

Representations of Habitants

120

WINTER SCENE, BLIZZARD, 1856
oil on canvas, 33.6 × 46.1 cm
LL: C Krieghoff/Quebec 56

The Thomson Collection (P-C-632)

Provenance
Possibly Thomas F. Bell, Philadelphia,
1857; Genevieve C. Hallowell,
Norristown, Pennsylvania; Kenneth R.
Thomson, Toronto, purchased 30 August
1984.

Exhibitions
Possibly Philadelphia, Pennsylvania
Academy of Fine Arts, 1857, Thirty-fourth
Annual Exhibition, no. 7, as "Winter
Scene," or no. 48, as "Winter Scene."

121

THE HABITANT FARM, 1856
oil on canvas, 61.0 × 91.5 cm
LR: C. Krieghoff/Quebec 1856

National Gallery of Canada, Ottawa, gift
of Gordon C. Edwards, Ottawa, 1923, in
memory of Senator and Mrs. W.C.
Edwards (2036)

Provenance
Possibly Thomas & Co., Philadelphia;
unidentified owner, New York; Watson Art
Galleries, Montreal; Gordon C. Edwards,
Ottawa, purchased 1916; NGC, gift, 1923.

Exhibitions
INAUGURAL EXHIBITION AGT 1926, no. 191;
KRIEGHOFF AGT 1934, no. 272; KRIEGHOFF
NGC/AAM 1934, no. 93; London, Western
Art League, London Art Museum, 9
January–3 February 1942, Milestones of
Canadian Art, no. 4; New Haven,
Connecticut, Yale University Art Gallery,
11 March–16 April 1944, Canadian Art
1760–1943; Richmond, Virginia, Virginia
Museum of Fine Arts, 17 February–20
March 1949, Painters of Canada, no. 45;
FRENCH IN AMERICA 1951, no. 88;
KRIEGHOFF MORGAN 1952; Bordeaux,
Musée Bordeaux, 1 May–31 July 1962, L'Art
au Canada, no. 19; KRIEGHOFF WILLISTEAD
1963, no. 21; COLONIAL PAINTING 1964, no.
30; KRIEGHOFF MQ 1971, no. 105.

Literature
Albert H. Robson, Canadian Landscape
Painters (Toronto: Ryerson Press, 1932),
21, (repr.); Eric Brown, "Canada's
National Painters," Studio, 103 no. 471
(June 1932), 323 (repr.); BARBEAU 1934,
43, facing 54 (repr.), 56, 106; ROBSON
1937, 24, [25] (repr.); Paul Duval,
"Canada's Two 'K's,'" Empire Digest 10, no.
5 (May 1948): 12 (repr.); "The Habitant
Farm ...," Gazette (Montreal), 12 January
1952, 18, (repr.); Arthur Lismer,
"Cornelius Krieghoff, 'Canadian Artist
Number One,'" Sun Life Review (January
1954): 15 (repr.); The Arts in Canada
(Ottawa: Department of Citizenship and
Immigration, 1957), 38 (repr.); NGC CAT
1960, 162 (repr.); Gilberte Martin-Méry,
L'Art au Canada (ex. cat.) (Bordeaux: Musée
Bordeaux, 1962), (repr. plate X); J. Russell
Harper, A Century of Colonial Painting: The

Seven Years War to Confederation (ex. cat.)
(Ottawa: National Gallery of Canada,
1964), 29 (repr.); HUBBARD 1963, 59;
JOUVANCOURT 1971 and JOUVANCOURT 1973,
63 (repr.); JUNEAU 1971, 58 (repr.); VÉZINA
1972, [52] (repr.), (repr. fig. 58);
Raymond Vézina, "Attitude esthétique de
Cornelius Krieghoff au sein de la tradition picturale canadienne-française,"
RACAR 1, no. 1 (1974): 54 (repr.); HARPER
FARM 1977, (repr.); Peter Mellen,
Landmarks of Canadian Art (Toronto:
McClelland and Stewart, 1978), 120, 121
(repr.); Jacques de Roussan, "Sur une
peinture de Krieghoff," L'Information médicale et paramédicale (Montreal) 30, no. 13
(16 May 1978), (repr.); HARPER 1979, 83
(repr.), 84, 88; JOUVANCOURT 1979, 101
(repr.); Alan E. Samuel et al., Treasures of
Canada (Toronto: Samuel-Stevens, 1980),
187 (repr.); NGC CAT 1994, 387 (repr.).

122

SETTLER'S LOG HOUSE, 1856
oil on canvas, 62.2 × 92.7 cm
LL: C Krieghoff/Quebec 1856

Art Gallery of Ontario, Toronto, purchased with funds from the Reuben Wells
Leonard Estate, Toronto, 1937 (2413)

Provenance
Probably Watson Art Galleries, Montreal;
R.W. Reford, Montreal, purchased before
1920; AGO, purchased through Percy F.
Godenrath, Ottawa, 1937.

Exhibitions
KRIEGHOFF AGT 1934, no. 236; KRIEGHOFF
NGC/AAM 1934, no. 114; DEVELOPMENT OF
PAINTING IN CANADA 1945, no. 59;
Toronto, Sportsmen's Show, Canadian
National Exhibition, mid March 1950;
FRENCH IN AMERICA 1951, no. 90;
KRIEGHOFF MORGAN 1952; Toronto,
Canadian National Exhibition, 22
August–6 September 1952, Exhibition of
Paintings and Sculpture..., no.43; Hamilton,
Art Gallery of Hamilton, 12 December
1953–21 January 1954, Inaugural Exhibition,

no. 30; KRIEGHOFF BAG 1961, no. 15
(repr.); KRIEGHOFF WILLISTEAD 1963, no.
16; KRIEGHOFF ROM 1975.

Literature
BARBEAU 1934, 107; ROBSON 1937, 28, [29]
(repr.); BARBEAU 1948, [29] (repr.);
Harold Walker et al, *50th Anniversary,
1900–1950, Art Gallery of Toronto* (Toronto:
[Art Gallery of Toronto], 1950), 27
(repr.); KRIEGHOFF GAZETTE MONTREAL
1952; GUTTENBERG 1954, 106; T.R.
MacDonald, *Inaugural Exhibition* (ex. cat.)
(Hamilton: Art Gallery of Hamilton,
1953), (repr.); Art Gallery of Toronto,
Painting and Sculpture (Toronto: Art Gallery
of Toronto, 1959), 33 (repr. fig. 17);
COOKE 1961, (repr. no. 15); AGO CAN COLL
1970, 234 (repr.); JOUVANCOURT 1971 and
JOUVANCOURT 1973, 67 (repr.);
JOUVANCOURT 1979, 101 (repr.); Ian
Trowell, "'Unquestionably Canadian,'"
Christian Science Monitor, 6–12 October
1986, (repr.); Art Gallery of Ontario,
Selected Works (Toronto: Art Gallery of
Ontario, 1990), 244 (repr.).

123

AFTER THE BALL, CHEZ JOLIFOU,
1856
oil on canvas, 61.0 × 91.5 cm
LR: C Krieghoff./Quebec 1856

The Thomson Collection (P-C-671)

Provenance
Possibly Thomas & Co., Philadelphia;
possibly W.W. Adams, Philadelphia, 1856;
Slater family, Philadelphia; George Slater,
Montreal, presumably by succession; Ward
C. Pitfield, Cartierville, Quebec, by January
1934; Grace Pitfield (wife of W.C. Pitfield),
by succession; Kenneth R. Thomson,
Toronto, purchased from the estate of
Grace Pitfield 9 February 1987.

Exhibitions
KRIEGHOFF AGT 1934, no. 229; as "After
the Ball Jolifoux" [sic]; KRIEGHOFF
NGC/AAM 1934, no. 102; KRIEGHOFF
MORGAN 1952; ELEVEN ARTISTS 1960, no. 6;
KRIEGHOFF BAG 1961, no 14.

Literature
BARBEAU CGJ 1934, 109 (repr.); BARBEAU
RSC 1934, [120] (repr.); CHAUVIN 1934, 6
(repr.); BARBEAU 1934, frontispiece
(repr.), 43, 44, 47, 109; BARBEAU 1936,
120–21 (repr.); ROBSON 1937, 22, [23]
(repr.); McINNIS 1941, (repr.); BARBEAU
1948, facing 13 (repr.); KRIEGHOFF STAR
MONTREAL 1952; GUTTENBERG 1954,
104–105; JOUVANCOURT 1971, facing 44
(repr.), 106; JOUVANCOURT 1973, facing 34
(repr.), 106; REID 1973, 66; HARPER 1979,
70; JOUVANCOURT 1979, 37 (repr.), 168,
170; REID 1988, 63.

124

BREAKING UP OF A COUNTRY BALL
IN CANADA, EARLY MORNING, 1857
oil on canvas, 61.2 × 91.4 cm
LL: C. Krieghoff/Quebec 1857
verso, on lining on canvas: The Morning
after a Merrymaking/in Lower Canada/C.
Kreighoff [sic] 1857

The Thomson Collection (P-C-304)

Provenance
Thomas F. Bell, Philadelphia; undisclosed
owner, New York City; C. Wilson
Spaulding, Cohocton, New York, gift c.
1935; Kenneth R. Thomson, purchased 8
April 1975.

Exhibitions
Philadelphia, Pennsylvania Academy of
the Fine Arts, end of April–May 1858,
Thirty-fifth Annual Exhibition, no. 178, as
"Breaking up of a Country Ball in
Canada, Early Morning."

Literature
HARPER 1979, frontispiece (repr.), 70.

125

PLAYTIME, VILLAGE SCHOOL, c. 1857
oil on canvas, 63.5 × 91.5 cm
LR: C Krieghoff

The Thomson Collection (P-C-174)

Provenance
Possibly Thomas & Co., Philadelphia;
Thomas F. Bell, Philadelphia; Slater fami-
ly, Philadelphia; George Slater, Montreal,
presumably by succession; Johnson Art
Galleries, Montreal; Ward C. Pitfield,
Montreal, purchased before January 1934;
Grace Pitfield (wife of W.C. Pitfield),
Montreal, by succession; Walter
Klinkhoff Gallery, Montreal, purchased
probably 1971; Kenneth R. Thomson,
Toronto, purchased through Leslie W.
Lewis, Montreal, 12 April 1971.

Exhibitions
Philadelphia, Pennsylvania Academy of
the Fine Arts, May 1858, *Thirty-fifth Annual
Exhibition*, no. 261, as "Snow Scene
(School Breaking Up)"; KRIEGHOFF AGT
1934, no. 230; KRIEGHOFF NGC/AAM 1934,
no. 103; KRIEGHOFF MORGAN 1952; ELEVEN
ARTISTS 1960, no. 5; Mexico City, Museo
Nacional de Arte Moderno–Instituto
Nacional de Bellas Artes–S E P, November
1960, *Arte Canadiense*, no. 88; KRIEGHOFF
BAG 1961, no 16.

Literature
BARBEAU CGJ 1934, 112 (repr.); BARBEAU
1934, facing 34 (repr.), 43–44, 47–48,
51–52, 106–107; CHAUVIN 1934, 6 (repr.);
BARBEAU 1936, 141 (repr.); ROBSON 1937,
20, [21] (repr.); BARBEAU 1948, frontispiece (repr.); GUTTENBERG 1954, 104;
MACLEAN'S 1955, 14–15 (repr.), portfolio
(repr. plate VIII); KRIEGHOFF GAZETTE
MONTREAL 1952; JOUVANCOURT 1971, facing 52, (repr.); JOUVANCOURT 1973, facing
35 (repr.); JOUVANCOURT 1979, 55 (repr.).

126

BRINGING IN THE DEER, c. 1859
oil on canvas, 52.0 × 84.5 cm
LL: C Krieghoff

The Thomson Collection (P-C-413)

Provenance
Unidentified owner, possibly Ireland;
Watson Art Galleries, Montreal; Harry A.
Norton, Ayer's Cliff, Quebec, purchased
for $2,000 15 November 1931; Miss Helen
Norton, Ayer's Cliff, presumably by suc-
cession, before September 1960; Mr. and
Mrs. David Molson, Montreal; G. Blair
Laing, Toronto; Kenneth. R. Thomson,
Toronto, purchased 28 April 1977.

Exhibitions
KRIEGHOFF NGC/AAM 1934, no. 95; ELEVEN
ARTISTS 1960, no. 9; TREASURES 1962.

Literature
BARBEAU 1934, 108; JOUVANCOURT 1971,
facing 68 (repr.); JOUVANCOURT 1973, facing 53 (repr.); HARPER 1979, 85 (repr.);
JOUVANCOURT 1979, 137 (repr.).

127

HABITANTS RETURNING FROM
TOWN, c. 1860
oil on canvas, 33.0 × 45.8 cm
LL: C Krieghoff./Quebec

The Thomson Collection (P-C-234)

Provenance
Watson Art Galleries, Montreal, before
December 1920; Lawrence Hart,
Washington, D.C.; Walter Klinkhoff,
Montreal, purchased probably 1972;
Kenneth R. Thomson, Toronto, pur-
chased through Leslie W. Lewis, Toronto,
21 June 1972.

128

A WINTER INCIDENT, c. 1860
oil on canvas, 33.0 × 45.8 cm
LR: CKrieghoff

The Thomson Collection (P-C-933)

Provenance
Unidentified owner, near Kingston, Ontario; unidentified owner, New Hampshire, by succession; Kenneth R. Thomson, purchased for $70,000 at auction, Sotheby's (Toronto), *Important Canadian Art*, 15 November 1995, lot 88 (repr.).

129

BARGAINING FOR A LOAD OF WOOD, 1860
oil on canvas, 36.2 × 47.7 cm
LR: C Krieghoff
verso, on canvas: Fr. Canadians. Bargaining for a Load of Wood/Quebec 1860 (now covered by lining)

The Thomson Collection (P-C-242)

Provenance
A. Norton Francis, Westmount, Quebec; Walter Klinkhoff Gallery, Montreal, purchased 1972; Kenneth R. Thomson, Toronto, purchased through Leslie W. Lewis, Montreal, 13 November 1972.

130

CLEARING LAND NEAR THE ST. MAURICE RIVER, 1860
oil on canvas, 61.3 × 82.0 cm
LL: C Krieghoff/Quebec 1860

The Thomson Collection (P-C-270)

Provenance
W.H. Stewart, Philadelphia; John Wanamaker, Philadelphia; Bethany Collegiate Presbyterian Church, Philadelphia, bequest 1922; Watson Art Galleries, Montreal, purchased through John Levy, New York, by December 1948; Mrs. M.E. Ramsay, Westmount; Walter Klinkhoff Gallery, Montreal, 1974; Kenneth R. Thomson, Toronto, purchased 29 May 1974.

Exhibitions
Probably Philadelphia, Pennsylvania Academy of the Fine Arts, May 1860, *Thirty-seventh Annual Exhibition*, no. 309, as "French Canadians clearing Land and burning Stumps near the St. Maurice, Lower Canada."

131

HABITANTS ON A TRIP TO TOWN, 1861
oil on canvas, 32.3 × 45.9 cm
LR: C Krieghoff/Quebec 1861

The Thomson Collection (P-C-64)

Provenance
Possibly Honourable John Sharples, Quebec City; possibly Lt. Col. F. Stanton, Quebec City, 1913; Continental Galleries, Montreal, before 12 December 1957; Kenneth R. Thomson, Toronto, purchased c. April 1970.

Literature
Possibly BARBEAU 1934, 112, as "Winter Scene"; JOUVANCOURT 1971 and JOUVANCOURT 1973, 132 (repr.); JOUVANCOURT 1979, 77 (repr.).

132

SLEIGH RACE ACROSS THE ICE, 1861
oil on canvas, 36.2 × 53.6 cm
LR: C Krieghoff/Quebec 1861

Montreal Museum of Fine Arts, Lady Allan Bequest, 1958 (1958.1177)

Provenance
Lady Marguerite E. Allan, Montreal; MMFA, bequest, 1958

Exhibitions
KRIEGHOFF WILLISTEAD 1963, no. 32; PAINTER AND THE NEW WORLD 1967, no. 256 (repr.); Montreal, Montreal Museum of Fine Arts, 25 November–5 December 1971, *Noël 71*; MACAMIC TO MONTREAL 1974; WINTER KING 1988, no. 22.

Literature
"Recent Acquisitions by Canadian Galleries and Museums," *Canadian Art* 16, no. 1 (February 1959): 45 (repr.); MMFA

CAT 1960, 24; *Montreal Museum of Fine Arts, Painting, Sculpture, Decorative Arts* (Montreal: Montreal Museum of Fine Arts, 1960), 138, (repr.); Anne-Marie Le Moyne, "Kane et Krieghoff," L'Œil, no. 178 (April 1967): 27 (repr.); CARTER 1967, (repr. no. 256); JOUVANCOURT 1971 and JOUVANCOURT 1973, 110 (repr.); VÉZINA 1972, (repr. fig. 61); CAVELL/REID 1988, 21 (repr.).

133

LOG CABIN, WINTER SCENE, LAKE ST. CHARLES, c. 1862
oil on canvas, 45.7 × 63.5 cm
LR: CKrieghoff.

The Thomson Collection (P-C-235)

Provenance
Nadeau family, Quebec City, purchased from the artist; René Nadeau, Quebec City, presumably by succession, until at least c. June 1944; Kenneth R. Thomson, Toronto, purchased through Leslie W. Lewis, Montreal, and Warda Drummond, Montreal, 10 July 1972.

Literature
HARPER 1979, 78, 82 (repr.), 83.

134

CROSSING CATTLE FOR LUMBERING PURPOSES, 1862
oil on canvas, 28.2 × 46.7 cm
LR: C Krieghoff 62
verso, on lower stretcher: Crossing Cattle for Lumbring purposes

McCord Museum of Canadian History, Montreal, bequest of Arnold Wainwright, Q.C., 1967 (M967.100.2)

Provenance
Unidentified Canadian family, England; Dominion Gallery, Montreal, 24 October 1951; Arnold Wainwright, Montreal, purchased before May 1962; MMCH, bequest, 1967.

Exhibitions
EVERYMAN'S CANADA 1962, no. 33; KRIEGHOFF MQ 1971, no. 85.

Literature
FAIRCHILD 1908, 73, as "Lumberer's Ferry"; HARPER 1962, 33 (repr.); JUNEAU 1971, 50 (repr.); VÉZINA 1972, (repr. fig. 48); HARPER 1979, 99 (repr.).

135

LOG HUT ON THE ST. MAURICE, 1862
oil on canvas, 33.4 × 46.5 cm
LR: CKrieghoff 62
verso, on canvas LR: On the St. Maurice

McCord Museum of Canadian History, Montreal, bequest of Arnold Wainwright, Q.C., 1967 (M967.100.15)

Provenance
John S. Budden, Quebec City; Lt. Col. J.F. Turnbull, Quebec City; Mrs. Lorenzo Evans, Quebec City, purchased by June 1917; Mrs. Florence Evans (daughter-in-law of Mrs. Lorenzo Evans) presumably by succession, c. 1944; Watson Art Galleries, Montreal, purchased for $2,500 23 February 1957; Roland Thérien, Outremont, purchased for $4,500 4 June 1957; Arnold Wainwright, Montreal, before May 1962; MMCH, bequest, 1967.

Exhibitions
EVERYMAN'S CANADA 1962, no. 32; KRIEGHOFF MQ 1971, no. 103.

Literature
NOTMAN 1865, plate 85, as "Log Hut on the St. Maurice"; BARBEAU 1934, 108; JUNEAU 1971, 58 (repr.); VÉZINA 1972, (repr. fig. 86), VÉZINA 1974, 57 (repr. detail).

136

CHEATING THE TOLL MAN, c. 1863
oil on canvas, 30.1 × 52.8 cm
LL: C Krieghoff

Montreal Museum of Fine Arts, George B. Cramp Bequest, 1914 (1914.94)

Provenance
George B. Cramp, Montreal; MMFA, bequest, 1914.

Exhibitions
KRIEGHOFF AGT 1934, no. 228, as "Toll Bar"; KRIEGHOFF NGC/AAM 1934, no. 2; Toronto, Canadian National Exhibition, 24 August–8 September 1934, *English Painting, Miniatures, and Sculpture; Canadian Painting and Sculpture …*, no. 276; KRIEGHOFF MORGAN 1952; MILESTONES 1961; KRIEGHOFF BAG 1961, no. 42 (repr.); PAINTER AND THE NEW WORLD 1967, no. 266 (repr.); KRIEGHOFF MQ 1971, no. 116 (repr.); MACAMIC TO MONTREAL 1974; Montreal, Galerie A, 12 October– 4 November 1977, *Winters of Yesteryear*; Montreal, Montreal Museum of Fine Arts, 18 December 1979–16 March 1980, *Cheating the Toll Man*; La Rochelle, France, Le Musée du Nouveau Monde, 15 June–15 July 1982, *Une autre amérique*, no. 167.

Literature
BARBEAU 1934, 112; KRIEGHOFF STAR MONTREAL 1952; MMFA CAT 1960, 23; JOUVANCOURT 1971 and JOUVANCOURT 1973, 20 (repr.); JUNEAU 1971, 72 (repr.); VÉZINA 1972, [167] (repr.); Alain Parent, *Une autre Amérique* (ex. cat.) (La Rochelle, France: Le Musée du Nouveau Monde, 1982), 114 (repr.); Luc Chartrand, "C'est la faute à l'histoire!," *L'actualité* 23, no. 17 (1 November 1998): 38–39, (repr.)

137

WINTER IN LAVAL MOUNTAINS NEAR QUEBEC (THE CRACK IN THE ICE), 1863
oil on canvas, 61.5 × 92.0 cm
LR: C Krieghoff/Quebec 63

The Thomson Collection (P-C-633)

Provenance
John S. Budden, Quebec City; James Gibb, Quebec City; Mrs. David A. Ross (widow

of J. Gibb), Quebec City, presumably by succession; John Theodore Ross (no relation), Sillery, Quebec, gift in lieu of payment by May 1923; Frances S. Stein (daughter of J.T. Ross), Victoria, B.C., gift before 1954; Kenneth R. Thomson, Toronto, purchased through Robert G. Ross, Montreal, 9 October 1984.

Exhibitions
Possibly EXPOSITION DE PEINTURES 1920; KRIEGHOFF NGC/AAM 1934, no. 138.

Literature
NOTMAN 1865, plate 45, as "Winter in Laval Mountains near Quebec"; BARBEAU 1934, 108.

138

HABITANT RETURNING FROM MARKET, 1863
oil on canvas, 44.2 × 64.6 cm
LR: C Krieghoff/1863

The Thomson Collection (P-C-450)

Provenance
Peter Arnold Shaw, Quebec City, from the artist; Harold Shaw (son of P.A. Shaw), Winnipeg, presumably by succession, by 1934; Mrs. D.B.W. Walcot (niece of H. Shaw), Montreal, or Mrs. H.L. Rutherfurd (niece of H. Shaw), Montreal, presumably by succession; Walter Klinkhoff Gallery, Montreal, purchased November 1977; Kenneth R. Thomson, Toronto, purchased 25 November 1977.

Literature
BARBEAU 1934, 107.

139

SETTLER'S HOUSE, LAVAL, 1863
oil on canvas, 33.0 × 45.6 cm
LL: C Krieghoff/1863
LR spandrel: In Laval

The Thomson Collection (P-C-673)

Provenance
Ward C. Pitfield, Cartierville, Quebec, before 1934; Grace Pitfield (wife of W.C.

Pitfield), Montreal, by succession; Kenneth R. Thomson, Toronto, purchased from the estate of Grace Pitfield 9 February 1987.

Exhibitions
KRIEGHOFF BAG 1961, no. 36.

Literature
BARBEAU 1934, 108.

Europe 1864–70

140

SILLERY COVE, QUEBEC, c. 1864
oil on canvas; 93.2 × 116.0 cm
LL: C Krieghoff. Quebec.

The Thomson Collection (P-C-585)

Provenance
John Ogilvy, Montreal, purchased from the artist; Alexander Pringle, Montreal, purchase; unnamed owners (A. Pringle's former cook and maid), Chateauguay, Quebec, by succession c. 1920; Mrs. Roberta Pringle, Montreal, by succession 1947; Watson Art Galleries, Montreal, purchased for $1,500 between 19 April and 12 May 1949; John A. MacAulay, Winnipeg, purchased for $4,500 14 January 1952; Carol (MacAulay) Taylor (daughter of J.A. MacAulay), Santa Barbara, California, by succession 1979; Kenneth R. Thomson, Toronto, purchased 19 March 1982.

Exhibitions
Ottawa, National Gallery of Canada, 15 April–20 May 1954; Toronto, Art Gallery of Toronto, 28 May–13 June 1954. *Paintings from the collection of John A. MacAulay, Q.C.*, no. 39; KRIEGHOFF BAG 1961, no. 26; THREE HUNDRED YEARS 1967, no. 118.

Literature
"Paris Exhibition of 1867—Contributions from Lower Canada," *Gazette* (Montreal), 15 December 1866, 2; "Quebec and the

Paris Exhibition," *Mercury* (Quebec City), 18 December 1866, 3; "Le tableau de M. Kreighoff [sic] …", *Journal de Québec* (Quebec City), 21 May 1867, 2; Abbé H.-A. Scott, *Grands Anniversaires: Souvenirs historiques et pensées utiles* (Québec: Imp. et Rel. de L'Action Sociale Ltée, 1919), 297- 99; BARBEAU 1934, 116, as "A Timber Depot at Quebec"; Ferdinand Eckhardt, *Paintings from the Collection of John A. MacAulay, Q.C.* (ex. cat.) (Ottawa: National Gallery of Canada, 1954), (repr. no. 39); R.H. Hubbard, ed., *An Anthology of Canadian Art* (Toronto: University of Toronto Press, 1960), (repr. plate 46); BARBEAU 1962, (repr. plate 27); ROMBOUT 1962, 45 (repr.), 46; HUBBARD/OSTIGUY 1967, 72, 73 (repr.); JOUVANCOURT 1979, 163 (repr.).

141

CHIPPEWA INDIANS AT LAKE HURON, 1864
oil on canvas. 64.6 × 90.3 cm
LL: C. Krieghoff/1864
verso, across top of frame: Autumn./Chipewa [sic] Indians/Lake Huron/Canada (now covered by lining)

The Collection of Power Corporation of Canada, Montreal

Provenance
William R. Watson Galleries, Montreal; Helen Norton, Coaticook, Quebec, purchased for $2,500 21 September 1933; Walter Klinkhoff Gallery, Montreal, purchased probably 1968; PCC, purchase, 1968.

Exhibitions
MAÎTRES CANADIENS 1989, no. 37.

Literature
BARBEAU 1934, 137, as "Midday Rest" or "Indians camping at foot of big rock"; JOUVANCOURT 1971, facing 118 (repr.), 133; JOUVANCOURT 1973, facing 98 (repr.), 133; HARPER 1979, 134 (repr.); JOUVANCOURT 1979, 211, 215 (repr.).

142

SPILL MY MILK, 1865
oil on canvas, 35.5 × 55.0 cm
LL: C Krieghoff. 1865

The Thomson Collection (P-C-115)

Provenance
William Scott, Montreal, by February 1867; unidentified owner, United States; Leslie W. Lewis, Hayne's Gallery, Toronto, 1948; unidentified owner, Toronto, purchased at auction, Ward-Price (Toronto), 29 November–3 December 1948; Kenneth R. Thomson, Toronto, purchased through Leslie W. Lewis, Toronto, and John Britnell Art Galleries, Toronto, for $13,000 at auction, Sotheby's (Toronto), *Important Canadian Paintings, Drawings, Watercolours and Prints of the 19th and 20th Centuries*, 25–27 May 1970, lot 51 (repr.).

Exhibitions
Montreal, Art Association of Montreal, 5 February 1867, *Fourth Exhibition, Oil and Water Colour Paintings, Statuary Bronzes, and other works of art …*, no. 82, as "Spill my milk."

Literature
"An Important Krieghoff Comes To Light," (advertisement for Ward-Price auction), *Globe and Mail* (Toronto), 26 November 1948, 3 (repr., as "The Habitant Farm: Winter"); JOUVANCOURT 1971 and JOUVANCOURT 1973, 137 (repr.); HARPER FARM 1977, 25 (repr.); HARPER 1979, 88, 90 (repr.), 162; JOUVANCOURT 1979, 95 (repr.).

143

William Notman
NOTMAN'S PHOTOGRAPHIC SELECTIONS, second series, 1865

Toronto and Quebec
CORNELIUS KRIEGHOFF'S DEATH OF THE MOOSE AT SUNSET. LAKE FAMINE SOUTH OF QUEBEC, plate 31
albumen print, 14.1 × 21.3 cm (image)

Ottawa, Vancouver, and Montreal
CORNELIUS KRIEGHOFF'S TRACKING THE MOOSE, LAKE FAMINE, SOUTH OF QUEBEC, plate 30
albumen print, 14.2 × 21.1 cm (image)

Art Gallery of Ontario, Toronto, purchased 1983 (83/315)

144

THE CARIBOU HUNTERS, 1866
oil on canvas laid on board, 33.0 × 45.7 cm
LR: C Krieghoff/1866

The Thomson Collection (P-C-745)

Provenance
Thomas A. McGinnis, Kingston, Ontario; Watson Art Galleries, Montreal, in exchange for a painting by Frederick Verner, November 1952; Dr. S.C. Duffy, Montreal, purchased for $1,000 31 October 1953; Kenneth R. Thomson, Toronto, purchased for $140,000 at Sotheby's (Toronto), *Important Canadian Art*, 7 November 1989, lot 69 (repr.).

145

WINTER SCENE IN THE LAURENTIANS—THE LAVAL RIVER, 1867
oil on canvas, 68.6 × 91.5 cm
LL: CKrieghoff 1867

The Thomson Collection (P-C-108)

Provenance
W. Darling Campbell, Quebec City; George Stephen (later Lord Mount Stephen); Lady Northcote (adopted daughter of Lord Mount Stephen), London, England, presumably by succession; Col. George Stephen Cantlie (nephew of Lord Mount Stephen), Montreal, by succession 1934; probably Walter Klinkhoff Gallery, Montreal, purchased probably 1970; Leslie W. Lewis,

Toronto, 1970; Kenneth R. Thomson, Toronto, purchased 26 January 1970.

Literature
HARPER 1979, 152 (repr.), 153.

146

CALLING MOOSE, "HURON" INDIAN, c. 1868

Toronto and Quebec
chromolithograph and varnish on board, 27.6 × 22.7 cm (image)

McCord Museum of Canadian History, Montreal, purchased 1977 (M977.90.1)

Ottawa, Vancouver, and Montreal
chromolithograph and varnish on paper on board, 27.9 × 22.8 cm (image)

National Archives of Canada, Ottawa, purchased 1922 (C-013470)

147

IN DOUBT OF TRACK, "IROQUOIS" INDIAN, c. 1868

Toronto and Quebec
chromolithograph and varnish on board, 27.4 × 22.7 cm (image)

McCord Museum of Canadian History, Montreal, purchased 1977 (M977.90.2)

Ottawa, Vancouver, and Montreal
chromolithograph on paper on board, 27.4 × 22.9 cm (image)

National Archives of Canada, Ottawa, acquired before 1930 (C-013471)

148

ALBUM OF CARTE-DE-VISITE PHOTOS, c. 1870

Toronto and Quebec
CORNELIUS KRIEGHOFF'S LAKE ST. CHARLES: TWO CANOES TIED TOGETHER (p. 19, Moulin) and VIEWING FROM STONE BLOCK,

LAKE MEMPHREMAGOG (p. 20, photographer unknown)
hand-coloured albumen prints, p. 19: 5.7 × 9.2 cm, p. 20: 5.6 × 8.8 cm

Ottawa, Vancouver, and Montreal
CORNELIUS KRIEGHOFF'S UNTITLED (3 FIGURES WITH A TOBOGGAN) (p. 5, Moulin) and SPEARING SALMON BY TORCHLIGHT (p. 6, Moulin)
hand-coloured albumen prints, p. 5: 5.8 × 8.8 cm, p. 6: 5.7 × 9.3 cm

The Thomson Collection (P-C-680)

Quebec 1870–72

149

THE NEW YEAR'S DAY PARADE, 1871
oil on canvas, 64.3 × 109.2 cm
LL: CKrieghoff

The Collection of Power Corporation of Canada, Montreal

Provenance
Robert Reford, Montreal, by January 1934; Canada Steamship Lines; PCC, purchase, 1981.

Exhibitions
KRIEGHOFF AGT 1934, no. 235; KRIEGHOFF NGC/AAM 1934, no. 113; CANADIANA 1942, no. 145; Quebec City, Museum of the Province of Quebec, 10 December 1942–31 January 1943, *Le Vieux Québec— Exhibition of Canadiana*, no. 122.

Literature
BARBEAU STAR MONTREAL 1934 (repr.); BARBEAU 1934, 47, 109; CHAUVIN 1934, 7 (repr.); BARBEAU 1936, 122 (repr.); BARBEAU 1948, 21 (repr.); BARBEAU 1962, (repr. plate 24); JOUVANCOURT 1971, 104, facing 128 (repr.); JOUVANCOURT 1973, 104, facing verso 111(repr.); HARPER 1979, 159 (repr.); JOUVANCOURT 1979, 75 (repr.), 162.

150

J.B. JOLIFOU, AUBERGISTE, 1871
oil on canvas, 55.9 × 92.1 cm
LL: CKrieghoff/1871

The Thomson Collection (P-C-431)

Provenance
Slater family, Philadelphia; George Slater, Montreal, presumably by succession; Johnson Art Galleries, Montreal; Ward C. Pitfield, Montreal, before January 1934; Grace Pitfield (wife of W.C. Pitfield), Montreal, by succession; Kenneth R. Thomson, Toronto, purchased 13 July 1977.

Exhibitions
KRIEGHOFF AGT 1934, no. 231, as "J.B. Jolifoux"; ELEVEN ARTISTS 1960, no. 8; KRIEGHOFF BAG 1961, no. 40;

Literature
BARBEAU 1934, 47, facing 62 (repr.), 109; COOKE 1961, (repr. no. 40); Hugh MacLennan, "Canada," American Heritage (December 1965), 32, (repr. detail); HARPER 1966, 131 (repr.); JOUVANCOURT 1971 and JOUVANCOURT 1973, 104, 141, 142 (repr.); HARPER 1977, 124 (repr.), 131; JOUVANCOURT 1979, 115 (repr.), 162, 218.

151

RETURN FROM THE HUNT, 1871
oil on canvas, 57.2 × 94.0 cm
LR: C Krieghoff/Quebec 71

The Thomson Collection (P-C-316)

Provenance
M.J. Boylen, Toronto; Murphy Corporation Limited, Nassau, Bahamas; Kenneth R. Thomson, Toronto, purchased 4 September 1975.

Exhibitions
Quebec City, Provincial Exhibition, beginning 12 September 1871; KRIEGHOFF CNE 1955, no. 7, as "Return from the Hunt"; KRIEGHOFF WIMODAUSIS 1957; KRIEGHOFF BAG 1961, no. 38.

Literature
"The Fine Arts," Gazette (Quebec City), 13 September 1871, as "Returning from Hunting"; MACLEAN'S 1955: 3 (repr. cropped, as "Habitant Farm"), portfolio (repr. cropped plate VII); CURATOR 1961; COOKE 1961, (repr. no. 38).

152

THE BLACKSMITH'S SHOP, 1871
oil on canvas, 56.5 × 92.1 cm
LL: C. Krieghoff 1871

Art Gallery of Ontario, Toronto, gift of Mrs. J.H. Mitchell, Toronto, in memory of her mother, Margaret Lewis Gooderham, 1951 (50/13)

Provenance
Mr. Lewis; George Lewis (nephew of Mr. Lewis), Toronto; Margaret (Lewis) Gooderham (sister of G. Lewis), gift; Ada (Gooderham) Grant-Suttie (daughter of M. Gooderham), Toronto, by succession 1933; Mrs. James H. (Eva C. Gooderham) Mitchell (sister of A. Grant-Suttie), by succession before 1949; AGO, gift, 1951.

Exhibitions
KRIEGHOFF AGT 1934, no. 209; KRIEGHOFF NGC/AAM 1934, no. 38; Toronto, Art Gallery of Toronto, November 1935, Loan Exhibition of Paintings Celebrating the Opening of the Margaret Eaton Gallery and the East Gallery, no. 118; KRIEGHOFF MORGAN 1952; KRIEGHOFF BAG 1961, no. 39; KRIEGHOFF WILLISTEAD 1963, no. 46; KRIEGHOFF ROM 1975; Montreal, Expo 67 (Quebec Pavilion), 1967; WINTER KING 1988, no. 32.

Literature
BARBEAU 1934, facing 50 (repr.), 60, 115; CHAUVIN 1934, 7 (repr.); ROBSON 1937, 30, [31] (repr.); "Paintings by Krieghoff Showing at Morgan's," Gazette (Montreal), 17 January 1952, 17; COOKE 1961, (repr. no. 39); Elizabeth Kilbourn et al., Great Canadian Painting: A Century of Art ([Toronto]: Canadian Centennial Publishing Co. Ltd., 1966), 6–7 (repr.); AGO CAN COLL 1970, 235–36 (repr); JOUVANCOURT 1971, preceding 127 (repr.); JOUVANCOURT 1973, facing 99 (repr.); HARPER 1979, 161 (repr.), 163; JOUVANCOURT 1979, 75 (repr.); CAVELL/REID 1988, 28–29 (repr.).

Exhibitions History

PREPARED BY ARLENE GEHMACHER

1847

Montreal, Montreal Society of Artists, mid January–mid February 1847, *Montreal Gallery of Pictures*. Included 48 paintings by Krieghoff. Catalogue checklist.

1911

Toronto, Art Museum of Toronto, 24 January–22 February 1911, *Loan Collection of Paintings by Deceased Canadian Artists*. Included 14 paintings by Krieghoff. Catalogue checklist (nos. 135–148a) with brief biography.

1926

Toronto, Art Gallery of Toronto, 29 January–28 February 1926, *Inaugural Exhibition*. Included 16 paintings by Krieghoff. Catalogue checklist (nos. 190–205)

1934

Toronto, Art Gallery of Toronto, 5–29 January 1934, *Paintings by Cornelius Krieghoff*. Included 78 paintings. Catalogue checklist (nos. 200–277) with introductory essay by Marius Barbeau.

Ottawa, National Gallery of Canada, 15 February–March 1934; Montreal, Art Association of Montreal, 16 March–22 April 1934, *Exhibition of Paintings by Cornelius Krieghoff 1815–1872*. One hundred sixty-three works. Illustrated catalogue checklist with introductory essay by Marius Barbeau.

Toronto, Canadian National Exhibition, 24 August–8 September 1934, *English Painting, Miniatures, and Sculpture; Canadian Painting and Sculpture; English Water Colours; Graphic and Applied Art; Photography*. Included 17 paintings by Krieghoff. Catalogue checklist (nos. 262–278).

1943

Montreal, Stevens Gallery, 2 November–11 December 1943, *Exhibition of Canadiana by Cornelius Krieghoff 1812–1872*. Included approximately 28 paintings.

1951

Toronto, Royal Ontario Museum, 7 November–25 May 1952, *Oil Paintings and Watercolours of Early Canada*. Included undetermined number of paintings by Krieghoff

1952

Montreal, Henry Morgan & Co. Ltd, Antique Salon, 16–23 January 1952, [*Cornelius Krieghoff*]. Twenty paintings.

1955

Toronto, Canadian National Exhibition, 26 August–10 September 1955, *Exhibition of Paintings and Sculpture*. Included 53 paintings by Krieghoff. Catalogue checklist (nos. 1–53) with brief biography

1957

Toronto, Wimodausis Club, Casa Loma, 4–7 November 1957, Antique and Treasure Mart [*Cornelius Krieghoff Paintings from the Boylen Collection*]. Approximately 53 paintings.

1958

Toronto, Royal Ontario Museum, 22 March–4 October 1958, *Krieghoff, Kane and Bartlett: Three Pioneer Painters of Canada*. Included undetermined number of paintings by Krieghoff.

1961

Fredericton, Beaverbrook Art Gallery, September 1961, *Cornelius Krieghoff, ca. 1815–1872.* One hundred nine paintings. Illustrated catalogue checklist with introductory essay by Edwy Cooke.

1962

Toronto, Royal Ontario Museum, 25 September 1962–25 September 1963, *Treasures of Canadiana.* Included 22 paintings by Krieghoff. Illustrated catalogue checklist.

1963

Windsor, Willistead Art Gallery, 6–31 January 1963; London, London Art Museum, 7 February–11 March 1963; Hamilton, Art Gallery of Hamilton, 5–31 March 1963, *Cornelius Krieghoff ca. 1815–1872.* Fifty-five works. Checklist with brief introduction.

1966

Toronto, Laing Galleries, 5–26 February 1966, *Cornelius Krieghoff: Paintings.* Twenty-six works. Illustrated brochure checklist with brief introduction and chronology.

1968

Toronto, Royal Ontario Museum, May–15 July 1968, *Paintings by Cornelius Krieghoff.* Twenty-six paintings and lithographs.

Brantford, Ontario, Glenhyrst, the Art Gallery of Brantford, 5–29 October 1968, *The World of Cornelius Krieghoff.* Thirty-seven paintings and lithographs. Illustrated catalogue checklist with chronology and essay.

1971

Quebec City, Musée du Québec, 29 September–31 October 1971, *Cornélius Krieghoff 1815–1872.* One hundred twenty-one paintings. Illustrated catalogue checklist with introductions by Jean Soucy and André Juneau. Bibliography.

Toronto, Royal Ontario Museum, 16 December 1971–12 March 1972, *Krieghoff and His Contemporaries.* Included undetermined number of works by Krieghoff.

1972

Montreal, McCord Museum, 30 November 1972–23 April 1973; Toronto, Royal Ontario Museum, 10 May–15 August 1973; Paris, Canadian Cultural Centre, 1973; Brussels, Canadian Embassy, 1974; London, Canada House, 6 March–1 May 1974; Ottawa, Public Archives of Canada, 12 June–2 September 1974, *Scenes in Canada: C. Krieghoff, Lithograph Drawings After His Paintings of Canadian Scenery 1848–1862.* Twenty-one lithographs and paintings by Krieghoff. Illustrated catalogue checklist with introductory essay by J. Russell Harper and commentary by Peter Winkworth.

1975

Toronto, Royal Ontario Museum, 18 September–1 December 1975, *Cornelius Krieghoff (1815–1872): Genre Painter of Early Canada.* Undetermined number of paintings and lithographs.

1979

Toronto, Royal Ontario Museum, 23 February–6 June 1979, *Life in Lower Canada—Cornelius Krieghoff and His Contemporaries.* Included undetermined number of paintings and lithographs by Krieghoff. Illustrated brochure with short essay.

Montreal, Montreal Museum of Fine Arts, 18 December 1979–16 March 1980, *Highlights of the Collections, Cornelius Krieghoff: Cheating the Toll Man.* Approximately eight paintings. Photocopy handout with chronology and essay by Laurier Lacroix and Nancy Volesky.

1982

Toronto, Royal Ontario Museum, 25 September 1982–25 September 1983, *People and Places: Early Canadian Painters.* Included 20 paintings by Krieghoff.

1983

Halifax, Dalhousie Art Gallery, 22 September–30 October 1983, *Selections from the Sobey Collections: Part I: Cornelius Krieghoff (1815–1872).* Thirteen paintings. Illustrated brochure catalogue with short essay by Linda Milrod.

1985

Quebec City, Musée du Québec, 12 June–22 September 1985, *Cornélius Krieghoff et le XIXᵉ siècle: la peinture au Québec (1830–1880).* Included 15 paintings and lithographs by Krieghoff.

1994

Toronto, Royal Ontario Museum, 10 September 1994–9 July 1995; Washington, D.C., The Art Gallery of the Canadian Embassy, 5 October 1995–6 January 1996, *Krieghoff's Canada: An Artist's View 1844–1872.* Thirty paintings and lithographs. Illustrated brochure checklist with short essay by Honor de Pencier (Washington only).

Bibliography

PREPARED BY LAURA BROWN

Books

Barbeau, Marius. *Cornelius Krieghoff*. The Canadian Art Series. Toronto: The Ryerson Press, 1948.

—. *Cornelius Krieghoff*. The Gallery of Canadian Art, no. 1 [Toronto]: McClelland and Stewart Limited, 1962.

—. *Cornelius Krieghoff: Pioneer Painter of North America*. Toronto: The Macmillan Company of Canada, 1934.

—. ["On Krieghoff."] *Cornelius Krieghoff*. In *Documents in Canadian Art*, 20–28. ed. Douglas Fetherling, reprint, Peterborough: Broadview Press, 1987.

—. "Merry-Making." In *Quebec: Where Ancient France Lingers*, 116–27. Toronto: The Macmillan Company of Canada Limited, 1936.

—. "Comment on s'amusait." In *Québec: Où survit l'ancienne France*, 125–37. Quebec: Librairie Garneau Limitée, 1937 (same as English version from 1936, reprinted in *La Presse*, [Montreal], 6 June 1936, 38).

Béland, Mario, ed. *Painting in Quebec 1820–1850: New Views, New Perspectives*, 29–32, 42, 338–47, 556–61. Québec: Musée du Québec, [1992].

—. *La Peinture au Québec, 1820–1850: Nouveaux regards, nouvelles perspectives*, 28–30, 338–47, 556–61. Québec: Musée du Québec, [1991].

Colgate, William. *Canadian Art: 1820–1940*, 1–2. Toronto: The Ryerson Press, 1943.

Fairchild, G.M., Jr. *From My Quebec Scrap-Book*, 121–27, 157. Quebec: Frank Carrel, 1907.

—. *Gleanings from Quebec*, 23, 66–74. Quebec City: Frank Carrel, 1908.

Francis, Daniel. *National Dreams: Myth, Memory, and Canadian History*, 100–105. Vancouver: Arsenal Pulp Press, 1997.

Harper, J. Russell. *Cornelius Krieghoff: The Habitant Farm/La Ferme*. Masterpieces in the National Gallery of Canada, no. 9. Ottawa: National Gallery of Canada, 1977.

—. *Krieghoff*. Toronto: University of Toronto Press, 1979.

—. *Painting in Canada: A History*, 121–31. Toronto: University of Toronto Press, 1966.

—. *Painting in Canada: A History*. 2d ed., 97–106. Toronto: University of Toronto Press, 1977.

—. *La peinture au Canada des origines à nos jours*, 121–31. Québec: Presses de l'Université Laval, 1966.

Hubbard, R.H., ed. *An Anthology of Canadian Art*, 16–17. Toronto: Oxford University Press, 1960.

—. *The Development of Canadian Art*, 58–60. Ottawa: Queen's Printer ("Published for the Trustees of the National Gallery of Canada"), [1963].

—. *L'évolution de l'art au Canada*, 59–61. Ottawa: Imprimeur de la Reine, 1964.

Jouvancourt, Hugues de. *Cornelius Krieghoff*. Montréal: Éditions la Frégate, 1971 (deluxe edition).

—. *Cornelius Krieghoff*. Toronto: Musson, 1973 (trade edition).

—. *Cornelius Krieghoff*. Montréal: Stanké, 1979 (trade edition).

Keating, Tom, Frank Norman, and Geraldine Norman. *The Fake's Progress being the Cautionary History of the Master Painter & Simulator Mr. Tom Keating as Recounted with the Utmost Candour & without Fear or Favour to Mr. Frank Norman Together with a Dissertation upon the Traffic in Works of Art by Mrs. Geraldine Norman*, 106–114, 238–40. London: Hutchinson and Co. (Publishers) Ltd., 1977.

Laing, G. Blair. *Memoirs of an Art Dealer*, 233–46. Toronto: McClelland and Stewart, 1979.

—. *Memoirs of an Art Dealer 2*, 29–44, 194–95. Toronto: McClelland and Stewart, 1982.

Lesage, Jules-S. *Notes et esquisses québecoises; carnet d'un amateur*, 52–58. Quebec: Ernest Tremblay, 1925.

Lord, Barry. *The History of Painting in Canada: Toward a People's Art*, 45–50.

Toronto: NC Press, 1974.

MacTavish, Newton. *The Fine Arts in Canada*, 15–17, 19–20. Toronto: The Macmillan Company of Canada Limited, 1925.

McInnes, Graham. *Canadian Art*, 21–22, 31–34. Toronto: The Macmillan Company of Canada Limited, 1950.

Morisset, Gérard. *Peintres et tableaux*. Vol. I, *Les arts au Canada français*, 209–220. Québec: Les Éditions du Chevalet, 1936.

—. *La peinture traditionnelle au Canada français*. 141–46. *L'encyclopédie du Canada français*, Vol. 2, Ottawa: Le Cercle du Livre de France, 1960.

—. *Coup d'œil sur les arts en Nouvelle-France*, 85–87. Québec: Charrier et Dugal, 1941.

Reid, Dennis. *A Concise History of Canadian Painting*, 62–68. Toronto: Oxford University Press, 1973.

—. *A Concise History of Canadian Painting*. 2d ed., 58–66. Toronto: Oxford University Press, 1988.

Robson, Albert H. *Canadian Landscape Painters*, 28–35. Toronto: The Ryerson Press, 1932.

—. *Cornelius Krieghoff*. Toronto: The Ryerson Press, 1937 (reissued with additions, Toronto: privately printed, 1976).

Roy, Pierre-Georges. "Les peintures de Krieghoff." In *Les petites choses de notre histoire*. Vol. 4, 168–71. Lévis, Quebec, 1922.

Scott, Abbé H.-A. *Grands anniversaires: Souvenirs historiques et pensées utiles*, 298–99. Québec: Imp. et Rel. de L'Action Sociale Ltée, 1919.

Spendlove, F. St. George. *The Face of Early Canada: Pictures of Canada Which Have Helped to Make History*, 73–76. Toronto: The Ryerson Press, 1958.

Vézina, Raymond. *Cornelius Krieghoff, Peintre de mœurs (1815–1872)*. Ottawa: Editions du Pélican, 1972.

Watson, William R. *Retrospective: Recollections of a Montreal Art Dealer*, 23–29. Toronto: University of Toronto Press, 1974.

Articles

Barbeau, Marius. "Cornelius Krieghoff (1815–1871 [sic])." *The Educational Record* 70, no. 3 (July–September 1954): 151–56.

—. "Krieghoff Discovers Canada." *Canadian Geographical Journal* 8, no. 3 (March 1934): 100–113 (French version: "Krieghoff découvre le Canada." In *La Presse* [Montreal], 7 April 1934, 49, and *Proceedings and Transactions of the Royal Society of Canada*, Section 1, 3d series, vol. 28 [May 1934] 111–18.)

—. "Krieghoff, A Pioneer of Canadian Art." *Saturday Night* 49, no. 10 (13 January 1934): 2.

—. "Lauded for Perfection of Detail." *Star* (Montreal), 17 March 1934.

Beaulieu, André. "Cornelius Krieghoff: Peintre de l'instant." *Columbia* 51 (1971).

Bénézit, E. "Cornelius Krieghoff." *Dictionnaire critique et documentaire des peintres, sculpteurs, dessinateurs et graveurs... Nouvelle Édition*. Tome sixième, 316–17. Paris: Librairie Gründ, 1976.

Budden, Heber, C. Maxwell, and J.-M. LeMoine. "Cornélius Krieghoff." *Bulletin des Recherches Historiques* 1, no. 3 (March 1895): 45–46.

Chauvin, Jean. "Cornélius Krieghoff, imagier populaire." *La revue populaire* (June 1934): 6–7.

Edelstein, Hyman. "The Krieghoff 'Mystery.'" *Jewish Standard* (Toronto), 1 October 1952: 7, 15.

Gauthier, Ninon. "Le marché de Cornelius Krieghoff: Une valeur sûre qui poursuit sa montée." *Le Collectionneur* 6, no. 21 (October 1987): 51–64.

Ghent, Percy. "In the Spotlight: Welcome Kreighoff [sic] Paintings Back to Canada." *Telegram* (Toronto), 18 June 1949.

Guttenberg, A. Ch. de. "Cornelius Krieghoff." *Revue de l'Université d'Ottawa*

24, no. 1 (1954): 90–108 (reprinted in Guttenberg, A. Ch. de *Early Canadian Art and Literature*, 148–67. Vaduz, Liechtenstein: Europe Printing Establishment, 1969).

Harper, J. Russell. "Krieghoff and Collectors." *Canadian Antiques and Art Review* 1, no. 4 (December–January 1979–1980): 14–18.

—. "A Sketch-Book of Cornelius Krieghoff." *Canadian Art* 9, no. 4 (Summer 1952): 163–64.

Jouvancourt, Hugues de. "Krieghoff, un pionnier de la peinture canadienne." *Le Collectionneur* 6, no. 21 (October 1987): 41–48.

"Krieghoff's Sketch-Book—A Discovery." *New Frontiers* [1, no. 2] (Spring 1952): 25–28.

Landriault-Racine, Denise, Denise Charpentier, and Claudette Côté. "Krieghoff est-il québécois?" *Au fil des événements* (Université Laval) 8, no. 13 (30 November 1972): 6–7.

Le Moyne, Anne-Marie. "Kane et Krieghoff." *L'Œil*, no. 148 (April 1967): 20–27, 50, 78.

Lévis, Léo G. "Un ami vient de me montrer [...]." *Bulletin des Recherches Historiques* 1, no. 2 (February 1895): 32.

Lismer, Arthur. "Cornelius Krieghoff— 'Canadian Artist Number One.'" *Sun Life Review* (January 1954): 15–19.

M., C. M. "Cornélius Krieghoff." *Bulletin des Recherches Historiques* 1, no. 4 (April 1895): 57.

MacDonald, Colin S. "Cornelius Krieghoff." *A Dictionary of Canadian Artists*. Vol. 3, part 1, 679–85. Ottawa: Canadian Paperbacks, 1971.

Magnan, M.H. "Peintres et sculpteurs du Terroir." *Le Terroir* 3, no. 8 (December 1922): 342–54.

Massicotte, E.-Z. "Un autre Krieghoff." *Bulletin des Recherches Historiques* 42 (1936): 88–89.

McNamara, Eugene. "The Krieghoff Plot." *Books in Canada* 10, no. 9 (November 1981): 12–14.

Morris, Edmund. "Art in Canada: The Early Painters." *Saturday Night* 24, no. 14 (21 January 1911): 25, 29 (reprinted in Morris, Edmund. *Art in Canada: The Early Painters*. [Toronto: s.n., 1911].)

Pfeiffer, Dorothy. "Cornelius Krieghoff." *Gazette* (Montreal), 12 July 1958.

"The Rebirth of a Fascinating Painter." *Maclean's*, 24 December 1955: 13–19; [46] (reprinted with additions in a portfolio format, 1955).

Rombout, Louis. "Cornelius Krieghoff." *Atlantic Advocate* 53, no. 4 (December 1962): 42–43, 45–48.

Roussan, Jacques de. "Sur une peinture de Krieghoff." *L'information médicale et paramédicale* (Montreal) 30, no. 13 (16 May 1978).

Schwartz, Joan M. "William Notman's Hunting Photographs, 1866." *Archivist/L'archiviste* No. 117 (1998): 20–29.

Shoolman, Regina Lenore. "Cornelius Krieghoff." *Canadian Forum* no. 170 (November 1934): 66–68.

Vézina, Raymond. "Attitude esthétique de Cornelius Krieghoff au sein de la tradition picturale canadienne-française." *RACAR* 1, no. 1 (1974): 47–59.

—. "Cornelius Krieghoff." *Dictionary of Canadian Biography*. Vol.X: 1871–1880, ed. Marc La Terreur, 408–14. Toronto: University of Toronto Press, 1972.

—. "Cornelius Krieghoff." Dans *Dictionnaire biographique du Canada*, Vol. X: 1871–1880, ed. Marc La Terreur, 449–55. Québec: Les Presses de l'Université Laval, 1966.

Wallace, W. Stewart. "Cornelius Krieghoff." *The Macmillan Dictionary of Canadian Biography*, revised, enlarged, and updated by W. A. McKay, 421. Toronto: Macmillan of Canada, 1978.

Watson, William R. "Bringing Home the Krieghoffs—Tracking Down 100 Lost Glimpses of Pioneer Life." *Toronto Star/Canadian Weekend Magazine*, 4 January 1975: 14–17.

Wheeling, Ken. "Cornelius Krieghoff and the Sleighs of the Canadian Habitants." *Carriage Journal* 3, no.3 (Winter 1995): 91–96.

Winkworth, Peter. "Cornelius Krieghoff: Scenes in Canada." *Connoisseur* 185, no. 745 (March 1974): 211–18.

Reviews

Marius Barbeau's *Cornelius Krieghoff: Pioneer Painter of North America*. Toronto: The Macmillan Company of Canada, 1934.

C., C. "C. Krieghoff, the Painter, Is Saved from Spite-Mongers." *Winnipeg Free Press* 19 January 1935, 10.

Chicoine, René. "La vie artistique." *La petite revue*, 15 February 1935, 7.

Colgate, William. "Krieghoff, Pictorial Historian." *Mail and Empire* (Toronto), 8 January 1935, 6.

Davies, Florence. "Early Canadian Painter Depicts Pioneer Life." *Detroit Michigan News*, 3 February 1935.

Grierson, Ronald. "Emptying the Demi-John." *Canadian Forum* 15, no. 174 (March 1935): 240.

H., E. W. "Marius Barbeau's Book on Krieghoff." *Ottawa Evening Citizen*, 31 January 1935.

Hébert, Maurice. "Quelques livres de chez nous: Cornelius Krieghoff." *Le Canada français* 24, no. 2 (October 1936): 162–65.

Jefferys, Charles W. "Cornelius Krieghoff." *Canadian Historical Review* 16, no. 3 (September 1935): 329–30.

Morisset, Gérard. "La vie artistique: Cornelius Krieghoff: Réflexions en marge du livre de Marius Barbeau." *Le Canada* (Montreal), 19 and 21 January 1935.

Van Gogh, Lucy. "Pioneer Painter." *Saturday Night* 50, no. 13 (2 February 1935).

W., E. "Cornelius Krieghoff." *Connoisseur* 96, no. 409 (September 1935): 176.

J. Russell Harper's *Krieghoff*. Toronto: University of Toronto Press, 1979.

Allodi, Mary. "Krieghoff." *Canadian Collector* 15, no. 2 (March–April 1980): 27–28.

Andreae, Janice. "Romanticism of Krieghoff Illuminating." *London Free Press* (London, Ontario), 8 December 1979.

Hammock, Virgil G. "Démêler le vrai du faux." *Vie des arts* 25, no. 99 (Summer 1980): 84.

Bell, Michael. "Krieghoff." *Queen's Quarterly* 87, no. 3 (Autumn 1980): 526–27.

Davis, Ann. "Krieghoff." *Quill and Quire* 45, no. 14 (December 1979): 24–25.

Mulhallen, Karen. "Behind the Christmas Card." *Canadian Forum* 60, no. 701 (August 1980): 32–34.

Silcox, David. "Krieghoff the Craftsman, Carr the Visionary." *Saturday Night* 94, no. 10 (December 1979): 67–69.

Vézina, Raymond. "Krieghoff." *University of Toronto Quarterly* 49, no. 4 (Summer 1980): 489–92.

Westfall, William. "Krieghoff." *The Canadian Historical Review* 62, no. 4 (December 1981): 538–40.

Wistow, David. "Krieghoff." *RACAR* 7, no. 1–2 (1980): 127–28.

Young, Mahonri Sharp. "Krieghoff." *Apollo* 117, no. 255 (May 1983): 414.

Hugues de Jouvancourt's *Cornelius Krieghoff*. Toronto: Musson, 1973.

Edinborough, Arnold. "Canadian Picture Books Come to Fore." *Financial Post*, vol. 67 (15 December 1973): 9.

Kritzwiser, Kay. "Cornelius Krieghoff." *Globe and Mail* (Toronto), 15 December 1973.

Raymond Vézina's *Cornelius Krieghoff, Peintre de mœurs (1815–1872)*. Ottawa: Editions du Pélican, 1972.

"Cornelius Krieghoff." *Le livre canadien*, no. 333 (December 1973).

Lamonde, Yvan. "Le regard étrange de Cornelius Krieghoff." *La Presse* (Montréal), 7 April 1973.

Leblond, Jean-Claude. "Krieghoff, peintre de genre." *Vie des arts* 18, no. 74 (Spring 1974): 86.

Robert, Guy. "Sur trois monographies : De Michelangelo à Krieghoff et Mondrian." *Le Devoir* (Montréal), 17 July 1976.

Toupin, Gilles. "Cornelius Krieghoff." *Livres et auteurs québécois* (1973): 259–63.

PHOTO CREDITS

INDEX